INCLUSIVE HOUS
AN AGEING SOCIE

Innovative approaches

Edited by Sheila M. Peace and Caroline Holland

First published in Great Britain in October 2001 by

The Policy Press
34 Tyndall's Park Road
Bristol BS8 1PY
UK

Tel +44 (0)117 954 6800
Fax +44 (0)117 973 7308
e-mail tpp@bristol.ac.uk
www.policypress.org.uk

British Library Cataloguing in Publication Data

A catalogue record for this book is available from the British Library

ISBN 1 86134 263 2 paperback

A hardcover version of this book is also available

Sheila M. Peace is a senior lecturer and **Caroline Holland** is a research fellow, both in the School of Health and Social Welfare, The Open University.

Cover design by Qube Design Associates, Bristol.

Illustration on front cover by Kate Foster.

The Policy Press works to counter discrimination on grounds of gender, race, disability, age and sexuality.

Printed and bound in Great Britain by Hobbs the Printers Ltd, Southampton.

Contents

List of tables and figures

Tables

Figures

Acknowledgements

In July 1998 we held a one-day conference – 'Lifetime homes to staying put schemes: the future of living arrangements for an ageing society' – hosted by the School of Health and Social Welfare at The Open University, on behalf of the British Sociological Association's study group on Sociology + Environment + Architecture. Our thanks go to Dr Tim Brindley of De Montfort University, for help in setting up that event. The meeting provided the initial impetus for this publication, as many of the contributors were speakers. They have been joined here by a number of other experts who have added to the breadth of our debate. We would like to thank all of the contributors for helping us to bring this exciting text together. But, of course, we would not get far without administrative support, and our thanks, in relation to both the conference and the text, go primarily to Pat Chalk. We would also like to thank others who have helped in various ways to prepare the book: Pauline Byrne, Linda Cambourne-Paynter, Tanya Hames and Samantha Marshall. Our special thanks go to Kate Foster, one of our authors, for letting us choose one of her wonderful pictures to incorporate in the cover of this book. These pictures were based on drawings made during her research and reflect her multiple talents. Finally, we are grateful for the comments of the anonymous reviewers of earlier drafts of the text.

Sheila M. Peace and Caroline Holland

Notes on contributors

Miriam Bernard is Professor of Social Gerontology and Head of the School of Social Relations at Keele University. Her research interests are primarily oriented around the development of new/healthy life-styles in old age and she has a particular interest in the lives of older women.

Simon Biggs is Professor of Social Gerontology at Keele University. He has worked as a Community Psychologist and in social work policy. His main interests include ageing identity, social theory, therapeutic approaches to work with older people, and interprofessional relationships.

Maria Brenton is a Visiting Research Fellow in the School for Policy Studies, University of Bristol. She works from home in Cardiff and is funded by the Joseph Rowntree Foundation to assist the Older Women's CoHousing project in London to realise a CoHousing Community. Her main research interests are preserving autonomy and independence in old age, older women and collaborative living arrangements.

Malcolm J. Fisk is Director of Insight Social Research, a company with expertise at the interface of housing and care, and regarding technologies that support independent living. He is also a Research Associate at the Centre for Social Research, Queen's University of Belfast.

Kate Foster completed her PhD in 1997 at the Dementia Services Development Centre at the University of Stirling. More recently she has studied environmental art at Glasgow School of Art and now practices as an artist-researcher.

Julienne Hanson is Reader in Architectural and Urban Morphology and Director of the Space Syntax Laboratory at the Bartlett School of Graduate Studies, University College London. She chaired Age Concern's Built Environment Study Group for the Millennium Debate of the Age and was recently engaged in research to develop a profile of the UK's housing stock for older people (EPSRC/EQUAL funded).

Caroline Holland is a Research Fellow in the School of Health and Social Welfare at the Open University, where her doctoral work looked at Housing Histories. She has previously worked with local authorities and housing associations in England, and is currently working on an ESRC-funded project,'Environment and identity in later life'. Her main research interests are in housing, environment and the life course.

Leonie Kellaher is Director of the Centre for Environmental & Social Studies in Ageing at the University of North London. An anthropologist and gerontologist of long standing, she has conducted extensive research into environmental settings for older people. Her most recent research included a study of'Cemetery as garden' (ESRC-funded); and a study of users' perceptions of living in residential care provided by Methodist Homes.

Mary Kelly is an architect and researcher working for a Northumberland-based national charity which provides help and support to people, particularly those on low incomes and in housing need, building their own homes and community buildings. She has previously worked with the Women's Design Service in London and with the Dementia Services Development Centre at the University of Stirling.

Paul Kingston is Senior Lecturer in Applied Health Studies and Gerontology, and Director of Undergraduate Studies, School of Social Relations, Keele University. He has a particular interest in the health dimension in later life: specifically, accidents, falls, retirement communities and quality of life. Other interests include adult protection and the vulnerability of adults. He is a co-editor of *The Journal of Adult Protection.*

Brian A. McGrail is currently an Associate Lecturer for both the Open University and the University of Highlands & Islands project, teaching social sciences and area studies. Prior to this he worked as a Research Fellow at the Open University on two ESRC-funded projects, including 'The virtual remake of high-rise housing'. His current research interests lie in the fields of surveillance, housing and theories of power.

Ruth Madigan is Senior Lecturer in Sociology at the University of Glasgow with particular interests in urban sociology and housing. She has published extensively in the fields of women's needs and design of housing and has more recently extended her focus to include disabled and older people's rights.

Mary Marshall is the Director of the Dementia Services Development Centre and Professor in the Department of Applied Social Science at the University of Stirling. Her research interests are in two main areas: design and technology for people with dementia, and hearing the voice of people with dementia about the services they receive.

Jo Milner is a Senior Lecturer in Applied Social Studies at the School of Social Work based in the University of Kingston-upon-Thames. Her main research interest centres on housing and disability issues, particularly as they relate to the building design needs of disabled people.

Sheila M. Peace is Senior Lecturer in the School of Health and Social Welfare at the Open University, where she has also been Sub-Dean (Research). She is both a geographer and a gerontologist with research interests in environment and ageing, residential care services and the regulation of care services.

John Percival, an experienced social worker, completed a PhD in 1998 on his ethnographic study of older people's social interactions in sheltered housing. As a freelance researcher he has recently worked on studies of: minority ethnic elders' management of long-term medication at home; and older people's changing uses and perceptions of space in the home environment.

Judith Phillips is a Professor in the School of Social Relations, Keele University. Her research interests include: residential and community care issues, carers in employment, retirement communities, spatial aspects of ageing, family and community life of older people and intergenerational solidarity.

ONE

Housing an ageing society

Sheila M. Peace and Caroline Holland

> An outstanding ground floor one-bedroom conversion with two reception rooms and direct access to a private rear garden. Excellent decorative condition and peacefully located within a short walk of the train station. (Estate agent advertisement in local paper)
>
> 36 small studio flats in a two-storey development consisting of six interconnecting blocks, each with its own communal kitchen, dining area and bathroom. This scheme is intended for very frail (though not confused) elderly people and can be considered a 'bridge' between sheltered housing and full residential care. There is a team of staff maintaining 24-hr cover rather than a single warden. (Local authority, extra-care scheme information leaflet)

Introduction

These quotations illustrate a point about the image of housing for older people in the UK at the beginning of the 21st century. The first, an estate agent's description of a property on the open market, emphasises its attractiveness, privacy and convenience: a place which sounds pleasant to stay in, nice to visit, easy to get away from. The second presents the property as a provision for a particular group – by implication needy people more concerned about being cared for than caring about the place where they live (but not presenting behavioural problems). This reflects attitudes to 'ordinary – age-integrated' and 'specialised – age-related' housing as much as the differences between the two places, raising issues about integration, segregation and the capacity of the environment – built and social – to support 'ordinary life'. Social exclusion is currently a major political issue. The divisions between people who are able to take part fully in the life of the community, and those who are hindered from doing so by material and cultural deprivation, are seen as harmful to the whole of society, and the present rhetoric is one of inclusion and enablement. Older people – particularly the very old – are among those groups which, by virtue of their relative economic disadvantage and increased propensity for long-term limiting conditions and disabilities, are most at risk from social exclusion and its consequences. Our particular focus in this book is the environment of old age, which can help or hinder the integration of older people within their communities. We will explore some of the ways in which forms of housing and attitudes to the housing needs of older people have changed and will continue to do so as the 21st century progresses.

Throughout our lives we all live somewhere, whether in a high-rise flat, a hostel, a family house, a retirement community, a maisonette, a doorway in a city, a bungalow, a group home, a village, a suburb, a town. These are all places that provide context for part of our daily life, which may be valued in different ways and to which individuals can develop a greater or lesser attachment. They are also places in which we can act out roles, express ourselves through our routines and our possessions, and exert varying degrees of autonomy and control over how we spend our time and who we relate to. Whether and when we are able to withdraw from others and seek solitude or anonymity, or choose to mix and interact – both within and without our living place – varies with the setting. Across our lives contexts will change and our acceptance of these changes will reflect many things about ourselves: our experience of households, power base, continuity of place, material circumstances, mental and physical health, generational history and relationships with others, including neighbours.

In this book we focus on housing arrangements that might enable people to live to the end of their lives, with their health and care needs met or supported, in places that are valued both by them and by other people. These presently include a whole range of environments (see Figure 1.1). We are part of an ageing population whose structure is changing and where there will be a great diversity of household types. Collective recognition of such changes has been slow. To date our thinking around 'accommodation and care' in later life has focused on very old people who are seen as unable to fit into mainstream housing and whose needs have been labelled as special, segregated or separate, rather than accepting accommodation and care as part of society's needs in general. It should be acknowledged that some people, more than others, welcome the prospect of 'being looked after' as their own physical strength diminishes; some older people also value the company of their peers above that of younger people. Yet housing which supports disability or frailty need not segregate people and efforts are being made on a number

Figure 1.1: Issues for inclusive housing in later life

The places

Age-related?	**Age-integrated?**
Adult foster care	Homelessness
Small residential care homes	Home sharing
Retirement communities	Terraced housing
Sheltered housing	Flats – high rise
CoHousing	Flats – conversions/adaptations
Shared housing	Semi-detached houses
Extra-care housing	Bungalows
Residential care homes	Detached houses
Long-stay hospital accommodation for older people	Hospices
Care housing for people with dementia	
Hospices	

The issues: people, support, finance, regulation, technology, design

Independent living
Financial matters
Lifetime Homes
Palliative care
Regulated accommodation
Assisted living
Smart housing
Personal care
Nursing care
Supported housing
Intermediate care
Continuing care
Household change

of fronts to maintain the integration of older people along with their independence. To set the context, we look first in this chapter at our changing population, the type of society that is developing, how this is affecting where people live and the experiences that many older people now face.

Who is an older person?

It has become general knowledge that the population of the UK is getting older. The proportion of people aged over 60 years of age increased across the world during the 20th century, but in some countries, including the UK, this was accompanied by a falling birth rate so that the average age of the whole population increased. Media representations of this trend have often portrayed this as a problem for younger people who will somehow have to support an ever-expanding and increasingly frail older generation. But, more recently, we have begun to see a wider recognition of the need to face the ageism, which disempowers a growing number of people (see for example *The Guardian*, 14 June 2000). To make any sense of what has been happening we need to look at what 'an ageing population' means and bring this knowledge to the field of housing. So, who is an 'older person'?

From 'early retirement', in the mid- to late-fifties, to 'super-centenarians', aged over 110 years, there is a potential age range of more than 60 years for people who are variously described as 'older', 'retired', 'elderly', 'senior', or 'pensioners'. In spite of the fact that some people have no work from which to retire, some retire earlier and others continue to work, the first time many older people feel they are really getting old is when they become eligible for a state retirement pension. Indeed, 'pensionable age', is frequently used in official documents as a defining category. In the UK this age has been set at 60 for women and 65 for men since the 1940 Old Age and Widows Pension Act, but from 2010 to 2020 this will be progressively harmonised to age 65 for everyone (DSS, 2001).

However, policy makers and writers on ageing have often needed to be more precise about who they are referring to: 60-year-olds who are still fit, active and possibly working, or frail people in their late nineties who need nursing care. Some have made a distinction, for example, between the 'young elderly' (aged up to 74) and the 'old elderly' (aged over 75) (Falkingham, 1998) – recognising that greater support is often necessary towards the end of life. However, the number of years during which people can expect relatively good health and mobility has increased. This has given many people, with reasonable incomes and lessening family responsibilities after their children have grown up, some time to do things they enjoy doing. Laslett (1989) defined this as a 'third age' of self-actualisation before the onset of the 'fourth age' of increasing dependency. The notion of the 'third age' has since been used as a convenient shorthand for older people who live an active lifestyle; therefore given the salience of genetic, cultural and other factors, advancing age in itself does not define dependency for individuals.

The characteristics, abilities, needs and aspirations of older people vary greatly, not just because they are all individuals or because of their chronological age differences, but also because of the different experiences that successive cohorts of people carry with them as they age. More recently, writers on ageing have incorporated elements of cohort histories into definitions of age groups. For example, Evandrou and Falkingham

(2000) have made a distinction within the 'baby-boom generations' of the second half of the 20th century. The 'first baby-boomers', were born during the period of austerity after the Second World War, but by the time they entered adulthood in the late 1960s/early 1970s, higher education was expanding, the employment market was buoyant and there was a general atmosphere of liberality. On the other hand, the 'second baby-boom' generation, born in the 1960s in a time of relative prosperity, came into the labour market in the late 1970s and early 1980s during a period of recession and contraction of the welfare state. The timing of these events in their lives will have affected the possibilities open to them when deciding where to live as they grow older. This demonstrates that a historical perspective is important to understanding the housing situations and aspirations of older people, among whom there are a whole range of collective (cohort and generational) as well as individual experiences.

Compared to earlier generations, older people in the 21st century increasingly expect to have a 'voice' about their own prospects, both as individuals, and collectively through such organisations as Age Concern and many locally-based pensioner forums and groups (Age Concern, 1999; Better Government for Older People, 1999). As an economic and electoral group of large and growing significance, we might expect that, in future, more older people will demand an appropriate input to policy processes and decisions and to research into ageing issues.

Demographic change

By 2021 it is projected that the average age of the population will have risen to 42 years (from 37 years in 1998) and, by 2008, the number of people in the UK who are aged over 65 will for the first time exceed the number of children under 16 years (Shaw, 2000). The rate of increase in the number of official 'pensioners' will be slowed somewhat by the changes in women's state retirement age coming into force after 2010; nevertheless, by 2021 it is expected that about 19% of the population will be of pensionable age (Shaw, 2000). The projected life expectancy of women will continue to exceed that of men, but the gap will narrow in this period. The differences between the life experience of men and women are reflected in the demographics of income, health status and likelihood of living alone or in a residential setting (Ginn and Arber, 1998).

Population projections also show a continuing increase in the proportion of older people from minority ethnic groups. Atkin commented regarding minority groups that "less than 20 per cent are aged over 45 and 3 per cent are over 65. The comparative figures for the white population are 22 per cent and 17 per cent respectively" (1998, pp 164-5). He also stressed the differences between various minority ethnic groups, showing that Bangladeshi and Pakistani communities are generally younger than Indian and Afro-Caribbean groups. There are also variations in ratios between older men and women, for example, Black and South Asian groups having more men than women over 65 years; this may have implications for informal caring relationships. Blakemore and Boneham (1994) have pointed out that, as successive cohorts of migrants of the late 1950s and 1960s reach retirement age, the numbers of older people within minority groups will rise. Successive cohorts will include larger numbers of British-born people of Black and Asian origin, adding to the diversity of experience of the older population.

The financial situations of individual older people vary enormously, however, the perception and very often the reality of old age has been one of limited incomes and reduced expenditure. To quote from a Joseph Rowntree Foundation (JRF) press release of 1998:

> Age is no longer synonymous with poverty, but 60 per cent of pensioners remain in the bottom 40 per cent of the income distribution. About one million pensioners have no income other than the state retirement pension and benefits. Their vulnerability is underlined by figures showing that they spend about half as much on food as those with private incomes. Older people with low incomes are also more prone to moderate anxiety and depression. (JRF, 1998)

Given that men and women tend to have different experiences within working life in relation to full-time and part-time working and levels of income, it is unsurprising that older women, especially single older women, fall within the group with the lowest incomes. Access to occupational pensions, social security benefits, continued employment and savings and investments all differ, and, as Falkingham showed, in 1997 over three times as many women pensioners as men were dependent on Income Support (1998, p 105).

Older people with low incomes include both renting tenants of property and owner-occupiers; for the latter, maintenance and improvements may have to become a low priority after paying everyday bills. People on low incomes – especially older women – are less able to take part in hobbies and activities which cost money, to afford transport, to improve their wardrobes, and so on (Ginn and Arber, 1998). This can affect their interactions with others, the amount and quality of time spent outside the home and, as the JRF release stated, the likelihood of reduced well-being.

Older people also vary enormously in their state of health. While the majority of older people may be relatively healthy and managing independently in the community, as people age they are at risk from age-related diseases and senescent changes, so that by the age of 75 most people will experience some physical symptoms of ageing (Briggs, 1993). The prevalence of disability also increases with age and the majority of people over 85 years have some degree of impairment. Consequently, given women's longer life expectancy, it is not surprising that they should be faced with a greater degree of chronic illness and functional disability. It is also true that older men have a higher mortality rate due to conditions such as heart disease and cancer, while older women cope with conditions such as diabetes, arthritis and osteoporosis (Ginn and Arber, 1998). Yet the perception of health is not entirely a matter of physical condition, and many older people can tolerate their symptoms and get on with their lives. The nature of the environment in which they live can have a profound affect on their ability to do so.

The changing nature of households

If the population is ageing how will people decide to live? The basic way of describing social units is the 'household', defined in the 1991 Census as:

> ... one person living alone or a group of persons (not necessarily related) living at the same address with common housekeeping – that is sharing at least one meal a day and sharing a living room or sitting room. (OPCS, 1993, p 2, para 4)

This provides a working definition for the purposes of assessment, but in many ways it disguises the dynamic nature of households. Members may join or leave these arrangements, become part-time or occasional members of the household, or, as 'insiders' or 'outsiders', take part in some joint activities and not others.

We know that the number of households in the UK is predicted to grow steadily to 3.8 million by 2021. At the same time, it is predicted that the average size of households will continue to fall, from 2.4 persons in 1996 to 2.2 persons in 2021 (King et al, 2000). In the UK people of all ages have tended to form or maintain independent households – supported by the increasing availability of separate housing from the middle of the 20th century, trends in the housing market and cultural changes towards increasing individualism (Wall, 1984). During the earlier 1900s members of different generations chose, or perhaps more often were forced, to live together as one household. By the end of the 20th century three-generation households were much less common and fewer older people lived with their adult children. For example, in 1971, 42% of women aged over 85 lived in two- or three-generational households; by 1991 this was down to 21% (Grundy et al, 1999). Many studies have shown that older people now prefer to live in their own homes, alone if necessary, rather than move in with their children or into residential care (Arber and Ginn, 1991; Grundy, 1999).

While the nuclear family has been a stereotype for the household for much of the 20th century, there has been a great rise in the number of people living alone at all stages of life. Although still associated with the lives of older people, the recent expansion in living alone has been greatest among younger age groups – particularly the under-forties. Hall et al report that, in 1991, people living alone formed 27% of all households in Britain, as compared to 18% in 1970, and that by 2020 they will form more than one in three households (1999, p 265). Evandrou and Falkingham (2000) have also estimated that successive cohorts will increasingly tend to live alone. For example, in their study, 50% of the 'second baby-boomers' may be expected to live alone at the age of 75, compared to 38% of the older cohort born in 1930 (p 29). We can therefore see that, as they age, younger groups will be even more likely to live alone in later life than the present population of older people – and living alone is one of the major factors which can lead people to seek alternative living arrangements.

Research has shown a geographical variation in the location of younger and older groups of people living alone, with those over pensionable age showing greater concentration in rural areas and traditional retirement areas, while those below pensionable age are more commonly found in urban areas, especially in London (Hall et al, 1999, p 272). This variation reflects generational changes in rural/urban living. However, Census analysis also shows that, among all people over 75 years of age, proportionally more men live in rural areas while proportionally more women live in urban areas (Denham and White, 1998).

So where are older people housed?

Individual older people live in all kinds of homes including 'mainstream' and 'specialised' accommodation that is owned, rented and licensed, in houses, flats, bungalows and so on, and across the range of locations. But, as a group, older people are found in proportionally larger numbers in particular types of accommodation, including property that is owned outright and housing rented from local authorities (see Table 1.1). This reflects changing trends in housing provision and access during the time period through which they have lived, and the historically weaker economic position of people relying on state pensions. The effects of these factors on housing opportunities can be seen in the position of successive cohorts of older people (Holland, forthcoming). For example, in 1983, people aged over 60 and living alone were most likely to be in local authority housing. But, by 1997, following the general expansion of home ownership and the Right to Buy policies of the 1980s, they were most likely to be owner-occupiers (Forrest and Leather, 1998; Statsbase, 2000), with older couples more likely to own their home than single people. Forrest et al (1995) estimated that, by 2001, 75% of older people would own their own home. These changes reflect the intermix of personal resources and opportunities, and wider societal issues of political ideology, housing policy and cultural trends (Peace and Johnson, 1998).

Both the value and the condition of the homes in which older people live vary enormously (Hancock, 1998), but around 20% of households

Table 1.1: Percentage of tenure by oldest household member

	A: Oldest member 60-74 years	B: Oldest member 75 years plus	All households with a member over 60 years (A + B)
% of all households	22.3	12.2	34.5
% of owner-occupier households	23.1	10.5	33.6
% of private tenant households	8.8	8.2	17.0
% of local authority tenant households	26.7	18.7	45.4
% of Registered Social Landlord tenant households	21.8	21.8	43.6

Source: DETR (1998)

headed by someone aged 75 or over are in 'poor' housing – that is, housing which is "unfit, in substantial disrepair or requiring essential maintenance" (DETR, 1998). In general, the English housing stock is older than that in France and Germany for example (DETR, 1998), and includes less flats and more owner-occupied properties. The age of property gives a crude guide to the likelihood of physical deterioration and deficient amenities and data for 1998 showed that 21% of the total housing stock at that time had been built before 1919 (therefore, more than 79 years old) and a further 19% pre-dated 1944. In contrast only 11% had been built after 1985 (DETR, 2000a). Furthermore, as part of the older housing stock becomes replaced over time, more recent housing, including that built during the housing expansion period of the 1950s and 1960s, will itself be ageing. Some of it, particularly certain houses built in the 1960s by non-traditional methods, may in time present costly maintenance and modernisation problems both for individuals and for housing providers.

The proportions of people living in houses built at different times vary quite considerably between tenures, although all tenures include some accommodation which is older and/or in poor condition. Many owner-occupiers live in ageing properties in need of repair and modernisation (DETR, 2000a); private rented dwellings of all ages (except post-1964) are in a noticeably worse state of repair than dwellings of the same age in other tenures (DETR, 1998). Around a quarter of long-leaseholders are aged over 65, and many of this group have experienced problems both with maintenance issues and with unreasonable service charges (Cole et al, 1998). Properties defined as in disrepair are most common in older London boroughs, large urban districts and older resort and university towns, and in the 56 most deprived authorities disrepair levels are twice the average rate (DETR, 1998).

Council tenants are most likely to live in accommodation built in the mid-20th century, while housing association properties were often built more recently – post-1980s. This reflects the history of social rented housing during this period. In the local authority stock, the newer dwellings (post-1964) tend to be in worse physical condition than dwellings of the same age in other tenures; this is largely accounted for by high levels of disrepair in purpose-built council flats (DETR, 1998).

In contrast to the majority of older people living in mainstream housing, just 9-10% of people of pensionable age live in what has been called 'special settings' – sheltered housing, 'extra-care' housing, residential care homes, nursing homes and hospitals. Yet, for people over 80 years of age, collective forms of accommodation-with-care became relatively common towards the end of the 20th century, with around 25% of people aged over 85 years living in residential care homes or nursing homes (see Table 1.2).

Finally, in addition to homeowners, leaseholders, tenants, licensees, residents or patients – we often fail to recognise the group of older people who are homeless (Crane, 1999; Crane and Warnes, 2000). Until recently their situation has been largely neglected. A large percentage of the country's homeless people live in London and figures from Shelter and the Peabody Trust have showed that around 100,000 people can be homeless there at some time each year (*Evening Standard*, 19 July 2000, p 4). Crane (1999) has shown that among them are a wide diversity of older people – alcoholics, people who have suffered family breakdown and ex-servicemen among them – staying in hostels, night-shelters and sleeping rough. The living environments of older people are as diverse as the population.

The impact of diversity

As people grow older, their housing reflects aspects of social diversity and of individual housing histories. For example, the relationship between gender, housing and quality of life in old age is related to a range of issues: social, psychological and physiological. As women have a longer life expectancy than men and as they have tended to marry men older than themselves it is more likely that they will become widows (Ginn and Arber, 1998) and, with increasing age, live alone. Men are more likely to live with their spouse. As we have also seen, older women are more likely than men to suffer from long-term limiting illnesses such as musculo-skeletal disorders. The consequent impact on ability to maintain daily activities can affect people in different ways. Given that having a limiting long-term illness in later life is a predictor of moving to a residential care or nursing home (OPCS, 1993, p 88), it is not surprising that most people living in specialised accommodation with care facilities are women (Peace, 1993).

Alongside gender, matters such as social class and ethnicity also have an impact on access to accommodation. Older people with low socioeconomic status who have lived in rented accommodation and who are not able to live with family, are more likely to move into institutional settings than those who have been owner-occupiers and in non-manual occupations (Peace and Johnson, 1998). Atkin (1998) also shows that, while some older people from minority ethnic communities are homeowners, in the main this is a much smaller proportion than in the white community. They are also more likely to be located in poor housing with less access to housing wealth: "Older minority ethnic communities are more likely to be in older, unmodernised, inner city housing which is damp and draughty, as well as lacking in central heating and other household amenities such as washing machines" (p 169).

However, people from black and minority ethnic groups are, on the whole, less likely to live in institutional or communal settings, including sheltered housing, than white people (Jones, 1994). In most minority ethnic groups, older people are also much more likely to live with their children: for example, the fourth Policy Studies Institute National Survey of Ethnic Minorities (Modood et al, 1997) showed that 31% Caribbean, 72% Chinese, and 70% African/Asian people aged 60-79, shared with a son or daughter, compared to 13% of white older people. Blakemore and Boneham (1994) have attributed this in part to a lack of information among black and especially Asian older people about benefits and services and in part to providers' assumptions about their needs and preferences. For example, before the first sheltered housing schemes for Asian people were opened in Leicester, Birmingham and elsewhere, it was generally assumed that older Asian people preferred to live with their families: once the schemes were opened, there were many applications to move in. Older people may have been living in overcrowded family housing without information concerning alternative accommodation (Askham et al, 1995). Demand relates to local conditions, availability and knowledge, and these factors need to be considered alongside the expressed preferences of older people in general and minority ethnic groups in particular. The Housing Corporation's (1998) document, *Black and minority ethnic housing policy*, suggests that black and minority ethnic community-based Registered Social Landlords (RSLs) frequently take a wider social perspective and have been leaders in 'Housing Plus' initiatives (The Housing Corporation, 1998). They have already initiated several assessments of minority ethnic older people's housing needs (for example, Jeffery and Seager, 1993; Bright, 1996; Bowes, 1998; Goodby, 1998; Steele, 1999), and might be encouraged to take a lead in addressing their needs and aspirations.

Living arrangements across the life cycle

In broad terms, the movement of households through a series of dwelling places has been conceptualised in relation to the requirements of the 'ordinary' life cycle. For example, newly-weds might move into a flat or small house; when their children grow up and leave home, couples might move from 'family' housing with three or more bedrooms into somewhere smaller and easier to manage; an older person living alone weighs up the positives and negatives of living alone. Progression through a series of 'suitable' settings is part of this pattern, although not inevitable. But, as we have seen, the social and demographic evidence suggests a more complex actuality in the ways people access 'ordinary' and 'special' housing.

'Ordinary' housing

The independence and autonomy of ordinary housing, taken for granted by most adults, may come under threat with advancing age. Older people value their independence and most tend to defend it as far as possible. What this means in terms of day-to-day living varies with individual circumstances. Most older people will, at some points in their lives, have lived in places which they have shared with other people – usually partners or close family, although some will have lived alone for much of their lives. Even though wartime arrangements may have led to different experiences (evacuation, co-residence, and so on), comparatively few will have shared with non-family groups for any length of time since. It is in this context – living either in families or alone being the norm – that they will have approached the idea of living communally. Forms of co-residence initiated by the residents themselves have been few in the UK and, to date, there has been very little alternative to choosing between individual mainstream housing on the one hand and 'specialised' accommodation for older people on the other.

We have already noted that older people may live in older property. Most will have the basic amenities of indoor toilet, bathroom and kitchen, but in houses the bathrooms and toilets will predominantly be upstairs and this may become problematic for those with mobility problems. However, the 1996 English Housing Condition Survey (DETR, 1998) showed that more than one third of the 44,000 dwellings still without an inside toilet at that time were occupied by older people. Also, many older people, living in private rented accommodation in particular, were among those who did not have central heating. Private tenants and those who are long-term residents in regulated tenancies figure prominently in the group of people aged over 60 years who live alone in poor housing.

Home maintenance may prove difficult for older people for a number of reasons including cost, access to support and personal frailty. But where essential maintenance is not undertaken people may be put, or put themselves, at risk of home accidents, particularly trips and falls (Davies and Pearson, 1999), which can lead to hospital admission. However, while many accidents at home are preventable, people may still need to accommodate their own problems in terms of mobility, or poor sight or hearing, in order to undertake their daily tasks and manage their home. Jarvis et al (1996) reported on the abilities of older people across Britain and found that, while a majority had little difficulty with self/personal care, there was a greater range of competencies with home maintenance tasks (such as washing dishes or cleaning windows) and with tasks related to mobility (such as getting in and out of bed or going up the stairs). In all cases competence did decline with increasing age and, in regard to some home tasks, could be seen as gender related. Unsurprisingly, couples coped more easily than those who lived alone.

An individual's ability to cope with everyday activities tends to be measured as Activities of Daily Living (ADLs), but these do not normally take into account the context of environment. Adapting home environments to facilitate everyday living is important in enabling people to remain in control and, at the present time, some of the people with the most need for help with these activities are living in the most difficult physical environments. In dealing with these issues, whether for people who are ageing, or permanently or temporarily disabled, the thrust of the Lifetime Homes movement has been to make environments themselves as barrier-free as possible. This has involved, for example, remodelling levels, fitting aids and adaptations, redesigning equipment and reconsidering access (Audit Commission, 1998, 2000).

'Special' housing

Some people reach a point at which they can no longer cope in their own homes and making adaptations is not an attractive option. For them specialised housing with some element of support or care, ranging from sheltered housing to nursing homes, has been the accepted solution. This usually means a move from living individually to living in some degree of co-residence. In the second half of the 20th century sheltered housing dominated what was seen as specialised 'housing' provision, whereas residential care homes and nursing homes (see Table 1.2) emerged through the different routes of workhouse provision and hospital reorganisation (Peace et al, 1997).

Local authorities took on large-scale developments of sheltered housing schemes, both by the conversion of existing buildings and by new-build developments, particularly after the 1960s. Two types of specialised accommodation were eligible for subsidy. 'Category 1' was conceived as self-contained dwellings such as bungalows for the 'more active' elderly, built to Parker Morris standards (MHLG, 1961), with limited communal facilities and possibly a warden. 'Category 2', or 'sheltered housing', was to be for less active people, comprising grouped flatlets with space standards less generous than Parker Morris, but with some communal facilities and a warden.

Between 1979 and 1989 England's total housing stock rose by 10%, but the number of sheltered housing units rose by 69% as public housing policy shifted from general needs to special needs provision. Within that increase, housing association provision rose by 150%, and private sector provision (mainly for sale) by 400% (Fletcher, 1991). A Department of the Environment study carried out in 1993 (McCafferty, 1994) indicated that, overall, there was by then a probable over-provision of sheltered housing, but an under-provision of very sheltered housing or extra-care housing which provided a higher level of personal support. Extra-care sheltered housing subsequently became the growth area, with housing associations funded to increase their provision in line with that of local authorities.

Sheltered housing was based on the idea that while older people need good quality housing they also have physical and social needs which call for a continuum of settings with levels of support to allow for increasing dependency. One of the original purposes of sheltered housing was to extend the amount of time that an individual could live independently in the community before moving to a residential care home, although there has been little evidence that this happened to any great extent. Sheltered housing has also come to be regarded as a 'home for life' rather than as an interim stage between 'ordinary' housing and residential options.

At the outset such housing was seen to provide companionship, access to emergency help and a mixed population with younger and fitter people able to give some assistance to older people, and to sustain an active community life. In practice the ageing of tenants has led to greater dependency on warden and care services, to some extent putting off younger retired people. Also some properties have become unattractive and 'hard to let' (Tinker et al, 1995). These may be bed-sits or very small flats, or they might be inconveniently located for services and facilities; for some, service costs have also been a deterrent. Nevertheless, in some areas the housing market is such that sheltered housing offers most of the affordable one-person-sized public sector housing available to older people.

During the period from 1981 to 1991, when the provision of sheltered housing was still expanding, the proportion of older people living in residential and nursing care homes actually increased. This increase was influenced both by financial and community care reforms in the 1980s and 1990s, which resulted in an expansion and then a contraction of all care home sectors (Peace et al, 1997; Laing & Buisson, 2000; and see Table 1.2). By the end of the 20th century, the residential care sector was continuing to evolve in response to the changing nature of the ageing population and socioeconomic factors, but was becoming squeezed between special housing and nursing homes (Davies, 1998; Royal Commission on Long Term Care, 1999; Laing & Buisson, 2000).

Table 1.2: Residential care home and nursing home places for older people, chronically ill and physically disabled people by sector, UK (1970-2000)

	Residential places*			Nursing home places†	
1 April	LA	Private	Voluntary	Private/ voluntary‡	
1970	108,700	23,700	40,100	20,300	
1975	128,300	25,800	41,000	24,000	
1980	134,500	37,400	42,600	26,900	
1985	137,100	85,300	45,100	38,000	
				Private	Voluntary
1987	135,500	114,600	42,200	52,000	8,300
1990	125,600	155,600	40,000	112,600	10,500
1995	79,700	169,300	56,700	193,400	17,900
1997	70,500	177,100	56,100	205,900	18,500
1998	68,000	180,700	53,500	203,200	18,200
2000	59,200	185,400	54,900	186,500	18,100

Notes: LA = local authority
* including residential places in dual-registered homes
† including nursing places in dual-registered homes
‡ private and voluntary nursing home places were listed together before 1987
Source: Laing & Buisson (2000)

What do we mean by independent living?

We can see from these developments that one of the ways to tackle the needs that some older people have for accommodation and a level of support with care tasks, is to define them as people with 'special needs'. Yet, many of these needs are similar to needs that we all have as children, when they are met in the main through family support. By adulthood most people become independent and want to do things for themselves in their own way. With spouses or partners, many people negotiate any support they need to get by without necessarily thinking of it as 'care'. It is often not until people are on their own again that a consciousness of their need for support rears its head and this may lead to a consideration of alternative lifestyles.

These issues are particularly important for those older people who now need assistance to enable them to live independently. What independence really means needs to be recognised in the context of people and their home environments. Many older people come to make a housing move at a late stage in their life, when new living arrangements may involve a degree of change for which they are not prepared. These changes may include moving from individual living to collective living; moving from a socially-integrated setting to a more separate setting; a change of tenure from owner-occupation to tenancy; spending more of their capital and income on themselves; coming to terms with technology in order to 'stay put'; and living more closely with people of their own age. Facilitating the opportunity for older people to make choices and to retain meaningful independence needs to acknowledge the diversity of living arrangements from which they may choose as they weigh up the advantages and disadvantages of living alone or with others. In particular, there is a need to understand the lives of the estimated 665,000 people aged 65 years and over in England and Wales who have significant dementia (Kirby et al, 1998), and of others who may find it difficult to communicate their wishes. As we reach for housing that will support and enable in later life, it is in the interests of all of us to find ways to challenge the institutional ageism that has contributed to the development of most currently available forms of housing and support. There are parallels to be drawn here to ongoing debates concerning the lives of people experiencing lifelong disabilities, where conflicting perspectives are offered by the *individual* and *social* models of disability (Marks, 1999).

Moving forward

In summary, people at any age may need support systems, for example help with financing and managing their housing, including setting-up costs and the costs of repairs and improvements; help with cleaning, laundry, shopping, preparing meals; and help with personal care. But in the case of older people, individual limitations are seen as leading to inevitable decline. The 'ageing enterprise' has become a growth industry with a heavily capitalised infrastructure while at the same time ageist attitudes permeate society as a whole. For these reasons there is a protective attitude towards older people which nevertheless devalues old age. We need to re-think.

In the chapters which follow, authors from a range of multi-disciplinary backgrounds – architecture, anthropology, geography, sociology, psychology, social policy and social work – discuss topics which have a direct bearing on how the housing and support needs of older people may be met in the future. They look at ways in which we might develop for our ageing society forms of inclusive housing which recognise our diversity (see Figure 1.1).

There are two parts to the book. In the first, **Policy and technology debates** we look at ways in which forms of accessible housing have been theorised, debated, defined, promoted and resisted. We begin with Julienne Hanson's overview in Chapter Two of the demand for housing among older people and the extent to which living environments have been created which predispose towards disablement for anyone less than fully fit and agile. She makes the case for a paradigm shift from the historic attitude which regards housing as a part of the welfare provision provided *for* vulnerable people *by* a beneficient state, to one where equal access to adequate housing is seen as a right.

The notion that people have a right to a barrier-free home is central to the movement for homes to be built to Lifetime Homes standards (that is, that they are flexible enough to be adapted to suit people as their physical requirements change due to ageing or disability). In Chapter Three Mary Kelly analyses existing housing standards and definitions of housing, which allow differing levels of accessibility and liveability. She profiles Lifetime Homes criteria and describes the benefits that could be derived from their wider implementation to the general housing stock.

Recent moves in these directions have been driven largely by the changing demographics and social structures already discussed in this chapter, and by the economics of providing care and support. We can see continuing shifts in public attitudes to issues of disability and citizens' rights, not least in the revised approach to building access produced by extended building regulations; issues which are explored in Chapter Four by Jo Milner and Ruth Madigan. But, as their study shows, the legacy of many years of specialised housing provision and the entrenched attitudes of many developers call into question whether further progress can be made without recourse to regulation.

Malcolm Fisk takes the concept of the barrier-free environment a step further in Chapter Five, looking at buildings that are equipped to offer active support and empowerment. He discusses the range of technologies already in common use and those that are currently feasible but not yet widely used. In essence these new technologies offer older people possibilities both for monitoring aspects of their own environment and for being monitored as part of a package of care or support. In Chapter Six Mary Marshall describes the particular application of both these possibilities in the case of older people with dementia. Dementia presents particular challenges to designers of living environments and, at the same time, details of design can have a strong impact on the quality of life of people living with dementia. Marshall describes a successful technology project, which was undertaken in central Scotland, and discusses possible reasons, including cost and resistance, for the failure of other local authorities to emulate it.

In Part Two – **New lives for old?** – authors with a considerable range of recent research experience address some of the issues that have arisen in various living environments in which principles of accessibility and social inclusion have been applied to bring people and places together to facilitate different degrees of autonomous living.

In Chapter Seven, the recent research of Brian McGrail, John Percival and Kate Foster is used to highlight developments and issues for three types of housing and care environments and to examine whether and how age-segregated environments affect older people's interactions within and beyond their immediate accommodation. Brian McGrail looks at a particular form of housing – the high-rise block – which has not hitherto been associated with accessibility or, indeed, with age-segregated housing. In his study of experimental applications of technologies to existing tower blocks, McGrail shows how the application of technologies may have profound implications for the future of urban housing provision in our increasingly aged society. John Percival considers the lives of people living in conventional sheltered housing accommodation in three inner London schemes, in a study which raises issues about the role of age-segregated housing in supporting or undermining self-esteem as people grow older. Kate Foster looks at shared housing for people with dementia. Her case study of three Scottish care houses, based on the notion of care within a household, describes housing which purports to offer high quality social care and an unusual level of engagement by residents. She describes what this means in practice for residents and questions the extent to which the concept of a 'home for life' is realistic within shared social environments.

In Chapter Eight Maria Brenton looks at another way of organising age-segregated congregate housing in her study of elective CoHousing communities in The Netherlands. These are communities based firmly on principles of self-determination and cooperation, and Brenton describes some of the elements which are essential to making such a scheme work – social relationships, financial arrangements and societal values among them. Decisions to opt for this arrangement are very much individually led, rather than relying on what society will offer.

This change of power and control is also seen in Chapter Nine where Judith Phillips, Miriam Bernard, Simon Biggs and Paul Kingston look at another type of age-segregated environment – the retirement community – which also demands a conscious change of lifestyle. Based on the continuing engagement of older people, the organisation of these communities places more emphasis on active lifestyles and participation in decision making than has been the case in traditional British sheltered housing for example. Until recently the idea of retirement communities has been slow to gather momentum in Britain compared to the United States (US) and parts of Europe, but in the current policy context this might be expected to change. Drawing on their ongoing study of some of the first such communities in England, the authors describe some of the ambiguities in these fledgling communities.

As this brief summary shows, the authors have approached the notion of inclusive housing from a number of directions and in different ways, describing various initiatives and innovations aimed at helping older people to retain both independence and social engagement. They describe aspects of social organisation and technological applications within the context of the built environment. In the penultimate chapter (Chapter Ten), Leonie Kellaher takes a critical look at the underpinning issue of whether it is possible to design a home for life. Considering aspects of the home environment that older people appear to regard as essential, she explores resistance to specially designed environments and asks whether and how the notion of lifetime homes can become more than an ideal.

Finally, in Chapter Eleven Caroline Holland and Sheila Peace consider the concept of inclusive housing: what it means, what it implies and what it demands. We expand on some of the issues that have been raised by the authors in this book and elsewhere. These include aspects of material and social environments, resources, technologies and issues around choice and self-determination. There are no easy answers to the development of a housing provision that is truly inclusive for all of us, but we hope that the chapters in this book will make a useful contribution to the necessary debate.

References

Age Concern (1999) *The millennium papers*, Reports of the debate of the age study groups, London: Age Concern.

Arber, S. and Ginn, J. (1991) *Gender and later life: A sociological analysis of resources and constraints*, London: Sage Publications.

Askham, J., Henshaw, L. and Tarpey, M. (1995) *Social and health authority services for elderly people from black and minority ethnic communities*, Studies in Ageing, Age Concern Institute of Gerontology, King's College London, London: HMSO.

Atkin, K. (1998) 'Ageing in a multi-racial Britain: demography, policy and practice', in M. Bernard and J. Phillips (eds) *The social policy of old age*, London: Centre for Policy on Ageing, pp 163-82.

Audit Commission (1998) *Home alone: The role of housing in community care*, Oxford: Audit Commission Publications.

Audit Commission (2000) *Fully equipped: The provision of equipment to older or disabled people by the NHS and social services in England and Wales*, Oxford: Audit Commission Publications.

Better Government for Older People (1999) 'It's in our hands', report of the conference 'Participation, politics and older people' held at Ruskin College, Oxford, 5-7 July.

Blakemore, K. and Boneham, M. (1994) *Age, race and ethnicity: A comparative approach*, Buckingham: Open University Press.

Bowes, E. (1998) *A way from home: The housing and care needs of black and minority ethnic elders in Tower Hamlets*, London: Labo Housing Association.

Briggs, R. (1993) 'Biological ageing', in P. Bond, P. Coleman and S.M. Peace (eds) *Ageing in society*, London: Sage Publications, pp 53-67.

Bright, G. (1996) *Caring for diversity: The housing care and support needs of older black and ethnic minority people*, London: Odua Housing Association.

Crane, M. (1999) *Understanding older homeless people*, London: Sage Publications.

Crane, M. and Warnes, A.M. (2000) 'Policy and service responses to rough sleeping among older people', *Journal of Social Policy*, vol 29, no 1, pp 21-36.

Davies, B. (1998) 'Shelter-with-care and the community care reforms – notes on the evolution of essential species', in R. Jack (ed) *Residential versus community care: The role of institutions in welfare provision*, Basingstoke: Macmillan, pp 71-111.

Davies, P. and Pearson, J. (1999) 'Gas in relation to other domestic risks', Business Strategy Group Research Report for the Health and Safety Executive, mimeo, Ipswich: HSE.

Denham, C. and White, I. (1998) 'Differences in urban and rural Britain', *Population Trends 91*, Spring, London: Office for National Statistics.

DETR (Department of the Environment, Transport and the Regions) (1998) *English Housing Condition Survey 1996*, London: DETR.

DETR (2000a) *Low demand housing and unpopular neighbourhoods*, Housing Research Summary 114, London: DSS.

DETR (2000b) *Living in Britain 1998*, General Household Survey, London: HMSO.

DSS (Department of Social Security) (2001) 'Change to the state pension age for women' (www.pensionguide.gov.uk)

Evandrou, M. and Falkingham, J. (2000) 'Looking back to look forward: lessons from four birth cohorts for ageing in the 21st century', *Population Trends 99*, Spring, London: Office for National Statistics.

Falkingham, J. (1998) 'Financial (in)security in later life', in M. Bernard and J. Phillips (eds) *The social policy of old age*, London: Centre for Policy on Ageing, pp 93-111.

Fletcher, P. (1991) *The future of sheltered housing – Who cares?*, London: National Federation of Housing Associations.

Forrest, R. and Leather, P. (1998) 'The ageing of the property owning democracy', *Ageing & Society*, vol 18, no 1, pp 35-63.

Forrest, R., Leather, P., Gordon, D. and Pantazis, C. (1995) *Home ownership in the UK: The potential for growth?*, London: Council for Mortgage Lenders.

Ginn, J. and Arber, S. (1998) 'Gender and older age', in M. Bernard and J. Phillips (eds) *The social policy of old age*, London: Centre for Policy on Ageing, pp 142-62.

Goodby, G. (1998) *The case for sheltered housing amongst black and minority ethnic elderly communities in west London*, London: Inquilab Housing Association.

Grundy, E. (1999) 'Intergenerational perspectives in family and household change in mid- and later life in England and Wales', in S. McRae (ed) *Changing Britain: Families and households in the 1990s*, Oxford: Oxford University Press, pp 201-28.

Grundy, E., Murphy, M. and Shelton, N. (1999) 'Looking beyond the household: intergenerational perspectives on living kin and contacts with kin in Great Britain', *Population Trends 97*, Autumn, London: Office for National Statistics, pp 201-28.

Hall, R., Ogden, P. and Hill, C. (1999) 'Living alone: evidence from England and Wales and France for the last two decades', in S. McRae (ed) *Changing Britain: Families and households in the 1990s*, Oxford: Oxford University Press, pp 265-96.

Hancock, R. (1998) 'Housing wealth, income and financial wealth of older people in Britian', *Ageing & Society*, vol 18, no 1, pp 5-33.

Holland, C. (forthcoming) 'Housing histories: older women's experience of home across the life course', Unpublished PhD thesis.

Housing Corporation, The (1998) *Black and minority ethnic housing policy*, London: The Housing Corporation.

Jarvis, C., Hancock, R., Askham, J. and Tinker, A. (1996) *Getting around after 60: A profile of Britain's older population*, London: HMSO.

Jeffery, J. and Seager, R. (1993) *Housing black and minority ethnic elders*, London: Federation of Black Housing Organisations.

Jones, D. (1994) *The numbers game – Black and ethnic minority elders and sheltered accommodation*, London: Anchor Housing Trust.

JRF (Joseph Rowntree Foundation) (1998) 'New indicators show extent of poverty and exclusion in late 1990s Britain', Press release 16 December, York: JRF.

King, D., Hayden, J., Jackson, R., Holmans, A. and Anderson, D. (2000) 'Population of households in England to 2021', *Population Trends 99*, Spring, London: Office for National Statistics.

Kirby, L., Lehmann, P. and Majeed, A. (1998) 'Dementia in people aged 65 years and older: a growing problem?', *Population Trends 92*, Summer, London: Office for National Statistics.

Laing & Buisson (2000) 'Care of elderly people market survey, 2000', in *Laing's Healthcare Market Review 2000-2001*, London: Laing & Buisson, p 169.

Laslett, P. (1989) *A fresh map of life*, London: Weidenfeld and Nicholson.

McCafferty, P. (1994) *Living independently: A study of the housing needs of elderly and disabled people*, London: HMSO.

Marks, D. (1999) *Disability: Controversial debates and psycho-social perspectives*, London: Routledge.

MHLG (Ministry of Housing and Local Government) (1961) *Houses for today and tomorrow*, Report of the Parker Morris Committee, London: HMSO.

Modood, T., Berthoud, R., Lakey, J., Nazroo, J., Smith, P., Virdee, S. and Beishon, S. (1997) *Ethnic minorities in Britain: Diversity and disadvantage*, Fourth National Survey of Ethnic Minorities, London: Policy Studies Institute.

OPCS (Office for Population Censuses and Surveys) (1993) *1991 Census: Household composition, Great Britain*, London: HMSO.

Peace, S.M. (1993) 'The living environments of older women', in M. Bernard and K. Meade (eds) *Women come of age*, London: Edward Arnold, pp 126-45.

Peace, S.M. and Johnson, J. (1998) 'Living arrangements of older people', in M. Bernard and J. Phillips (eds) *The social policy of old age*, London: Centre for Policy on Ageing, pp 56-75.

Peace, S.M., Kellaher, L. and Willcocks, D. (1997) *Re-evaluating residential care*, Buckingham: Open University Press.

Royal Commission on Long Term Care (1999) *With respect to old age: A report by the Royal Commission on Long Term Care*, London: The Stationery Office.

Shaw, C. (2000) '1998-based national population projections for the United Kingdom and constituent countries', *Population Trends 99*, Spring, London: Office for National Statistics.

Statsbase (2000) website of the Government Statistical Service (www.statsbase.gov.uk).

Steele, A. (1999) *A study of the housing and care needs of older people from the black and minority ethnic communities in Derby*, Derby: Methodist Homes.

Tinker, A., Wright, F. and Zeilig, H. (1995) *Difficult-to-let sheltered housing*, London: HMSO.

Wall, R. (1984) 'Residential isolation of the elderly: a comparison over time', *Ageing & Society*, vol 4, no 4, pp 483-505.

Part One
Policy and technology debates

In the first part of this text we raise a number of key issues around the future development of accommodation for people in later life. In describing new initiatives in housing design and regulation, the authors consider macro and micro approaches, and the extent to which mainstream housing can encapsulate accommodation-and-support throughout the life span by experiments in Lifetime Homes and through regulatory frameworks for building guidance. The chapters describe the tensions that exist between the values underpinning universal design, the demands of market forces, and the rights of people whose needs present a special challenge to the generally accepted parameters of housing. Considering how these needs might be met, the authors move on to examine what we mean by 'smart' homes and how technological advances might strengthen personal autonomy, relieve environmental press and prolong independent living. They also raise important ethical issues about these innovations.

TWO

From 'special needs' to 'lifestyle choices': articulating the demand for 'third age' housing

Julienne Hanson

Introduction

It is customary to think of housing for older people as housing for people with 'special needs', but, as society ages, older people's living arrangements will undoubtedly become a major component within mainstream housing. What is more, older people are quite unlike any other 'special needs' category because they are 'our future selves'. This chapter argues that pressures in the UK may already be precipitating a fundamental shift in how housing and care are conceived, produced, procured and experienced by older people. The emerging, more inclusive approach to housing has the potential to transform radically the way in which everyone's 'lifestyle choices' are configured and constrained. In particular, policy decisions and design strategies that are being implemented now could affect the extent to which older people are either incorporated into the mainstream or continue to be 'architecturally disabled' by the residential settings of the future. However, deep-seated social forces may prevent this important debate from receiving adequate public attention, so that the emerging emphasis on offering the next generation of older people a wider spectrum of lifestyle choices could turn out to be largely illusory, particularly for the poorest and most disadvantaged in society.

Medical and architectural disability

In his most recent edition of *Designing for the disabled*, sub-titled *The new paradigm*, Selwyn Goldsmith (1997) sets out his theoretical position on the relationship between 'medical disability' and 'architectural disability'. Medical disability describes a process by which individuals are disabled in that they cannot do things because their bodily functions are impaired. Within the population, there is a continuum running from the most able-bodied and active individuals to the most severely disabled people. Architectural disability refers to how the physical design, layout and construction of buildings and places can confront people with hazards and barriers that make the built environment inconvenient, uncomfortable or unsafe for everyone to use, and may even prevent some people from using it at all. When the built environment is sufficiently generous to meet the needs of all or most medically disabled people, people will not be architecturally disabled by the building. When normal provision is not so accommodating, the people who are not architecturally disabled will be those not inconvenienced by their environment, whereas all those who are inconvenienced will be architecturally disabled, regardless of their physical or medical condition.

Most architectural disability originates in one of two deficits: difficult changes of level or insufficient space. Because of these generic design defects, the built environment is capable of discrimination as harmful and undermining of people's self-esteem as the denial of equal opportunities or verbal abuse. It is not only medically disabled people that are discriminated against by buildings in this way, buildings can also disable children, adults with babies in pushchairs, larger, taller or smaller people, those carrying heavy loads and older people. Some features of buildings may even be inconvenient for average, able-bodied people. Almost everyone experiences problems in using the built environment at some time in their lives. Indeed, one design manual has suggested that as many as 90% of individuals may be architecturally disabled in some way or other (Wylde et al, 1994, p 8).

The process of growing older can make us all vulnerable to impairment and, by implication, to medical or architectural disability. As we age chronologically we experience functional ageing and its associated decline in biological efficiency. The list of impairments associated with ageing is extremely wide and most people cannot predict in advance which problems will affect them. The physical process of ageing varies from individual to individual – it may begin early in the middle years or late in old age. Growing older may be perceived as a mild inconvenience associated with niggling, non-specific symptoms, or it may be experienced as traumatic and severely disabling. Once it is underway, the process can be rapid or slow.

Advances in medicine can help to alleviate some of the worst effects of ageing, but, as these changes take place, some older people become less confident in their abilities or feel more exposed to the risk of an accidental injury, disabling impairment or long-term illness. We may become less resilient and adaptable. We may feel that our independence is threatened, less able to live life to the full, that our horizons are narrowing or that we have to change the habits of a lifetime. Mobility is the most widespread problem associated with growing older and many older people find it difficult to go out alone, climb the stairs, get out of bed or use the bath (Jarvis et al, 1996).

However, lowered physical performance or functional competence may not be simply the inevitable by-product of growing older, it could also be a product of architectural disability or 'environmental deprivation'. This is a state induced by "the necessity of dealing with environments built for younger people" which may render the older person more vulnerable, or more docile and accepting of environmental constraints (Lawton, 1974, p 257). Lawton warns that either a drop in competence or an increase in environmental pressure could account for the apparent negative effects of ageing. More positively, he asserts that small changes in the older person's physical environment may produce a substantial reduction in environmental pressure, so that "the payoff for effective environmental intervention is very high for older people in poor mental or physical health" (Lawton, 1974, p 259). It would appear that this particular form of architectural disability is eminently treatable by 'environmental therapy', with good prospects of improved functional competence and enhanced quality of life.

The picture is therefore not one of unmitigated gloom. Modern healthcare promotes a more positive perception of later life, particularly by stressing the importance to older people's self-esteem of maintaining a full, independent and active life in their own home. Older people enjoy a lifetime of accumulated experience, wisdom and memories. The 'grey vote' and the 'grey purse' are set to become increasingly powerful mechanisms for change as our society ages. This may enhance the power that older people yield and the esteem in which they are held. One important arena for the exercise of 'grey power' could be through greater advocacy for health-engendering, architecturally enabling and non-discriminatory environments.

Older people and disability

Because some of the medical problems faced by people in later life are shared with people who are medically disabled, it is tempting to treat the needs of older people and the needs of disabled people as synonymous, but this would be a dangerous supposition for at least three reasons. First, while it is undoubtedly the case that the risk of medical disability increases with age (Tinker, 1997, pp 71-2), many people remain quite fit and healthy throughout their life. Second, while we *hope* that we may not be disabled in the normal course of events, everyone *expects* to grow older.
Finally, at a very pragmatic level, although the generic problems of architectural disability – changes in level and insufficient space – may adversely affect both people with mobility problems and people in later life, older people are particularly disabled by the condition of the surface underfoot. Falls are the most common environmental problem encountered by older people, and these often result in a fracture that is sufficiently serious to lead to hospitalisation (HASS, 1983; Davies and Pearson, 1999). A fall may sound innocuous, but it can have serious repercussions for the older victim, which reverberate well beyond the accident itself. For example, half of older women and a quarter of older men aged 65 and over who fall and break a hip die within six months. Follow-up studies among older patients show that most falls are due to slipping, tripping or stumbling on level, but poorly maintained surfaces, or to tripping over small objects left around the home (Stell, 1998). Older people need 'walkable' environments.

Macro- versus micro-approaches to design: the genesis of 'special needs'

The degree to which the built environment disadvantages its users and the strategies that are employed to counter architectural disability are different, not just among different groups of users, but in different parts of the world. Goldsmith traces these differences to social attitudes and to the different legal frameworks which result from fundamentally different value systems (Goldsmith, 1997, pp 243-9). For example, the self-help culture that dominates the American way of life has resulted in civil rights legislation that guarantees equality of opportunity for all citizens.

According to this ethos, access to buildings is a matter of civil rights. Eliminating architectural discrimination does not stop at taking the barriers out of the built environment but extends to realising people's lifestyle aspirations. In a US context, living independently is treated as synonymous with the autonomous control of a person's lifestyle – the right to live as one chooses, rather than as an issue of physical independence and the ability to cope alone.

The UK, on the other hand, has no civil rights or written constitution. Its citizens do not have any entitlements other than those granted legally, and even these can be overturned by subsequent legislation. The UK attitude to disability of all types has been exemplified by a culture of welfare provision intended to ensure that disadvantaged individuals and groups are identified and then adequately supported (Goldsmith, 1997, p 244). Special environments have been provided for disabled people wherever possible, so that the designer can respond sensitively to the needs of the particular types of disabled people who will use the building. Goldsmith contrasts these different socio-cultural attitudes – of normalisation and enablement (US) as opposed to specialisation and pragmatism (UK) – as 'macro-environmental' and 'micro-environmental' approaches to design (Goldsmith, 1997, p 92).

A macro-approach to the built environment starts from the assumption that accessibility is a right for everyone – what Goldsmith terms a 'treat-as-normal' starting point (Goldsmith, 1997, p 19). Macro-environmental design aims to extend the parameters of normal provision until no one is excluded. So far as the built environment is concerned, this means that no one should ever be prevented from using a building or public place because of its inappropriate design. The specification can be 'got right' and it is a single definitive package of measures which meets everyone's needs; therefore everyone can be accommodated by normal provision, and the concept of 'special needs' is rendered otiose. Everyone who is disadvantaged by design should be emancipated by a macro-approach to design; everyone becomes a mainstream client.

The micro-approach originates from a 'treat-as-different' assumption (Goldsmith, 1997, p 19). It assumes that people, be they people with mobility problems, sensory impairments, learning difficulties, mental health problems or older people, have special needs which are best served by environments that are designed to meet their specific requirements. To those who adopt a micro-environmental paradigm, offering people the special facilities they so evidently require appears to be a pragmatic response to a practical problem. A 'tailored' micro-approach might involve the adaptation of a house so that it is specifically geared to the needs of an individual inhabitant. A 'categoric' micro-approach would mean special provision for each distinct group of users; blind people, single young people, older people, and so on. Either way, people who need specially adapted environments are treated as 'them' rather than 'us'. They become welfare clients.

The two approaches may start from different societal attitudes and people may feel strongly that one approach is 'better' than the other, but, as Goldsmith points out, insofar as the built environment is concerned they are not mutually exclusive. It is always open to the designer to provide some augmented accommodation or upgrading in order to include the few users whose particular requirements do not fall within the extended scope of 'design for all', even within a macro-approach. This view acknowledges that, however inclusive the provision, there will always be a few whose needs cannot be met by even the most people-friendly building and who therefore require supplementary provision.

This is an important concession, as it can be very cost-effective to design for, say, 90-95% of a building's potential users but extremely costly to cater for the remaining 5-10% whose needs may be unique and thus cannot be specified in advance. This stance is best exemplified by the approach known as 'universal design' that has been widely adopted throughout continental Europe in recent years. The implication of universal design is that there are 'generic needs' as well as 'special needs', and that a design that satisfies generic needs will be one that is appropriate for most people.

Sheltered housing: a micro-approach to third age housing

All welfare or social housing is seen as secondary housing – housing that is for special needs as opposed to primary, mainstream housing. Because the approach is micro, different special needs groups compete with one another for scarce resources. The Housing Corporation (1995) recognised 11 special needs groups, one of which is frail older people. Each of these groups can expect their needs to be met by special, purpose-designed housing, and there exist numerous small, independent initiatives in designing sensitive buildings that are tailored to the precise requirements of each client group. Until very recently, there has been little or no exchange of ideas – particularly among the smaller, independent providers. So, there has been no collective multiplier effect (itself a macro-effect) through which designers and managers of all types of housing could identify generic design issues, share innovations and experiences with one another, or listen to feedback from residents.

Housing for older people who cannot, or prefer not to, occupy mainstream housing is one of the earliest, largest and most developed 'special needs' housing sectors in the UK, originating in the medieval almshouse, the workhouse and the Poor Law Commission. Older people's housing is therefore set firmly with a micro-environmental approach to design. Sheltered or 'warden-assisted accommodation' has been provided for rent by local authorities since the mid-1960s, as part of a drive to release family council housing. Now widespread and more varied in quality, sheltered housing (local authority, RSL and private developments for rent and sale) is the most common form of specialised housing for older people in Britain today.

Most sheltered housing is designed on the assumption that its occupants are still reasonably fit and active (Smith, 1989), and this is particularly the case in sheltered housing for sale. If its occupants become too infirm to cope with their sheltered environment they may be expected to move on to a residential care home, a nursing home or into the geriatric ward of the local hospital. As Robson et al (1997) have recently observed, "some commentators in describing the various categories of housing which are available, seem to hold out the expectation that people will actually pass from one category to another" (p 8). This is one of the most obvious drawbacks of a micro-approach to the design of third age housing. Homes that are closely tailored to a resident's needs at retirement may be unable to respond to their requirements in later life. People who are inconvenienced by their environment are architecturally disabled: they may not be medically disabled at all. Yet they may still have to move, and some older people find the move to a new home environment that provides a more intensive level of personal or medical care distressing or even traumatic.

It is a disturbing fact that many surveys of older people have revealed a significant proportion who have ended up in what they perceive to be the wrong place. In Butler's study of sheltered housing (Butler et al, 1983) and Tinker's study of very sheltered housing (Tinker, 1989), about a quarter of those questioned would have preferred to stay where they were. Studies of residential care homes have also identified a proportion of older people who do not need to be in residential care (Peace et al, 1997). It has even been suggested that only a small proportion of the older residents in nursing homes actually need 'round-the-clock' skilled care, which implies that many others could live more independently if they were supported by a package of domiciliary care or home visiting (Valins and Salter, 1996). As well as the personal cost to the victims of these 'mistakes', financial and social costs are also incurred because traditional skilled nursing home care is particularly expensive to provide. Despite the best of intentions, a micro-approach to the provision of welfare and social housing for older people is failing some of its clients and, some would say, society at large.

Recent trends in older people's housing in the UK are equally clear and well known. There has been a sharp decrease in local authority residential provision and an even greater decrease in geriatric medical provision (Leather, 1999). However, this has been balanced by increased provision in the private and charitable sectors. The role of government has changed from that of being a major provider to that of a purchaser and regulator of provision. Within these policy constraints the micro-approach has flourished, leading to a proliferation of niche-market housing schemes designed for older residents, or perhaps more accurately, aimed at older customers. The problem of humane provision that ensures continuity of care is resolved by devising more and more special purpose housing, but looked at from a local or regional perspective, provision is partial and piecemeal. Many older people do not experience their housing circumstances such that they feel 'in control' or able to exercise reasonable choice as to the type of life they lead. This is another unfortunate by-product of 'thinking micro'.

The traditional model of 'sheltered' housing is no longer able to cope, becoming submerged under a multitude of independent initiatives. Recent design guidance (Robson et al, 1997, pp 8-9) suggests that there are now seven 'levels' in the "housing and care ladder":

1. *Staying put:* in non-specialised and non-adapted mainstream housing, including ageing-in-place or living with relatives.
2. *Retirement housing:* independent dwellings which have been purpose-built or adapted for fit and active older people, who may need some support but can generally look after themselves.
3. *Category 1 sheltered housing:* purpose-built, self-contained dwellings for the more active older people, normally built to mobility standards and grouped together on one site, with a warden in attendance but with minimal communal facilities.
4. *Category 2 sheltered housing:* purpose-built, self-contained dwellings for physically frail older people, normally built to full mobility and

wheelchair standards and grouped together under one roof, with a warden attendance and access to shared facilities and amenities.

5. *Category 2.5 or 'extra-care' sheltered housing:* similar to Category 2 but with extra personal care available when needed, and with an option available to take meals in the company of other residents.
6. *Category 3 homes:* residential care homes for those older people who may be mentally or physically frail and in need of constant personal care or supervision.
7. *Nursing homes and geriatric units:* for older people who are sick or very frail and need qualified nursing care.

Even this list is not comprehensive, as it omits the specialist micro-provision for dementia sufferers and hospices which offer palliative care to those who are terminally ill. It also omits more creative and informal arrangements such as 'granny annexes', private hostels and hotels catering to an older clientele, house-sharing (such as that run by the Abbeyfield societies) and 'fostering' with an unrelated carer.

From 'special needs' to 'lifestyle choices'

Consistently, research has shown that most older people prefer to live independently in their own homes, that is, within ordinary, mainstream housing, for as long as possible (Tinker, 1994, pp 57-82). Government policy encourages people to remain in their own home, supported where necessary by domiciliary services that complement the care provided by family and friends. Whether one looks at it emotionally or financially, the family home is the biggest single investment that many people make in their lives. Even for those living in rented or social housing, the home may be a focus for their hopes, dreams, achievements and memories. Most people's homes connect them into a social network of neighbours, relatives and friends. It is this that many older people value most and are most fearful of losing. Above all, a home of one's own is the symbol of full adult status and of the ability to lead an independent life, necessary attributes of being part of mainstream society.

As we grow older, most of us would prefer to remain first-class citizens in ordinary, mainstream housing. Most older people also want a home which is comfortable to live in and convenient for people to visit. Conversely, they also want the houses of their relatives, friends and neighbours to be easily 'visitable'. But ordinary, mainstream houses in the UK are ill-suited to growing older as most were not designed with accessibility in mind; they may be too big, too inconvenient, too expensive to run, or in the wrong place. Some older houses may allow little or no scope for upgrading to improve accessibility. Many new houses are designed as 'little boxes', built on two storeys and to space standards that do not accommodate older people's lifestyles. It is a sad fact that in later life some people still feel so constrained by their home environment that they experience its influence as almost wholly negative and disabling, compelled to regret 'that it should come to this'.

Nevertheless, what would suit most older people best, if they are not to suffer architectural discrimination, is conveniently designed ordinary housing, *not* special housing. Where people do consider an alternative to mainstream housing, this should spring from a positive lifestyle choice to live that way, rather than from a decision forced by present home circumstances being (or being deemed) insufficiently supportive and enabling.

The way to achieve change for the better has to be *paradigmatic*, that is, to substitute a macro-approach to design for the current micro-approach. Admittedly this requires an unprecedented shift away from our current preoccupation with 'dismembering' the housing stock into innumerable special needs groupings, but it is one which captures the spirit of the age. Moreover, there are good practical reasons why such a paradigmatic shift might be engineered by a consideration of older people's living arrangements, for older people will become a majority in society rather than a 'special' group. If anything, it will be the able-bodied, young, strong and independent adult male – the yardstick against which all previous design solutions have been measured – who will be in relatively short supply. If any constituency of building users is able to effect the shift from special needs to lifestyle choices, it should by rights be older people. Within the context of an ageing society, a macro-environmental approach may even be politically and economically inevitable.

Macro equals 'mainstream'

Within existing mainstream housing the current thinking is still micro. It is best exemplified by 'care and repair', 'ageing in place', 'staying put' and 'handy-person' schemes. The common denominator of all these initiatives is the emphasis that they have placed on enabling older people to live an independent life in their own homes within the community, through physical modifications and the provision of specialised aids and equipment.

At best, this process is geared to tailoring older people's homes to suit their individual requirements, organising the process by which the necessary repairs are carried out and ensuring that these are made to a sufficiently high standard to represent 'good value for money'. But, as one survey showed (Allen et al, 1997), some assessments of older people's needs may be rudimentary and the adaptations technically-led, aiming to put the home into a good state of repair rather than to help the occupant to achieve a more fulfilling way of life. Waiting times can be protracted, so that, "by the time we got there, they'd died" (Allen et al, 1997, p 49). A lack of foresight may be shown about progressive problems, so that earlier adaptations may conflict with an older person's subsequent requirements. Often the client's ideal solution is undermined by compromises that balance regulations, resource management and the agenda of the provider, who may be concerned that, once adapted, the property will be of little use to anyone else. The opportunity is rarely taken to make adaptations less client-specific or to modify the home environment so that it could suit a wide range of future occupants, although as one special needs housing officer has observed:

> "Possibly the adaptations could be done in a more generic way rather than very specifically, just for that person. That we could look at something which is going to be a bit more useful – it may be a bit more costly initially, but its going to be a bit more useful in the future for possibly ... for somebody else." (cited in Allen et al, 1997, p 54)

As far as new homes are concerned, the design standard for a macro-approach has been set by the Lifetime Homes movement, an assertively inclusive approach that was launched by the Joseph Rowntree Foundation in 1989 (see Chapter Three of this book). It takes as its starting point the view that most of the difficulties that are currently experienced in mainstream housing could be eliminated by simple design modifications to ensure that no one is the victim of architectural discrimination. The Lifetime Homes standard is based on 16 generic principles ranging from "wide doors and hallways" to "easy access to the bath and WC" (see Table 3.1 in Chapter Three, p 65). This standard could substantially enhance the capacity of ordinary, mainstream homes to accommodate the majority of risks which expose people to architectural disability, and residents should find that houses which incorporate these principles are more flexible and spacious than a normal family house.

A more radical, macro-community approach has been adopted by the

Habinteg Housing Association, which builds mixed developments of 75% family lifetime homes and 25% wheelchair dwellings. Having consulted their clients who asserted that they did not want to be located together in "a cripples' corner", Habinteg scatters the wheelchair homes throughout their developments so that residents with mobility problems are fully integrated within their local community. Residents appear to appreciate the anonymity of just being neighbours in an environment which does not draw attention to any difficulties or personal problems which they may have themselves, or that a family member may be experiencing (Habinteg, 1997, 1998).

From a purely financial point of view, adopting a macro-approach to the provision of new homes makes sound business sense, as it will undoubtedly lower the demand for subsidies later on to adapt today's new housing to any problems that its occupants may encounter in the future. More older people should be able to remain for longer within mainstream housing and to spend less time in care settings. A groundswell of opinion is emerging that there is no good reason why tomorrow's public purse should pay for today's design defects.

However, newly built homes account for just a fraction of the total housing stock. Because of the many design problems which beset older housing, it would be difficult, although not impossible, to shift to a macro-approach in the case of existing homes. Of approximately 20.4 million existing dwellings (DETR, 1998, p 13), about 69% are owner-occupied, 17% are local authority dwellings, 9% are in the private rented sector and 5% are owned by RSLs. Few of these homes were built with accessibility in mind, but all will fall into one of four possible categories when measured against a 'macro-environmental design standard' able to accommodate the widest possible client group. They include homes that:

- accommodate the widest possible group without any modifications at all;
- require minor modifications, such as the incorporation of aids and appliances or alterations to internal, non-load bearing partitions;
- need changes to the construction, structure or layout of the home;
- are unable to be adapted at all, or only by carrying out such major and expensive alterations that to adapt the home would not be cost-effective.

At present, we do not know what percentage of existing homes falls into each of these categories, although this could, in theory, be determined by a national audit of the housing stock.

If it were possible to determine the status of older dwellings in this way, a macro-approach to supporting the long-term, changing social needs of an ageing society would aim to upgrade all existing homes to a new 'generic' macro-environmental design standard based on universal design criteria, wherever it is feasible to do so. This would both increase the numbers of older houses that would suit most people's needs (and hence consumer choice) and would also identify those homes which could not be so adapted. The magnitude of the task would be considerable and the investment required substantial, but it could well prove more cost-effective in the long term than the partial, piecemeal and temporary arrangements that frame current adaptations.

Macro equals 'retirement community'

The civil rights legislative framework that governs the delivery of housing and care for older people in the US has led to a very different conceptualisation of macro-environmental provision from the mainstream orientation that has been described above. In the US, less emphasis has been placed on the need for older people to remain independent in their own homes, supported by care in the community. Rather, a greater emphasis has been given to guaranteeing older clients an appropriate balance of skilled nursing and personal care in the group residential setting of their choice, that is, as a member of an age-specific 'retirement community'. Legislation stipulates that older people should have the right to choose a safe, skilled, supportive and protected environment that suits their needs and their budget; that they should have access to the information which enables them and their relatives to make informed choices; and that people should retain control over their lives once they are there. For those who continue to live at home beyond the point where assistance is required, the entitlement to domiciliary services is limited and life may be a struggle.

However, retirement communities in the US have suffered from a number of drawbacks that have resulted in a growing unwillingness on the part of families to entrust their older relatives to care. Regimes are often medically-driven and perceived as institutional. The residential environment may be designed to comply with a 'prosthetic' model for care in which appropriate space standards and levels of functional care are offered but the need to imbue domestic life with meaning is ignored. Few conventional retirement communities are organised according to the alternative 'therapeutic' model which stresses the importance of the home as a means to personal growth and rehabilitation (Lawton, 1974), and many are unwilling or unable to offer the older resident an open-ended commitment to lifetime care.

'Assisted living' is now widely accepted in the US as a progressive, radical compromise between the retirement community and the traditional nursing home. Normally, it consists of a number of self-contained apartments, often located in a landscaped, parkland setting, which have at their core a facility such as a 'wellness' centre, nursing home, health campus or hospital, where primary healthcare is available for residents. A professional level of personal and medical care in a 'homely' group setting aims to maximise the capacity of every resident to live independently, but with a fallback position of 'round-the-clock' skilled care on site for those who need it. This avoids the trauma of moving older residents in a succession of placements that offer increasing levels of care. Assisted living therefore aims to combine independent living with high quality care in a way that claims to be cost-effective and is tailored to the evolving needs of each client.

Both the residential environment and the management strategy are intended to be resident-centred – the shift in ethos has been described elsewhere as from 'high tech' to 'high touch' (Valins and Salter, 1996, p 13). The 20 core directives that underpin the assisted living model for housing and care have been summarised (Regnier et al, 1995, pp 222-51) as follows:

1. A residential setting which offers clients a uniquely-prescribed package of health and personal care services.
2. Privacy, autonomy and independence.
3. Choice and control.
4. A therapeutic environment.
5. A residential model, housing with services, not institutional medical care.
6. A commitment to 'ageing in place'.
7. Community integration, a building and policy of outreach which fits into and builds links to its surrounding context.
8. Apartments which are a complete home, supporting all aspects of domestic life.
9. An environment which offers clients multi-sensory stimulation.
10. Strong indoor–outdoor physical, visual and psychological connections.
11. Functionally and behaviourally responsive amenities and common areas.

12. Flexible and creative regulations and oversight.
13. Decentralised management and decision making.
14. Supportive family, staff and resident relationships.
15. Uniquely-prescribed services for each client.
16. Risk management, so that residents can safely exercise independence.
17. Continuing care for the physically and mentally frail.
18. A sensitive humane philosophy of care, delivered by trained staff.
19. A reduction of the cost burden by augmenting formal care with self-care and family support.
20. The development of subsidising mechanisms that shift the care burden from nursing homes to assisted living.

Public policy in the UK tends to be against building for large concentrations of older people in one place (Bookbinder, 1991). However, one assisted living retirement village – Hartrigg Oaks – has been designed recently for the Joseph Rowntree Foundation as an experiment that aims to widen the lifestyle choices open to older people in the UK. The development comprises 152 one- and two-bedroom bungalows with a residential and nursing home at its core. Residents pay an entry fee which is refundable if they leave or die, plus an annual service charge which gives an entitlement to home services such as cleaning, laundry, shopping, food preparation, gardening, personal care or the administration of medications. A resident who requires a more intensive level of personal care or who needs round-the-clock nursing care, may have to move to the 'care centre' at the heart of the development, but they should not have to move out of Hartrigg Oaks because of an architectural or a medical disability.

For those residents who are fit and well, Hartrigg Oaks is an expensive way to live until the level of support that is available is actually needed, but for those (moderately wealthy) older people who are concerned about how they will cope with increasing frailty, the assisted living approach may offer peace of mind: "... you either have a happy life and lose your money or a lousy life and get your money's worth" (Kohler, 1996, p 17). The design of the physical environment plays a major role in helping residents to 'age in place' and, insofar as assisted living aims to be enabling, inclusive and non-discriminatory, it is a macro-environmental approach for those who have chosen this lifestyle (issues which are discussed in more detail in Chapter Nine). However, most older people cannot afford these developments at present unless they are heavily subsidised; preserving 'affordability' is a continuing issue for the assisted living movement in many countries.

Recent published examples from the US (AIA, 1997) suggest that widening access by driving down capital and continuing costs, may be driving up the physical size and architectural scale of the latest generation of assisted living communities. This is done to justify the expensive skilled nursing facility required by a small minority of residents towards the end of their life, which is crucial to the open-ended undertaking that no one's rights to continuing care will be infringed. As Regnier et al have observed, "in assisted living, the smaller the number of residential units, the more difficult it is to provide in-depth, twenty-four-hour care" (1995, p 28) and, elsewhere, "the single largest challenge architects face in designing these facilities is creating an attractive residential setting that is large enough to meet economy-of-scale requirements for efficient, functional service production" (p 90). This leads to a paradox, in which the rights of the few to skilled nursing care may conflict with the expectations of the many that they will continue to live in a domestic residential setting. As the building grows larger, there is a risk that it will become more institutional in its appearance and in its management style, and that it will be experienced as such by its residents.

The architectural strategy to minimise this risk is to cluster the apartments into smaller units which form the basic building blocks of a physical and organisational hierarchy, but this may in principle exacerbate rather than ameliorate the tendency to institutionalisation (Hanson and Hillier, 1987). Research carried out in the UK on housing that has adopted a similar design strategy of breaking down the group home into smaller self-contained and autonomous units is either ambivalent or cautious about the ability of such segmentation to induce independence and informality among residents (Peace and Harding, 1980; Booth and Philips, 1987; Brearley, 1990). Some negative effects, such as increased workload, isolation and stress have also been noted in the case of care staff (Wright, 1995).

Within the UK, the concept of 'extra-care' grouped housing has been developed particularly by housing associations and some private sector providers of older people's housing as a more cost-effective alternative to assisted living (Hanover Housing Association and Anchor Trust are among the leading Registered Social Landlord providers of such housing for rent, while Bovis has pioneered the approach within the private rented sector). The principal ingredients of extra-care are:

- grouped, fully independent one or two-bedroom flats;
- generous communal daytime living facilities and grounds;
- location in the heart of a thriving locality, to achieve maximum integration within the local community;
- a flexible, round-the-clock, onsite management service which takes care of building maintenance, advice and support to residents and the delivery of personal care;
- local partnerships with social services departments and domiciliary healthcare teams;
- packaging personal savings and public subsidies to widen access and increase affordability.

The key difference between extra-care and assisted living is that the extra-care service does not include a specialist nursing unit. It does not promise to cope with every condition that arises from declining health. The concept is, perhaps, closer to the European paradigm of universal design than the US's fully inclusive framework of normalisation and enablement in that it is acknowledged that extra-care housing can respond to the problems of 90-95% of older people, but the remaining 5-10% may be excluded because of a medical condition. Residents who need intensive nursing care go to the local hospital, as they would if they were living in mainstream housing, but the design of the home environment and the level of domiciliary support from the local community healthcare team following discharge from hospital, are usually sufficient for rehabilitation.

Extra-care apartments are designed from the outset to accommodate a range of age-related impairments. They are based on the premise that good design can minimise the medical conditions and architectural disabilities associated with ageing. The aim is to provide an enabling environment in which older people can come to terms with increasing frailty, while continuing to enjoy active, independent and fulfilling lives. Residents can join the community with a degree of security that they can 'age in place'. Residents are encouraged to remain independent, mobile and connected to mainstream society if they so wish (Tinker, 1997).

Because the service does not extend to close nursing care, which is provided 'in the community' as if the client were living independently in mainstream housing, the continuing, shared costs of care are reduced and the building can be smaller and more domestic in scale. But the smallest schemes often cannot afford generous common amenities and the service charge to residents may be correspondingly high. Depending on the extent of the shared facilities, most extra-care housing comprises between 40 and 60 bed spaces. The most popular building layout for new-build schemes takes the form of a separate, group retirement court, but other extra-care schemes have been developed from remodelled sheltered housing, some more successfully than others. In general, however, there seems to be a lower inherent risk than in the assisted living communities of the US that UK extra-care schemes will become impersonal and institutional, in either building morphology or management style.

Macro equals 'all-age communities'

Some local authorities are now beginning to develop a radical approach to community-based care that is even more macro-environmental and inclusive in that it is:

- based on the concept of an 'all-age community'; and
- able to support a wide variety of incomes and tenures.

This approach can be illustrated by the Holly Street Comprehensive Estate Initiative in the London Borough of Hackney (Hammill, 1998; Holly Street Comprehensive Estate Initiative, 1998). Holly Street is one of the largest housing regeneration projects of its kind in the world. It took shape in 1991, in a proposal to demolish one of Hackney's most notorious 1960s system-built housing estates. The area has now become a mixed-tenure residential neighbourhood of streets and squares, containing a mixture of mainstream housing for sale in shared-equity ownership, self-build housing and housing association rented homes. The tenants of the old estate were involved in the design of the new neighbourhood from its inception. Having appreciated all too well that architecture can discriminate or stigmatise by its appearance and imagery as well as in its layout and detailed design, most people wanted to live in ordinary houses on an ordinary street, in a neighbourhood that would not be perceived by others as either municipal or obviously experimental. Many of the tenants had moved onto the estate with young families in the 1960s and then 'aged in place', and the area had an unusually high concentration of older residents who had survived the decline of the area into a 'sink estate'. The intention was that they could form the nucleus of a more stable and buoyant local community, if only they could be persuaded to stay.

Today, Holly Street can be conceived of as having all the ingredients of assisted living, but embedded within a traditional urban neighbourhood rather than isolated in a parkland setting. The various combinations of housing and care which meet the needs of more able and more dependent older people co-exist in one locality, and the boundaries between the different forms of housing and care are almost invisible to the passer-by on the street. Local residents can still choose (or can be placed in) the appropriate package of housing and care by moving within the locality, thus lessening the trauma of dislocation from home, family and social network.

The older residents of Holly Street have been offered a wide choice in selecting their future housing. They could exchange their council house for one of the smaller dwellings in the new, mainstream housing. If necessary, they could work with an occupational therapist to tailor their new home to their needs before moving in. Embedded within the urban fabric of Holly Street is a tower with residents aged over 50 – one of the original tower blocks on the old estate that has been completely refurbished and provided with a 24-hour concierge service, CCTV surveillance and remote sensing that alerts the care team of any sudden changes in a resident's daily routine. One third of the flats are planned to wheelchair standards and all the residents are offered a choice of internal fixtures and fittings. Thus, although the tower was not designed explicitly to comply with Category 1 sheltered housing, it provides an equivalent level of care. Holly Street also contains a Category 2 sheltered housing scheme with a resource centre on the ground floor that provides a day centre, lunch club and range of personal services for local residents, and a Category 2.5 scheme of 40 apartments for frail older people. (Other ideas concerning high rise blocks are given in Chapter Seven.)

Pooling housing and care at a neighbourhood scale holds out the potential to provide a seamless service in which each and every resident can choose the package which most accurately reflects their current and future needs. It can be conceived of as a dispersed or 'virtual' assisted living community that is fully incorporated within its surroundings. But, this can only succeed if there is a commitment to:

- a collaborative culture among housing, social services and health service agencies and professions locally;
- entering into a partnership with local communities and the individuals who make up that community;
- an integrated approach to location, transport, services, amenity, long-term financial viability and environmental sustainability, as well as to housing and health;

• planning ahead rather than implementing coping strategies.

This inclusive macro-environmental approach could even begin to challenge 'special needs' categories in favour of an approach that integrates housing, health and care to suit everyone's needs. In an inclusive approach to housing and care, old, young, able-bodied and disabled should all be enabled to live together as neighbours if they so wish, in ordinary, well-designed homes that are flexible in tenure and supported by a wide range of health and personal services.

This would undoubtedly be a radical departure from the pragmatic, divisive, 'treat-as-different' way of designing the special and sometimes exclusive forms of housing and care that we are used to in the UK. However, it does imply one important continuity with the way that we are accustomed to conceptualise, plan and design the built environment. In the long-standing debate about whether local communities should be homogeneous or heterogeneous in their social composition, UK thinking usually advocates a heterogeneous, balanced approach which mirrors local demographic trends, whereas in the US it is normally assumed that a community is a 'community of interest' and therefore homogeneous in its social, economic, ethnic and cultural make-up (Rapoport, 1980-81, pp 65-77). In all probability, the way in which 'macro' is interpreted in the UK and the US will reflect these divergent social tendencies. This is a more fundamental distinction than the rather obvious policy contrast that was drawn earlier between a welfare tradition and a history of civil rights legislation. It suggests that, in the UK, the residential setting of a macro-approach will strive to remain balanced and integral with mainstream housing whereas in the US we have already seen that a macro-approach results in distinctive, age-specific retirement communities which remain separate from mainstream society.

It was observed earlier that a micro-approach can operate at an individual level (a tailored approach) or at the level of the group (a categoric approach). It follows that a macro-approach can, in principle, involve generic adaptation so that the whole of the environment is geared to meet most individuals' needs, or involve a categoric approach, which would still imply special provision that reflects the distinctive lifestyle aspirations of society's constituent groups. If we do eventually switch to a macro-approach within the UK – and the pressure of public opinion as society ages may already be working to effect just such a shift – we shall also need to decide (or, more likely, fail to take clear policy decisions about) how the balance is to be maintained between 'generic' and 'categoric' groups within society at large. This is likely to exert a major influence both on the types of lifestyle choices that are available to people in the future and how integrated or segregated they are likely to be within mainstream society.

Lifestyle choices: the power to choose

It seems obvious and wholly beneficial that designers should help more people become mainstream customers by adopting design strategies that seek to eliminate or minimise architectural discrimination and disability (Goldsmith, 1997). The assumption is that architecture that is inclusive and emancipatory will, of itself, empower more people to choose how they would like to live. Instead of being allocated to one of a small range of special residential settings on the basis of externally-ascribed criteria such as health status, competence or temperament, older people should be enabled to elect their preferred 'lifestyle' by selecting the domestic milieu which best expresses their self-identity (Giddens, 1991).

This may well be, but it would be wise to exercise caution. The idea of offering older people ways to express their independence, dignity, identity and lifestyle through universal design and community-based services is, in many ways, reminiscent of a much older notion within welfare service provision, that is, the idea of 'community care' which precipitated mental health services provision out of the hospitals in the 1960s and 1970s.

It is not appropriate here to evaluate the success or failure of 'care in the community', since this has been undertaken comprehensively elsewhere (for example, Baldwin, 1993), but it may be apposite to note the role that these changes in institutional structures may play with respect to wider social transformations. As Townsend has observed:

> Despite the powerful movements in favour of community care, the emergence of that sector cannot be said to have properly materialised. This is not easy to explain. The failure to achieve a shift in priorities has to be explained partly, as I have implied, in relation to the powerful vested interests of certain branches of the professions, unions of hospital staffs and certain sections of the administration.... The failure to shift the balance of health and welfare policy towards community care has also to be explained in relation to function of institutions to regulate and confirm inequality in society, and indeed to regulate deviation from the fundamental social values of self-help, domestic independence, personal thrift, willingness to work, productive effort and family care.

> Institutions serve subtle functions in reflecting the positive structural and cultural changes taking place in society. (Townsend, 1981, p 22)

This is not to suggest that the clearly articulated desire to dissolve the categories of welfare provision that relied on a division of the world into 'them' and 'us' is so much empty rhetoric, but to admit that the changes that are actually occurring in housing and care for older people may be an outward and visible manifestation of a redefinition of class, culture and identity that is currently taking place in late modern British society.

As the more traditional, rigid and reliable social groupings that were based on family and social class give way to more amorphous, ephemeral and risky groupings based on shared attributes and values, it is inevitable that there will be some losers as well as winners in the redistribution of power and resources. Those older people who can afford to reap the benefits of a macro approach to environmental design will probably feature among the winners, whether they live within the mainstream or as part of a retirement community. Those who remain trapped in poor quality, architecturally disabling housing are more likely to lose out if the pragmatic, welfare-oriented 'special needs' paradigm is jettisoned in favour of 'lifestyle choices' based on inclusive design. It is therefore important that we acknowledge the role that people's home circumstances play in the expression of individual and social difference, and that changes in housing and care that rather obviously benefit the better-off are monitored and evaluated to ensure that the needs of the poorest, least articulate and most disadvantaged in society are not forgotten.

References

AIA (American Institute of Architects) (1997) *Design for ageing 1996-7 Review*, Ageing Design Research Program of the American Institute for Architectural Research, Washington DC: AIA Press.

Allen, C., Clapham, D., Franklin, B. and Parker, J. (1997) *The right home? Assessing housing needs in community care*, Cardiff: Centre for Housing Management and Development/Department of City and Regional Planning/Cardiff University.

Baldwin, S. (1993) *The myth of community care: An alternative neighbourhood model of care*, London: Chapman and Hall.

Bookbinder, D. (1991) *Housing options for older people*, London: Age Concern England.

Booth, T. and Philips, D. (1987) 'Group living in homes for the elderly: a comparative study of the outcomes of care', *British Journal of Social Work*, vol 17, pp 1-20.

Brearley, P.C. (1990) *Working in residential homes for elderly people*, London: Tavistock.

Butler, A., Oldman, C. and Greve, J. (1983) *Sheltered housing for the elderly: Policy, practice and the consumer*, London: Allen and Unwin.

Davies, P.F. and Pearson, J. (1999) 'Gas in relation to other domestic risks', Business Strategy Group Research Project for the Health and Safety Executive, mimeo.

DETR (Department of the Environment, Transport and the Regions) (1998) *English House Condition Survey 1996*, London: HMSO.

Giddens, A. (1991) *Modernity and self-identity: Self and society in the later modern age*, Cambridge: Polity Press.

Goldsmith, S. (1997) *Designing for the disabled: The new paradigm*, Oxford: Architectural Press.

Habinteg (1997) *Homes for a lifetime*, Habinteg Housing Association Annual Report.

Habinteg (1998) Personal communication to the author by Mike Donnelly, Chief Executive of Habinteg Housing Association.

Hammill, P. (1998) Personal communication with Patrick Hammill of Levitt Bernstein Associates, Project Architect for the redevelopment of Holly Street, June.

Hanson, J. and Hillier, B. (1987) 'The architecture of community: some new proposals on the social consequences of architectural and planning decisions', *Architecture and Behaviour*, vol 3, no 3, pp 249-73.

HASS (Home Accident Survey Systems) (1983) *Elderly: Accidents to the elderly, a study of a sub-set of the Home Accident Surveillance Systems (HASS) data for 1983*, London: Consumer Safety Unit, Department of Trade and Industry.

Holly Street Comprehensive Estate Initiative (1998) 'Holly Street Information Pack', London: Levitt Bernstein Associates.

Housing Corporation, The (1995) *New funding arrangements for special needs schemes*, Circular 05/95, London: The Housing Corporation.

Jarvis, C., Hancock, R., Askham, J. and Tinker, A. (1996) *Getting around after 60: A profile of Britain's older population*, London: HMSO.

Kohler, M. (1996) cited in an article by R. Bayley, 'Retiring gracefully', *Search*, issue 26, Winter, pp 16-17.

Lawton, M.P. (1974) 'Social ecology and the health of older people', *American Journal of Public Health*, vol 64, no 3, March, pp 16-17.

Leather, P. (1999) *Age file: A fact file about older people in England*, Kidlington: Anchor Research.

Peace, S.M. and Harding, S.D. (1980) *The Haringey Group-living Evaluation Project*, Research Report No 2, London: Centre for Environmental and Social Studies in Ageing, University of North London.

Peace, S.M., Kellaher, L. and Willcocks, D. (1997) *Re-evaluating residential care*, Buckingham: Open University Press.

Rapoport, A. (1980-81) 'Neighbourhood heterogeneity or homogeneity: the field of man environment studies', *Architecture and Behaviour*, vol 1, no 1, pp 65-77.

Regnier, V., Hamilton, J. and Yatabe, S. (1995) *Assisted living for the aged and frail*, New York, NY: Columbia University Press.

Robson, D., Nicholson, A.M. and Barker, N. (1997) *Homes for the third age: A design guide for extra care sheltered housing*, London: Spon.

Smith, M.E.H. (1989) 'The needs of special groups', in *Guide to housing*, 3rd edn, London: The Housing Trust, pp 361-7.

Stell, I. (1998) 'Older people, morbidity, and the environment: medical aspects', Paper delivered to interdisciplinary module on housing and the environment for older people, Age Concern Institute of Gerontology, King's College, London, 13 January.

Tinker, A. (1989) *An evaluation of very sheltered housing*, London: HMSO.

Tinker, A. (1994) *The role of housing policies in the care of elderly people, in caring for frail elderly people*, Paris: OECD Publications.

Tinker, A. (1997) *Older people in modern society*, 4th edn, London: Longman.

Townsend, P. (1981) 'The structured dependency of the elderly: creation of social policy in the twentieth century', *Ageing & Society*, vol 1, no 1, pp 5-28.

Valins, M. and Salter, D. (1996) *Futurecare*, Oxford: Blackwell.

Wright, F. (1995) *Opening doors: A case study of multi-purpose residential homes*, Age Concern Institute of Gerontology Studies in Ageing, London: Age Concern Institute of Gerontology.

Wylde, M., Baron-Robbins, A. and Clark, S. (1994) *Building for a lifetime: The design and construction of fully accessible homes*, Newtown, CT: Taunton Press.

THREE

Lifetime Homes

Mary Kelly

Introduction

> We must consider our needs in later life in order to provide maximum choice, ensuring independence, mobility and comfort without leaving behind the essential aspect of aesthetics. It is no original idea but everyone must recall that the lifecycle begins in the womb and ends in the grave. In between these two unavoidable points there are enumerable [sic] stages of development. As Darwin has taught us, we are constantly within a process of 'selective evolution'. Some have the good fortune to be born healthy and remain that way for a long time. Some have the misfortune to be born with disabilities and others may acquire them somewhere along the way. (Bieber, 1988, p 31)

Today, designing with only the young and fit as target users and buyers of homes is a narrow and short-sighted approach. Designing with the needs of later life in mind extends consumer choice and widens the potential client group – which makes good business sense and provides a challenge to architects and designers. Older people do not generally become more mobile and active than they were when younger, but a product or element designed to suit an older person will generally be just as useful to a younger person.

In Britain, decisions about the standards, planning and design of social, low-cost or rented housing have rarely been made in consultation with the people who are going to live in them. Such decisions have almost always been made by housing professionals, managers, developers, architects and planners. Statistics show that few of these professionals are women, have serious disabilities or are from minority ethnic groups. They are also unlikely to have experienced old age and may be unused to conducting and combining many of the everyday routines of housework and childcare. But this has not prevented professionals from designing housing without finding out what people's different needs are, or how they might like to use the space(s) within their homes. As a result, there are many examples of social housing in which the design and layout create problems and inconveniences for the people who live there.

One of the objectives of recent project and research work has been to demonstrate to housing providers that people's differences – such as their levels of income, culture, ethnicity, age and mobility, and whether they have responsibilities for children or other dependants – create different priorities for them. What is regarded as adequate housing by one person may not be considered adequate by another, and this indicates that a choice of types of accommodation should be available.

Unfortunately recent surveys into the condition and standards of existing housing stock in Britain show that most new-build low-cost accommodation fails to reflect the needs of a large proportion of the population (DETR, 2000). Whether through inadequacies of internal space or of the planning of facilities, both in the home and within the larger community, the tasks of daily living can be made very difficult for a large number of people. Evidence of this is revealed in the amount of money spent each year on adaptations to existing housing and in the cost of having to move to other, more flexible or appropriate buildings or locations. While accepting that the cost of improvements due to inherent limitations in much existing housing are a largely unavoidable expense, great savings would be made if people who wished, or chose to do so, could continue to live in their current homes.

The question of choice and issues around quality in the design of social housing in Britain must be considered against the realities of the overall, increasingly inadequate, supply of affordable rented accommodation. Cutbacks in investment in social housing have increased pressure on local authorities and housing associations, which may find that they are focusing on meeting rising demands rather than on the quality of the housing provided. Although this is understandable, in the long term it only creates a continuing cycle of disadvantage. Homeless people and overcrowded households frequently find that the new-build housing they are offered has deficiencies in quality as well as poor local amenities. For many people the long-term effects of living in poor housing perpetuates social disadvantages and inequalities which have already been created by differences in gender, wealth and opportunity, and from which it is hard to escape without assistance. In the search for 'value for money' and short-term housing solutions, the costs of extra welfare benefits or medical expenses resulting from inadequate standards or unsuitable housing are rarely calculated or taken into account by housing providers.

Current pressure for sustainability should influence policy makers and housing providers to acknowledge that the provision of adequate and widely usable housing is an essential part of any community. The provision of housing by numbers as a short-term measure to meet demand is no longer an affordable or sustainable option. More attention must be given to the fact that homes and their surroundings are vital personal and community resources that enable individuals to lead healthy, productive and independent lives. Providing the right long-term environments for individuals and communities to flourish will be an investment for future societies.

The concept of 'lifetime homes' was first proposed by the Helen Hamlyn Foundation in October 1989 (Helen Hamlyn Foundation and Rowe, 1989), and has since been developed further through the work of the Joseph Rowntree Foundation's (JRF) Lifetime Homes Group. This group of housing experts (including a Lifetime Homes Technical Working Group) was founded to provide advice to the JRF and to devise criteria that would ensure that new housing developments would meet the needs of both current and future occupants. 'Lifetime homes' were originally termed 'multi-generational housing' in order to promote the theme of 'a home for life'. While not aimed at any particular age or client group, Lifetime Homes address the different needs of families and households by house design that creates accessible homes, which will adapt to the changing needs of all the people who live in them as they age and change, and to meet the varying needs of different occupiers of that same home.

Housing today: current guidelines and standards

New development of any sort, whatever its use or tenure, must meet the standard criteria set out in building regulations in relation to structure, services, energy efficiency, components, fixtures and fittings, and so on. Part M of the building regulations deals specifically with the design of access and facilities for disabled people, but until October 1999, this related solely to public buildings. Thus, the guidelines followed by those designing and developing housing projects until that time were very much dictated by the interests of those who funded and briefed the work. This chapter considers the position of some major players in housing development: The Housing Corporation, Scottish Homes and local authorities.

The main players

The Housing Corporation

Until the late 1980s, most new social housing was developed by and for local authorities. Changes in central government policies and funding, particularly through the 1988 Housing Act and the 1989 Local Government Act during the latter years of the Conservative government, imposed restrictions on local authority housing. New affordable or social housing for rent was subsequently provided primarily through the development programmes of various housing associations – known as Registered Social Landlords (RSLs) since 1996, which exist throughout the UK. Private sector housing for sale and for rent is provided by different contractors, some operating locally, some nationally.

Funding for social housing is provided in part by The Housing Corporation in the form of a Social Housing Grant (SHG) (formerly a Housing Association Grant [HAG]), perhaps combined with private sector finance. The Housing Corporation approves applications from competing housing associations and allocates funding according to how well bids meet the regional development priorities and answer criteria set out in the Corporation's own Scheme Development Standards (The Housing Corporation, 1996, 1998). These standards set out spatial provisions and other features required to meet the needs of housing users. The features are listed as either 'essential' or 'desirable', and are set out in relation to the different activities and uses that might take place, including the accessibility of internal and external environments. The standards are generally considered to be more demanding than those required under building legislation, but do not apply to all housing providers, only to those RSLs seeking Housing Corporation funding.

Scottish Homes

Scottish Homes – the equivalent to The Housing Corporation in Scotland – produced its own guidance on designing housing for older people and disabled people (Scottish Homes, 1996a). A consultation and review concluded that there are quality issues for older people which also apply to housing in general (Scottish Homes, 1996b). The view of Scottish Homes was that there should be a general requirement for dwellings to make allowance for disability, within the following criteria:

- access;
- circulation space, including wheelchair turning circles, in all parts of the dwelling;
- rooms should accommodate a reasonable amount of furniture and still allow sufficient space for people to move around;
- good kitchen design and allowance for appliances;
- storage needs.

Local authorities

There are different guidelines for the design and development of new housing but, with the exception of those aspects of the building regulations[1] which apply to all proposed development, there are no mandatory standards (for space or accessibility, for example) which apply specifically to proposals for new dwellings. However, some local authorities have introduced guidelines for housing developers and providers that espouse higher standards of space and accessibility than those currently required under planning and building legislation. Local authorities will often use their Unitary Development Plan (UDP)[2] or 'local plans' to set targets and standards. The London Borough of Islington, for example, states that a proportion of any new dwellings provided should be acceptable for use by people with disabilities with the remainder being to 'mobility' standard. This means that they should be accessible on the ground floor for wheelchair users and provide an independent living option for ambulant disabled people. Since RSLs, rather than councils, are now the main providers of new-build social housing, the council planning department has encouraged those working within the Borough to go beyond The Housing Corporation's scheme development standards and build to the higher UDP standards. Also, prior to the extension of Part M of the Building Regulations in 1999, the Borough tried to extend the design standards set to cover all sections of the built environment.

The London Borough of Haringey's UDP also required a higher percentage of new dwellings to be wheelchair accessible than was demanded by The Housing Corporation. While, Glasgow City Council (1992) have produced guidelines to 'barrier-free housing'[3] which not only endorse the Scottish Homes requirement for 20% of new dwellings to be 'barrier free' (a figure higher than that currently demanded under the Building Standards [Scotland] Regulations), but also emphasise the need to eliminate barriers that prevent ordinary houses from being occupied or visited by disabled people.

> The concept [of barrier free housing] should be used as an instrument to expand the realms of what is considered 'normal'. People with special needs must be completely integrated into the community without the stigma of specialised aids and features fitted as an afterthought. (Glasgow City Council, 1992, p 1)

Supporting Lifetimes Homes initiatives

Guidelines produced by local authorities cannot be enforced by law and developers will often use this fact as justification for not incorporating them into their own proposals. Their frequently argued case against complying with such guidelines is that the additional costs and space required would restrict their ability to undertake cost-effective or competitive new development in that local authority area. It may also be suggested that the requirement to comply could force their withdrawal to another locality (by implication, perhaps, to one with less demanding standards). Faced with the potential loss of new housing, in a climate where council stock has dwindled to leave affordable housing in very short supply, most local authorities accept that, in many cases, they will be unable to enforce their own guidelines without being held responsible for losing valuable new housing.

However, local authorities can influence developments by RSLs by giving priority to those that incorporate recognised Lifetime Homes standards, since local authority priorities are taken into account by The Housing Corporation when assessing bids for SHGs. Portsmouth City Council has already adopted this approach; while a review of practice in Derby (Reeves, 1996) demonstrates the various actions that local authorities can take, using their position as landowners and planning authorities, to encourage the private sector to develop to Lifetime Homes standards, and thus secure accessible housing.

Working with developers and others as active partners enables local authorities to be proactive at introducing elements which developers may not choose to include if developing alone. For example, a proposal for new housing in Berwick-upon-Tweed involved an innovative partnership between the local council and a local housing association, financed through a 'ground-breaking' government initiative to aid social housing projects (*The Berwick Advertiser*, 19 March 1998). The proposal was to provide 250 new houses and the refurbishment of others where appropriate, with 50 jobs safeguarded or created over five years. The council decided on the number of homes, their location, the standards to which they would be built and the rent to be charged:"All the bungalows and houses, and 25% of the flats, are to be built or refurbished to Lifetime Home standards" (*The Berwick Advertiser*, 19 March 1998).

The need for standards

Space standards

The continuing problems of access to and within homes, the gradual erosion of space standards over the years and the adverse effect that this has had on the usability of different dwellings, have contributed to the 14 criteria developed by the Lifetime Homes Group (see Table 3.1 on page 65). In 1981 the Parker Morris standards (MHLG, 1961) ceased to be mandatory for public sector housing, although they remained a requirement of The Housing Corporation until April 1982. Since then, The Housing Corporation has not stated floor-space requirements as one of the essential criteria for new developments, and this has been followed by a gradual decline in the number of new homes built to match the old standards.

This has not gone unnoticed by residents. During workshops held in 1998 by the Women's Design Service to explain plans for new housing on an estate being renovated in London, women residents expressed concern that some proposed housing units did not appear to provide enough space, nor did they seem appropriately designed, to accommodate either their children's needs or their own needs as child-carers. One of their objections was that, in order to maximise density of housing, the individual sites had become so narrow that it was necessary to increase the number of storeys. This would cause the women (many of whom were single parents) extra costs to cover the stairs and extra work to clean them, as well as causing difficulties of access and lack of flexibility in use. Additionally, lack of space overall often means that insufficient space is allocated for families to sit and eat together; bedrooms have no space for a desk for children to do school work and there is an acute lack of storage space throughout. This erosion of internal space standards and inappropriate layouts is unfortunately not unique.

Since the removal of minimum design standards for housing, it has become increasingly difficult to defend them against the counter pressures that currently exist. Private sector house builders have to respond to demand from a large proportion of potential homeowners who may be on low incomes, but for whom current rental shortages mean they have no option but to buy. For housing associations the pressure has been to minimise their dependence on grant support. For both, there are severe pressures to reduce costs and, subsequently, standards.

Many housing associations adopted an informal benchmark of 10% below Parker Morris standards for their new developments, but in 1994 Karn and Sheridan found that 40% of the property assessed in their research had fallen below even this lesser requirement (Karn and Sheridan, 1994). Guidelines issued by many RSLs, in addition to The Housing Corporation, require only that dwellings must "be suitable for their intended purpose" (The Peabody Trust, 1993), or that they should be "capable of sensibly accommodating the necessary furniture and equipment associated with specific room activities and be suitable for the particular needs of intended user groups" (The Housing Corporation, 1998, p 9). Although a list of essential furniture generally accompanies such requirements, it is easy to see how a failure to specify minimum space will often result in rooms that are not only too small, but consequently inflexible and impractical. Figure 3.1 illustrates typical house plans showing the limited circulation possibilities in this type of arrangement.

Usability standards

In addition to the cost of having to adapt existing housing which fails to reflect the lifestyles of a large proportion of the population, most housing, both existing and proposed, is categorised according to its potential users. Thus, as most current housing is not designed for easy living in later life, flats and houses designed specifically for older people are provided as 'sheltered' or 'supported' housing, while buildings designed specifically for people with disabilities are categorised as 'special needs'. People who do not have identifiable 'special needs' are then lumped together as having 'general needs'.

This affects everything from the location to the appearance of new dwellings, and limits the scope for people to live independently or to move home easily. This has been especially true for tenants subject to the lettings policy of their landlord, who might designate particular housing types as being appropriate for particular 'needs groups'. Until very recently dwellings and other buildings designed for older people or for those with

Figure 3.1: Typical house plans showing circulation routes through living areas

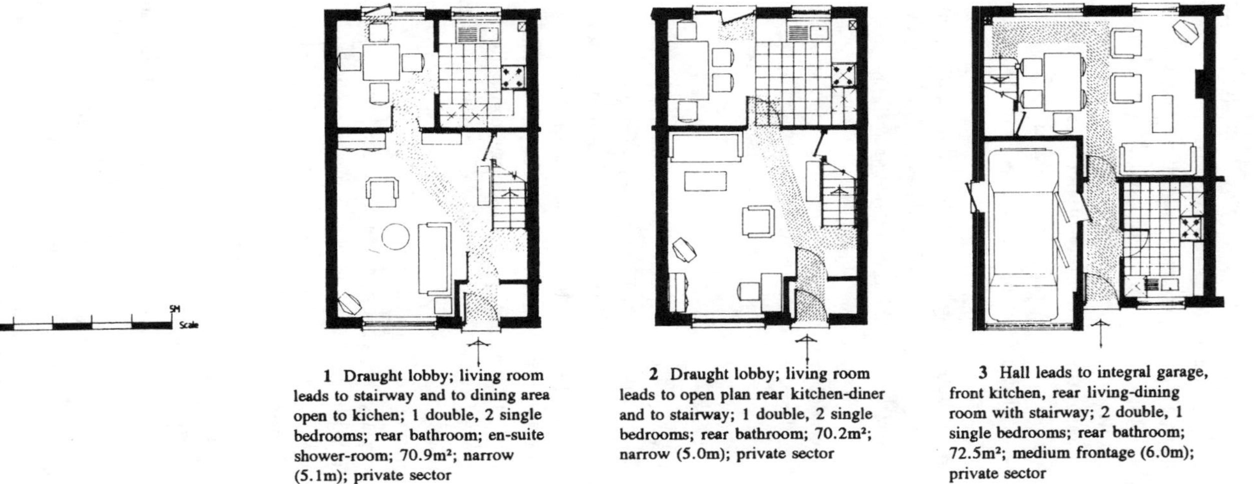

1 Draught lobby; living room leads to stairway and to dining area open to kichen; 1 double, 2 single bedrooms; rear bathroom; en-suite shower-room; 70.9m²; narrow (5.1m); private sector

2 Draught lobby; living room leads to open plan rear kitchen-diner and to stairway; 1 double, 2 single bedrooms; rear bathroom; 70.2m²; narrow (5.0m); private sector

3 Hall leads to integral garage, front kitchen, rear living-dining room with stairway; 2 double, 1 single bedrooms; rear bathroom; 72.5m²; medium frontage (6.0m); private sector

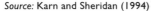

Source: Karn and Sheridan (1994)

special needs would generally be located together, rather than being integrated with the general needs provision of any new development.

Unless and until all dwellings are made more accessible to and usable by all people, buildings will continue to exclude some people completely, and make it difficult for others to use them safely and comfortably. Design anomalies range from the positioning of electrical sockets so close to the floor that they are convenient only to small and curious children, to the thresholds, steps, awkward or narrow spaces and 'standard' fixtures and fittings that present obstacles to anyone who does not fit the stereotype: male, fit, of average height, right-handed and aged between 18 and 40.

> In our anxiety to leave the housing market as free as possible we allow short-term costs to dominate our policies. We watch complacently as every year we add, to the country's housing stock, dwellings whose inflexibility makes them even less suitable for any but the young and agile than their predecessors of ten or twenty years before. (Rowe, 1990, p 3)

There is arguably a lack of originality and an inconsistency of design and style in much new housing provision, which leads to dreariness, a lack of local character and an overall blandness. This is apparent, not only in the look of housing but also in its location and planning. New housing can be isolated from town centres and from where other things are happening; thus, cars are needed to go shopping, to school, to the doctor, to socialise and to make use of local services and facilities. The detached house 'model' has been favoured by developers, and encouraged through marketing. This, in turn, has led to a decline in the design of shared spaces, so there are fewer opportunities for social and community interaction. In addition, work is changing, with little job security, an increase in people commuting over fairly long distances and in people working from home.

Quality of life standards

In a recent study to find what sustains well-being and quality of life during the ageing process, between 27% and 43% of 1,500 interviewees aged 65 and over said that practical provisions could help to better maintain their independence at home. Most mentioned aids and adaptations such as grab-rails, higher chairs, trolleys and other improvements (JRF, 1997). While acknowledging that "building a Lifetime Home does not normally

Table 3.1: Lifetime Homes standards criteria

Criteria	Notes
Access	
A parking space that can be widened to 3.6m allowing a wheelchair user to get out of a car	Does not apply to all car-parking – only that immediately adjacent to the dwelling
Distance between parking space and entrance to be kept to a minimum – with level or gently sloping path	Ground slope requirement does not apply to vehicular route from road to parking space
A level area outside the front door, no steps and a low threshold (maximum 15mm); a covered main entrance	Would apply to pedestrian access
Halls and doorways wide enough for a wheelchair to manoeuvre	Turning circles not essential within hallways
Inside the home	
Space for wheelchair to turn in all ground-floor rooms	Not essential in hallways
The sitting room or family room to be at entrance level	
A ground-floor WC suitable for a wheelchair user with space and plumbing for a future shower	Provision of side transfer space adjacent to WC pan can double as space for the shower gully
A stairway suitable for adding a stair-lift; a suitably identified space in a downstairs room and the room above for potential installation of a through-floor lift with upper-floor joists trimmed to fit the lift	Provision for a vertical lift may interfere with furniture layouts but should not interfere with communication space
Sufficient space in a downstairs room for a bed or for conversion to a bedroom	
Bath and bedroom ceilings strong enough to support a hoist at a later date; within the wall provision for future floor-to-ceiling connecting door for the hoist	Most roof truss manufacturers have confirmed that their design will allow for domestic loading for a hoist spread across the trusses
Turning space in the bathroom for a wheelchair and walls capable of taking adaptations such as handrails	Careful selection of the critical areas should be sufficient rather than full ply lining of walls
Bathroom layout to allow ease of access, preferably with a side approach to the bath and WC. The wash basin should also be accessible	
Fixtures and fittings	
Low window-sills; living room glazing at 800mm or lower, with windows that are easy to open and operate	
Switches, sockets and service controls to be at a height usable by all – between 600mm and 1200mm from finished floor level	

Source: Sangster (1997)

require higher space standards" (Sangster, 1997, p 7) the Lifetime Homes Group has stated that, where space is tight, the incorporation of their standards requires more careful thought. In 1997 the Group produced a publication illustrating a range of plans to adapt existing homes and design new housing to meet their criteria (Brewerton and Darton, 1997). Table 3.1 shows the essential features of Lifetime Homes that can be applied to the majority of general needs houses, flats and bungalows with relative ease and at little additional cost.

It should be noted, however, that the Lifetime Homes standards criteria (see Figure 3.2) make no reference to storage needs – an aspect of design highlighted by tenants and others in their dissatisfaction with current accommodation and their wish to move (Karn and Sheridan, 1994). This point was confirmed in an audit of housing association stock built in the 1970s and early 1980s, undertaken by a team including the author of this chapter (Housing 21, 1997). This revealed that one of the most appreciated aspects of design, in what was otherwise often unsatisfactory accommodation, was the amount and disposition of storage provision in both flats and bed-sits. In contrast to the Lifetime Homes criteria, both The Housing Corporation and Scottish Homes make specific reference to preferred areas for storage.

Planning ahead

There is an increasing number of RSLs who are considering how innovative design can be used to plan ahead for the increasing frailty of some of their tenants and for changing needs generally: from the specification of materials and finishes and, more recently, cabling for interactive computer links, to the integration of new schemes within the general community. Recent analyses of the costs and benefits of designing Lifetime Homes (Cobbold, 1997; Sangster, 1997) have concluded that, in the general view, the more such design becomes normal practice the less such features will be thought of as special or different, and the less they will add to 'standard' costs.

Habinteg Housing Association (see also Chapter Two, pages 40-1) and North Housing Association, for example, have both incorporated many of the Lifetime Homes features into their standard house designs while maintaining total cost indicators and value for money criteria. For Habinteg, the link between poverty and poor access to housing is the basis for the association's work. Habinteg considers that priority should be given to the design and building of accessible housing within the

Figure 3.2: Typical plan illustrating Lifetime Homes criteria

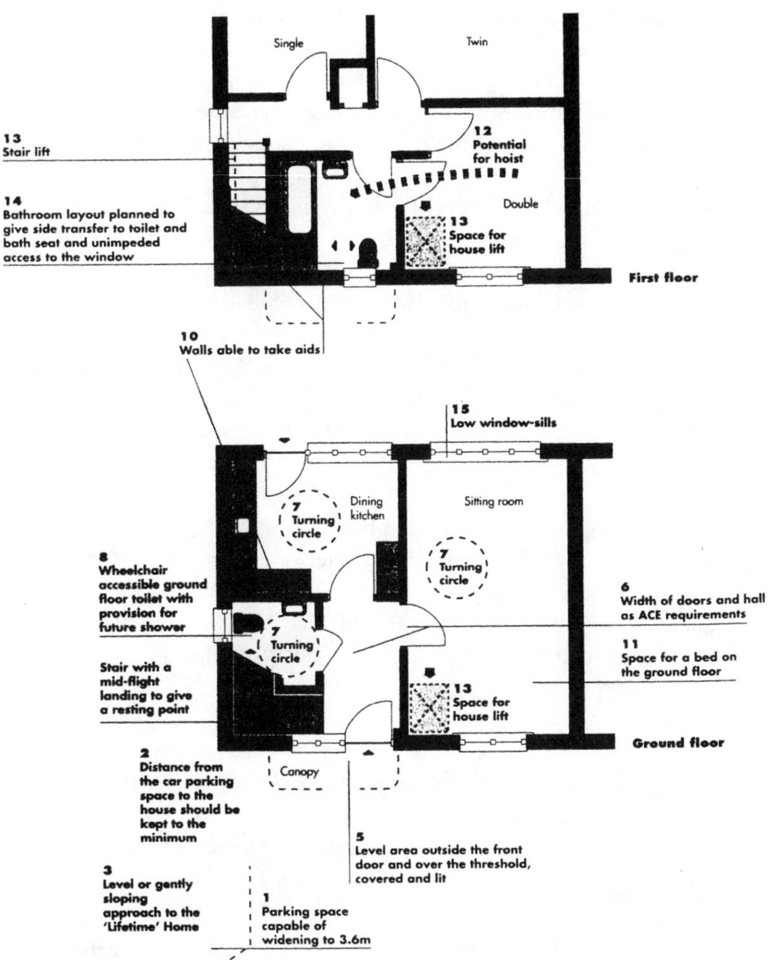

Source: Karn and Sheridan (1995)

mainstream, and that this can be done effectively through careful planning. The principles the association would like to see adopted include:

- *The right place:* Thoughtful choice of location: amenities, gradients, services and transport.
- *The right design:* Level access, wider doors, more space, care in layout of kitchens and bathrooms, care in the specification and placing of equipment (including switches, door and window ironmongery and kitchen furniture).
- *Getting out and about:* Access to all dwellings – including those not occupied by households with a disabled member – and access to the area/community outside.
- *Variety:* A range of housing fully suited to wheelchair users, including two-, three- and four-bedroom homes.
- *Loose fit fine-tuning:* Flexible planning of interiors which can be easily fine-tuned to suit individual needs.
- *Back up:* Provision of support and care services for those households who want and need it.

Edinvar Housing Association in Edinburgh adopted its own 'barrier-free' housing policy in 1985, using their experience as providers and managers to produce their own design guide (Martin, 1992; see also Glasgow City Council above, pages 59-60). They elucidate that house design should meet the requirements of different people at various stages of life, because unless

> ... fit or favoured with every faculty in good order you are especially handicapped by conventional design. The result is that our housing is best fitted for a minority of the population and scant attention is paid to design detailing which could make the home a more accessible and usable place for the majority. (Martin, 1992, p 3)

Edinvar has set out four categories of 'barrier-free' housing design:

1. *Negotiable:* The most basic permissible standard. Wheelchair access to lowest dwelling level, with assistance up steps, and free movement on that level. No confirmed access to WC.
2. *Visitable:* Preferred minimum standard. Wheelchair user has unassisted access to lowest level of dwelling with free movement on that level. 'Accessible' WC (one that can be used with the door open) to be

available but 'usable' WC (that is, one that can be used independently with the door closed) is preferred.

3. *Livable:* Allows unassisted access to lowest level of dwelling to independent wheelchair user with free movement on that level. A 'usable' bathroom or shower room, WC and a room suitable for use as a bedroom should be available.
4. *Universal:* A house or flat designed specifically for a wheelchair user and meeting standards set out in The Housing Corporation's scheme development standards 'wheelchair standard' or the Scottish Housing Handbook, Bulletin 6 – 'Housing for the disabled'.

From October 1999, building regulations were extended to cover new dwellings:

> ... to allow people to be able to invite disabled people to visit them in their own homes, and for home owners to be able to remain in their own homes longer as they become less mobile as they get older. (DETR, 1998)

The press release from the DETR announcing the changes in March 1998 went on to state that:

> ... the benefits of these changes will be considerable – more than ten million people will benefit. In particular, there will be direct benefits of increased convenience, accessibility and sociability for disabled people. The measures will also help significantly those people who are temporarily disabled through accident or injury, the elderly and those with young children in prams and pushchairs. (DETR, 1998)

While the changes addressed many of the features acknowledged to make accessibility difficult, the measures described (see Chapter Four in this book) did not go far enough towards the recommended size and space requirements, or other dimensions, as recommended by the Lifetime Homes Group. The requirements for access are not as demanding as the essential criteria given by the Group, nor even as demanding as those listed as essential items in The Housing Corporation's scheme development standards.

It has been claimed by the construction industry that the additional costs of incorporating the new standards into all new homes would have a negative effect. However, interviews with designers, carried out by the

Lifetime Homes Group (Sangster, 1997), showed that these additional costs were primarily in relation to the provision of a ground-floor toilet. Their analysis of costs at that time concluded that an additional minimum cost of £90 would apply to new two-bedroom social housing while £100 would be the likely minimum cost of incorporating the standards into a new privately developed two-bedroom dwelling. The same analysis determined that the maximum costs to new social housing and to private housing would be £1,377 and £1,224 respectively. However, they emphasised that the costs shown would only apply if no downstairs toilet was to have been originally provided. If it had been, the maximum additional cost would have been £69 for social housing and £59 for private housing. The DETR press release (1998) made a point of saying that it would be "better and more cost effective for new homes to be designed and built with proper facilities ... than to rely on later piecemeal adjustments".

As a balancing view, a study undertaken for the JRF (Brewerton and Darton, 1997) concluded that the consequent savings through the incorporation of Lifetime Homes standards, of not having to undertake adaptations, not delaying moves into residential care, reducing the need for temporary residential care and in home care costs, would amount to £248 for every new dwelling built between 1996 and 2025.

A home for life

> A house is generally taken to be synonymous with a dwelling or physical structure whereas a home is not. A home implies a set of social relations, or a set of activities within a physical structure whereas a house does not. The home as a social concept is strongly linked with the notion of family.... The word 'home' conjures up such images as personal warmth, comfort, stability and security, it carries a meaning beyond the simple notion of shelter. (Watson, 1988)

It is also true to say that 'home' for most people is not solely constituted by the boundaries of their own physical space, but also where that home is located and how it enables or encourages interactions and socialisation with others in the surrounding community, as well as further away. It is important to ensure that, in designing a 'home for life', a form or dwelling is not created that can become as proscriptive as it is intended to be liberating. It is therefore crucial to avoid creating accessible, usable homes wherein freedom of use ends at the threshold.

A truly adaptable, responsive and usable home can only be achieved if other factors, such as the surrounding community and services, as well as the interests and needs of their occupiers, are taken into consideration. For many, the concept of a 'home for life' implies that the occupier will not want to move, or that the home of an earlier stage of their life will remain the home of their old age – a pattern of living no longer as relevant as it may have been even 10 years ago. Designing all new dwellings to Lifetime Homes standards as a minimum would ensure that the broadest range of needs could be met, making it easier for individuals with different needs to move in and out, and to use the buildings as creatively and individually as they pleased – without their activities being circumscribed by the physical constraints of their house.

> "As a disabled person I could find a place, spend a lot of money adapting it and then stay there for the rest of my life but I'm young, I want to have fun and move around, go where I want and where the work is like everyone else." (Berkowitz, 1998)

Integration and flexibility without blandness

Adaptable housing should be able to accommodate people from a wide range of backgrounds, ages and cultures without becoming bland. For example, a positive benefit of homes designed to meet Lifetime Homes criteria may be the provision of housing to meet the requirements of an extended family. This can be accomplished by designing large spaces that can later be subdivided into separate units or flats to accommodate a changing family, while also giving greater freedom to let. ASRA (Greater London) Housing Association has a scheme whereby a house with two large living rooms and two kitchens may be separated into a maisonette and a flat at a later stage, and there are similar proposals by Labo Housing Association and Mitali Housing Association (both in London).

Another option is to consider rehousing families or groups within the extended family into smaller dwellings near to each other, known as 'sensitive allocation'. This policy is considered as the way forward by some RSLs who have developed general needs and sheltered housing on the same or adjacent sites. Housing associations considering this approach include the Asian Special Initiatives Housing Agency in Rochdale, Spitalfields in London and Derby People. It is important to remember, when designing for larger families, not only to consider the numbers involved, but also the greater age range of family members. Designing to incorporate Lifetime Homes criteria will ensure that these needs are more likely to be met.

Recent surveys of housing services for Asian people in the London Boroughs of Brent, Harrow, Ealing and Tower Hamlets found that there were no specialist residential projects designed for older Asian people in any of the boroughs. A majority of respondents said they would prefer to live in self-contained accommodation with built-in support and care services to meet their specialist needs. Those who were in inappropriate housing, ranging from high-rise blocks to temporary accommodation, felt trapped in their own homes, afraid to go out for fear of attack and cut off from support (JRF, 1996).

The logic of Lifetime Homes is that housing built to enable more mobility, through greater space standards, better planning and provision of fixtures and fittings (such as taps, WCs, cupboards and so on), storage and ease of access, would enable greater numbers of people to remain in their own homes without the need for segregated housing or the expense of later alterations and adaptations. Locating new housing within the community and in relation to local services would ensure that accessibility was extended beyond the front door. Finally, the importance of designing with appropriate materials and energy use in mind should not be underestimated. This should ensure that such housing provision remains easy and affordable to live in and use, as well as to maintain and to run. So, the provision of new dwellings that combine flexible, usable and adaptable building forms with long-term affordability will encourage neighbourhoods to evolve and flourish. Thus they represent the best way to achieve community sustainability.

Today less than half of households conform to the image of the traditional nuclear family. Social and demographic changes in the postwar period, such as greater longevity, later marriages, child-free lifestyles and increasing rates of divorce, separation and remarriage have resulted in more diverse households and 'family' formations. We know that changes in work practices, evolving lifestyle choices, family groupings and so on, all illustrate the desire to live more flexibly and to move more often – to where there are jobs and schools for example. This chapter proposes that *all* homes should be designed to be 'lifetime' or 'life cycle' homes, not just those which may be developed in specific areas (usually designated 'special needs' housing) in order to take advantage of additional funding opportunities. Neighbourhoods will change. Housing should not be planned for a particular age or group, but in such a way as to be responsive to the different people who do, and will, live there. It would be folly to predetermine the demographics of an area by designing housing which may exclude others. We do not want to design ghettos where 'accessibility' alone determines tenure or ownership, but rather to plan for a wide range of social, cultural and economic activities to be accommodated within the houses and neighbourhoods in which we choose to live.

Notes

[1] The 1991 Building Regulations (amended 1998) are the minimum legal standards laid down by Parliament to secure the health and safety of people in or about buildings. They also cover energy conservation and access and facilities for disabled people. The regulations are laid before Parliament and supported by Approved Documents that reproduce the legal requirements and give practical and technical advice on how to satisfy these requirements.

[2] Each local authority is required to produce a UDP which details strategies for dealing with environmental, social and economic conditions in the borough by addressing various issues, including housing. Once officially adopted by the local council, the UDP becomes the statutory land-use plan for that borough for the next decade.

[3] Scottish Homes (1996a) guidance and definition states that 'barrier-free housing' is not 'special needs', but a set of criteria that should be applied to *all* housing to allow easy adaptation to the design criteria generally needed by ambulant older or disabled people, and to allow wheelchair access.

References

Berkowitz, A. (1998) Commenting on the new Lifetime Homes criteria issued by the DETR, 'From the edge', BBC2, 21 April.

Bieber, M. (1988) 'Designing and building for a lifecycle', in E. Midwinter (ed) *New design for old: Function, style and older people*, London: Centre for Policy on Ageing.

Brewerton, J. and Darton, D. (1997) *Designing lifetime homes*, York: JRF.

Cobbold, C. (1997) *A cost benefit analysis of Lifetime Homes*, York: JRF.

DETR (Department of the Environment, Transport and the Regions) (1998) DETR News Release 178/ENV, 9 March, London: DETR.

DETR (2000) *Living in Britain 1998, General Household Survey*, London: The Stationery Office.

Glasgow City Council (1992) *An approach to barrier free housing: An aid to briefing*, August, Glasgow: Special Initiatives Group, Glasgow City Council Department of Architecture and Related Services.

Helen Hamlyn Foundation and Rowe, A. (1989) One day seminar at the University of Kent, 7 October, held under the joint auspices of the Helen Hamlyn Foundation and Andrew Rowe, MP for Mid-Kent.

Housing 21 (1997) *An audit of court remodelling proposals*, June, London: Housing 21.

Housing Corporation, The (1996) *Housing for older people*, London: The Housing Corporation.

Housing Corporation, The (1998) *Scheme development standards*, 3rd edn, August, London: The Housing Corporation.

JRF (Joseph Rowntree Foundation) (1996) 'Housing and mental health care needs of Asian people', Social Care Research Paper No 79, York: JRF.

JRF (1997) 'Living well into old age', Social Care Research Paper No 95, York: JRF.

Karn, V. and Sheridan, L. (1994) *New homes in the 1990s: A study of design, space and amenities in housing association and private sector production*, York/Manchester: JRF/Manchester University.

Karn, V. and Sheridan, L. (1995) *Housing quality: A practical guide for tenants and their representatives*, York: JRF.

Martin, F. (1992) *Every house you'll ever need: A design guide for barrier-free housing*, Edinburgh: Edinvar Housing Association.

MHLG (Ministry of Housing and Local Government) (1961) *Houses for today and tomorrow*, Report of the Parker Morris Committee, London: HMSO.

Peabody Trust, The (1993) *Peabody design criteria*, London: The Peabody Trust.

Reeves, D. (1996) 'Accessible housing', Strategic Papers on Planning No 29, Strathclyde: University of Strathclyde.

Rowe, A. (ed) (1990) *Lifetime homes, flexible housing for successive generations*, Helen Hamlyn Foundation, London: Milgate Publishing Ltd.

Sangster, K. (1997) *Costing lifetime homes*, York: Joseph Rowntree Foundation.

Scottish Homes (1996a) *The design of barrier free housing*, Edinburgh: Scottish Homes.

Scottish Homes (1996b) *The physical quality of housing: Housing for older people and disabled people*, Edinburgh: Scottish Homes.

Watson, S. (1988) *Accommodating equality: Gender and housing*, London: Allen and Unwin.

FOUR

The politics of accessible housing in the UK

Jo Milner and Ruth Madigan

Introduction

Current social and legislative trends within the UK and Europe relating to housing design and quality reflect opposing influences. While there has been an ongoing policy shift towards deregulation overall, *re*regulation has emerged and grown within two key areas: first, energy efficiency in terms of consumption and sustainability within the home; and, second, access in terms of the flexibility of housing to cater for the wider needs of a heterogeneous public, including older and disabled people (Karn and Nystrom, 1999). This chapter will focus on *access*. Considerable pressure from key interest groups to make the built environment more inclusive has challenged all those involved in housing policy and practice to rethink the traditional design and function of housing.

Given, on one hand, the nature of the existing stock of housing and pressures towards obvious marketability in new developments, and, on the other hand, the impetus towards implementing human rights, encouraging citizenship and increasing inclusivity, moves towards wider accessibility raise many issues. These issues include finance, quality criteria, flexibility, choice and appropriate levels of regulation. We examine some of these in this chapter and look at ways in which recent legislative and regulatory moves towards wider accessibility have been interpreted by various interest groups.

A key objective of our analysis was to review in depth the wider politics of the leading interest groups which represented different positions within the debate on the extent to which regulatory frameworks are necessary to ensure the development of more user-responsive housing. This debate begs a central question: to what extent is it possible to legislate for good 'inclusive' design which meets the widest number of people's design needs, without compromising the degree of design flexibility and choice necessary to achieve this goal? This reflects a major paradox within the 'regulation versus deregulation' argument.

In this chapter we begin by charting the developments in housing policy that have shaped the regulatory frameworks for housing quality standards, and we identify and chart the most significant socioeconomic and environmental influences to impact on access within the context of housing quality and design. We consider the evidence drawn from our own assessment of responses to the proposal in 1995, to extend Part M and Part T of the English and Scottish building regulations, with the aim of incorporating access standards in all new private dwellings. These regulations were subsequently amended in 1998 to require that all new housing meet the minimal standard of 'visitability'. We then move on to identify the key factors which led to the repositioning of the formerly discrete concept of 'accessibility' into the central debate on the future of housing quality criteria.

Housing quality and deregulation

Within the European house-building industry, significant social and economic indicators have influenced the trend towards deregulation (Karn and Nystrom, 1999, p 126). Among these is the belief that consumer choice and preference create market demand, which should be commodified rather than compromised by prescriptive regulation, financial subsidies or incentives. This policy perspective holds that any increase in government regulation will not only raise costs to the state and the construction industry, but also to potential house purchasers or tenants. In its place, self-regulation, supported by a greater emphasis on consumer information and advice, is perceived as a more favourable option. By the same token, increased compliance with regulatory mechanisms, such as minimum technical standards, may also lead to greater financial risk, by forcing investment in 'unpopular', 'uniform', less innovative, design solutions and technological developments.

In their comparison of the European regulatory frameworks, Karn and Nystrom (1999) suggest that "perhaps the most significant example of the effects of de-regulation is that of the social rented sector in England and Wales" (p 146). Clearly, therefore, it is important to examine the development and outcome of the trends in the UK that led to this low level of public control over the housing quality criteria, not only in private sector housing, but also in social housing.

Until relatively recently, the Parker Morris report (MHLG, 1961) was considered the benchmark against which floor-space and amenity standards within new public sector housing was measured. The report, entitled *Homes for today and tomorrow*, addressed criticisms of declining standards of local authority (LA) housing built in the 1950s. But, as the title suggests, the main objective was to establish a blueprint for the future, by offering an up-to-date definition of, not only the main function of each room, but also related activities, furniture sizes and layout. The average measurement for each living space was then combined with the required circulation space and storage to comprise a total aggregate floor area. However, as Goodchild and Furbey (1986) noted, it is important to point out that this calculation was based on *minimal* recommended criteria for housing quality: "Parker Morris standards assume a 'tight fit' between space and activities with little scope for possible changes in living patterns or for flexibility in coping with the varied preferences of different households" (p 80).

By 1969 Parker Morris standards were mandatory for all new public sector housing. Although the private house-building sector was not similarly bound, in 1967 the National House Builders' Registration Council (now the National House Building Council [NHBC] in England and Wales, and the Scottish House Building Council in Scotland) developed a system of voluntary accreditation, which became strengthened when adopted a year later by building societies as a 10-year guarantee of design quality. The National House Builders' Registration Council quality criteria were largely confined to minimal recommended room sizes and amenities, such as the inclusion of central heating and sound insulation, and fell short of the Parker Morris dimensional requirements by omitting reference to overall floor area, activities and furniture requirements (Goodchild and Furbey, 1986, p 82).

In the 1970s and 1980s there was a drive towards the deregulation of quality standards and, by 1981, the mandatory requirement was repealed to reduce overall development costs, although Parker Morris standards were still encouraged as a mark of good practice[1]. Local authority planning departments were exhorted to exercise greater leniency towards private house-building developments which fell significantly short of the Parker Morris criteria, with the aim of increasing the supply of more 'low-cost' starter homes to enable first time buyers to enter the housing market.

During the 1980s, as the number of new starts in LA house building significantly declined, the housing association (HA) sector emerged to take over as the main provider of new social housing. Initially, the principal guidelines relating to housing quality criteria were set out by The Housing Corporation in the 1983 document *Design and contract criteria*, which largely equated with the Parker Morris standards. However, by 1987, as the Housing Association Grant (HAG) gradually reduced and the bidding process for funding became more competitive, cost efficiency was rewarded and prioritised by The Housing Corporation above adherence to housing quality criteria. By the early 1990s, a drop in HA quality standards in England[2] began to be identified by a number of research reports (for example Walentowics, 1992; Karn and Sheridan, 1994) which documented the steady decrease in the quality of space and amenity standards. Karn and Sheridan (1994) showed that 68% of HA properties built in 1991/92 fell below Parker Morris standards by more than 5%. Further research showed a concomitant reduction in storage, circulation space, amenities and even standards of construction materials and workmanship (Bowron, 1992, quoted in Goodchild, 1997).

Although the private house-building industry may have escaped the level of scrutiny directed at the quality of Registered Social Landlord (RSL) housing design, they were criticised about the low floor-space standards of the 'starter home' properties which proliferated in the early 1980s. Difficulties began to arise at the point of resale, when owners found, not only that their properties were hard to sell, but also that their homes had significantly depreciated in value. This depreciation was largely due to one-off incentives, such as the inclusion of white goods such as cookers or washing machines in the original price or reduced solicitors' fees (Goodchild, 1997). Although there was a shift away from building 'starter homes', given their lack of popularity, this was not reflected in the rhetoric of private developers who still maintained that they fulfilled an important market niche – particularly in times of recession (Goldsmith, 1997, p 349). Yet the downward trend of the effects of the deregulation of quality standards continued and, by 1994, the NHBC dropped minimum storage space from its quality criteria.

The level of concern raised about the negative impact of deregulation on the quality of housing (Scottish Federation of Housing Associations, 1995), re-ignited the debate about the differences between the long-term aims of the private house-building sector compared to those of the social housing sector. Social housing has, not only a higher level of occupancy per living space than owner-occupied housing (by means of rationing through allocation procedures), but also has to serve a wider range of people – increasingly people with health and support needs – who have little opportunity to move into more suitable housing should their circumstances change. Social housing needs to have low a capital cost, require little building and/or amenity maintenance or replacement, sustain low rents and be as flexible and sustainable as possible throughout its life cycle. In the 1970s, LAs forced to comply with internal Parker Morris standards often used system-build construction techniques and built to higher densities in order to recoup costs (Goodchild and Karn, 1997). Their experience offers evidence that *external* quality criteria must also be taken into account.

All of which leads to the "classic contradiction which has affected so much of the debate on housing design" described by Sim (1993, p 187): should initial cost considerations outweigh the long-term benefits to be gained from compliance with quality standards? And, if so, what threshold of quality control is appropriate? From the early 1990s, these questions became as pertinent for the private house-building sector as they were for the social housing sector, due to the emergence of the most significant factor to date on the call for the reregulation of the quality standards for all new housing – the disability movement.

The trend towards reregulation and the disability movement

The final two decades of the 20th century saw a growth of awareness of disability rights on an international scale, with disabled people increasingly calling for recognition of a model of disability which takes account of the 'disabling' effects of social and environmental barriers (Barnes et al, 1999). Within the context of building design, disabled people assert that policy processes have for too long been informed by traditional 'special needs' perceptions of their requirements (Imrie, 1996). The 'social' model of disability presents a challenge to the very core of professional practice and professional belief systems, evidenced by the move towards 'inclusive' design, which expands traditional design parameters to accommodate a greater range of users.

The movement's achievements are reflected in recent developments in policy – particularly the 1995 Disability Discrimination Act, which challenges discrimination within a number of areas including education, employment and access to goods, facilities and services. The phased implementation of the Act led, in 1999, to the extension of the building regulations (Approved Document Part M in England and Part T in Scotland), which now require that all newly built homes will be accessible as defined by the criteria of 'visitability'. This level of accessibility can be better understood when located within the incremental classification system of four key definitions of accessible housing (negotiable, visitable, liveable, universal) developed by Edinvar Housing Association (see Martin, 1992, p 13 and Chapter Three of this book, pp 68-9).

Both the European Manual for an Accessible Built Environment (CCPT, 1990, p 21) and the Access Committee for England (ACE, 1992) have outlined largely similar classifications systems. However, the European Manual distinguishes between the concepts of 'adaptability' and 'visitability' – a difference which was not identified by Edinvar (Martin, 1992) or ACE (1992) at this point, and perhaps anticipated the emergence of the Lifetime Homes criteria.

The requirement to comply with the minimal criteria of 'visitability' under Part M/T of the building regulations comprise the following prescriptions as set out by the Centre for Accessible Environments (CAE):

- level entry to the principal, or suitable alternative entrance;
- an entrance door wide enough to allow wheelchair access;
- WC provision on the entrance or first habitable storey;
- adequate circulation and wider doors within the entrance storey;
- switches and socket outlets at appropriate heights from floor level;
- level or gently sloping approach from car-parking space to the dwelling or, where this is not possible, easy-going steps, but not a stepped ramp;
- where a lift is provided in flats, a minimum lift capacity and dimensions will be recommended;
- where a lift is not provided, the common stair to be designed to suit the needs of ambulant disabled people (Langton-Lockton, 1998).

The concept of 'visitability' was first launched in 1985 by the Prince of Wales Advisory Group on Disability, which comprised representatives of the then Department of Environment, the NHBC, the Centre for Non-Handicapping Environments (now the CAE) and Barratt's Housebuilders (Goldsmith, 1986). The term 'visitability' (originally known as 'X-housing') derived from the concept of 'mobility' housing detailed by the Housing Development Directorate in 1974 (DoE, 1974). It grew from awareness that, as the Parker Morris space and amenity standards did not take disabled people's needs into account, there was a need for ordinary housing which allowed for minimal access by disabled people. The 1974 criteria rest on, first, an accessible entrance, second, that the principal living room, the kitchen, and at least one bedroom should be wheelchair accessible and, third, that the bathroom and WC should be at entrance level although not necessarily wheelchair accessible (Goldsmith, 1997, p 343). Interestingly, although the current 'visitability' standard is based on single, two-storey, or flatted accommodation, and the 'mobility' standard is based on the presumption that two-storey accommodation would be unsuitable for disabled people, comparison shows that the core 'visitability' criteria have changed little in three decades.

However, the lifetime homes concept embraces the twin concepts of 'accessibility' and 'adaptability'. It rests on the philosophy of sustainability, flexibility and adaptability of design which caters for the changing needs of the population throughout their life-course, and enables older and disabled people to 'stay put' as and when their mobility needs change (see Chapter Three, pages 61-6, for details of the design criteria). Although Lifetime Homes criteria equate with the 'liveable' classification as defined by Edinvar (Martin, 1992), they fall far short of the 'universal' level of classification, which would allow wheelchair users fully independent living and unmitigated access to all living areas within a home. Comparison of the 'visitable' and lifetime homes concepts (which both emerged prior to the development of the 1995 draft proposal extending Part M/T of the building regulations) begs the question, why was the former concept favoured over the latter? And, indeed, why did it take just under three decades to move from the 1974 'mobility' housing guidelines to the implementation of the largely similar 'visitability' design criteria as a legislative measure in 1999?

Attitudes of the private house-building industry towards reregulation and accessibility

The main answer to these questions can be traced back to the ongoing strength of opposition by the private house-building industry to any attempt to regulate for the inclusion of even minimal access criteria into mainstream housing. While there was some support from the NHBC for applying the principle of 'visitability', this was lacking for Lifetime Homes criteria. A key argument was that Lifetime Homes would not cater for the bottom end of the market, leaving a gap currently filled by 'starter homes'. According to Goldsmith (1997) the principle of 'visitability' was favoured because it "was less onerous" (p 338) and therefore a more acceptable compromise.

Property development has a number of key characteristics which have shaped the attitudes and roles played by house-builders. A report (University of Reading and DEGW, 1996) undertaken on behalf of the then Department of Environment and the Royal Institute of Chartered Surveyors, argued that the housing development process significantly differs from the 'normal manufacturing process' as:

- it has a high capital value;
- its production time is far longer than most other manufactured goods;
- delay is very costly and, in times of recession, unlet or unsold buildings can have a crippling effect on corporate finances;
- the process of design and development must not be prolonged unnecessarily;
- the finished development must be marketable (University of Reading and DEGW, 1996, p 11).

This combination of factors has reinforced the strongly conservative attitudes of volume house-builders in particular, as they opt for traditional designs in case new designs or variations may involve extra expense or financial risks. Given this level of caution and the pursuit of maximum profits, the public regulation of space and amenity standards is likely to be weighed up as an added value variable to be set in the context of prevailing market conditions and customer preferences. Research by Imrie and Hall (1999) found that access considerations were largely dismissed as of little importance by developers in both the UK and Sweden, and when offset against other competing priorities were often dropped. They concluded that a key difficulty for property developers in responding to disabled people's access needs is that "access is seen as contributing little or nothing to a building's valuation or marketability" (p 10).

Yet, while the construction industry defends the development of 'starter homes', strong evidence suggests that negative publicity arising from their widespread development has turned a proportion of the public against newly built housing. *Kerb appeal*, the report of research undertaken on behalf of the Popular Housing Forum in 1998 (summarised in Housing Market Report, 1998), found that of the 58% of the public (n=819) who would consider purchasing a home, only half would consider buying new houses. Furthermore, perceptions of new houses tended to be polarised towards either end of the housing market spectrum. New homes at the lower end tended to be seen as 'boxy', 'cramped' or 'all the same', while at the upper end as 'expensive' and 'custom-built'. This finding is further reinforced by a study undertaken by the University of Reading (URBED et al, 1999), which examined public needs and aspirations for urban housing. The feedback from three workshops offered evidence that "in general the feeling was that new housing was cramped, poorly built and lacked storage". Such was the strength of opinion that one participant exclaimed: "What pisses me off about modern buildings is the meanness of their proportions". In a summary the report pointed out, "It was also widely felt by participants that new housing lacked 'soul' and was 'samey'", adding, "one of the key themes to emerge was 'an aversion to risk'". However, of the large number of risks identified, including 'crime and personal safety' or 'noise and disturbance', one of the most often mentioned was 'lack of space' (pp 12-37).

These findings indicate contradictory responses to the current debate on design parameters to meet the needs of demographic change and an ageing society (DETR, 1998; Christie and Mensah-Coker, 1999). While the private sector argues that potential market opportunities may be restricted by the requirement of a minimal floor-space threshold, recent research has shown that 'increased floor-space' is a priority in terms of public attitudes to new dwellings. How do these views relate to the extension of the building regulations?

Accessible new housing: a review of the responses to extend Part M/T

In early 1995, draft proposals to extend Part M of the English and Part T of the Scottish building regulations were sent out for consultation. Until this point, although physical access for disabled people had been required for all new public buildings, private housing was not included. The new proposals centred on the concept of 'visitability' as discussed above, enabling wheelchair access, with implications for the design of the threshold to the dwelling, the width of doors and corridors and the size of the WC.

The English responses to the consultation numbered well over 1,000; two thirds comprised employees of house-builders and MPs acting on their behalf in an organised campaign against the proposed changes. The remaining third included members of the public; national and local disability organisations; HAs; LA planning, social service, building control and access representatives; private house-building organisations; professional, technical and academic institutions; and architects. The Scottish Office received just under 100 responses and thus was able to undertake two rounds of consultation. Analysis of both the English and Scottish replies (from which the quotations here are taken) revealed that the majority fell into five main interest groups: representatives from the construction industry and private house-builders, LAs and related professional bodies, HAs, disability organisations, and the design professions. We look here at some of their arguments.

The construction industry and private house-builders

A significant proportion of the responses from the construction industry, including volume house-builders, was strongly opposed to any changes to the legislation. These respondents argued that the proposals would result in an overall increase in expense for both house-builders and consumers – particularly those requiring low-cost 'affordable' homes. They suggested that the requirement for increased circulation space, level or ramped thresholds, larger door widths and the provision of a downstairs toilet in smaller homes, would increase the overall floor area and the width of frontages to buildings. This would lead to lower density developments and raise house prices. The rate of building would be slowed down, given the need to adapt steep gradients on site and redesign popular house types, and this would also impact on house-builders' profits.

However, the overriding concern, provoking most vociferous comment, was a preoccupation with ramps. The proposals were widely interpreted as requiring ramps over level thresholds, and it was claimed that ramps and other forms of 'surgical hardware' would have a negative impact on the appearance of buildings and their subsequent marketability. As one large house-building company noted:

> "Most houses adapted with ramps, rails or other specific requirements for disabled people, will not sell in the open market without prior agreement that the builder will remove the offending adaptations after the house has been legally transferred to the purchaser, where he so wishes."

This point was reiterated by another volume house-builder:

> "The proliferation of ramps, kerbs, steps and handrails will give an 'institutional' feel to the developments, which is contrary to the image house-builders need to create to sell to owner-occupiers. The provision of these measures will reduce the appeal of new houses and increase the

> cost to developers. This is unlikely to be fully recovered by reduced land cost and still less from increased house prices. This will inevitably make the most severely affected house types non-viable."

In the words of another representative of the house-building trade, "large-scale ramping, ugly handrails and significant areas of hard landscaping are completely at odds with the concept of good design". The overall argument was that, as the proposal would only benefit a minority of the population (who were wheelchair users), and given the number and scale of detrimental implications, it should be either diluted or dropped.

Local authorities and related professional bodies

The majority of responses from LAs were in favour of the proposals, and tended to raise a number of technical points relating to the definition and consistency of the key terms and the details outlined. Cost and feasibility were also significant considerations, particularly in terms of the practical application of the recommendations; for example, there was concern about weatherproofing when installing a level threshold. A fairly typical reply from a LA identified this as a potentially problematic area:

> "To achieve a practical and efficient threshold detail to replace the traditional slip step ... is a challenge to our building industry. It requires understanding by and education of the trade skill operatives involved.... Any degree of failure that permits water ingress at an external door threshold will be completely unacceptable to the householder."

Cultural differences in terms of approaches to building design also began to emerge. Several Scottish LAs highlighted the Scottish tradition of construction with a suspended wooden floor, which may add to the height of the entrance from the ground, requiring more steps. Nevertheless, one respondent argued that a change in this pattern of design might be advantageous:

> "The predominant use of timber-frame construction for new housing in the countryside, with the associated under building, seems to result in steps to all access doors with their inherent danger to occupants. The introduction of the Technical Standard should result in more appropriate solutions, eliminating some of the steps and providing better and safer access and egress, especially in bad weather."

Despite strong reservations over threshold detailing, most LAs supported unassisted access to a dwelling entrance.

Many councils had already made a policy or party commitment to the legislation in principle, and thus were keen to ensure policy compliance in the future. The LAs which raised issues about enforceability pointed out that they were worried about loopholes allowing house-builders to 'design out' access requirements; for example, by using the exemptions for sites with steep gradients, the high threshold for lift provision within blocks of flats, individually designed housing, and alterations and extensions such as 'granny annexes'. Several LAs advised that this initial move towards increasing regulatory frameworks should be taken a step further. According to one:

> "As meeting the increased corridor width will reduce the apartment size, it is unlikely that the peripheral dimensions of the dwelling will expand to accommodate this, so therefore there is a need to consider reintroduction of the space standards in the building regulations."

The Royal Town Planning Institute argued for a clearer and more integrated role for the planning system supported by stronger regulations. It was suggested that policy and design guidance should complement Part M:

> "... to ensure that the principles of accessibility are extended from the inside of the dwelling to the external environment as a whole.... Policy guidance might set out minimum disabled access performance criteria, such as paths, widths, ramps, kerb crossings, the frequency of accessible crossings along a road, tactile surfaces etc. It might also embrace parts of DB32 [DoE, 1992] and cover access to public and private transport. Access policies would thereby become a legitimate feature of local plans and Unitary Development Plans, but within a clear policy framework."

In summary, while most LAs supported the concept of unassisted access and its implications for internal and external design, given their role (particularly in building control and planning departments), those who did support the measures tended to argue for stronger regulatory mechanisms to reinforce compliance.

Housing Associations

Housing Associations largely favoured the proposal but pointed out that the requirements were not far-reaching enough. They stressed the difference between 'visitability', with limited unassisted access for visiting wheelchair users, and design for 'occupancy', enabling 'staying put' if mobility problems developed. It was recommended that a more 'holistic' design approach should be adopted which embraced the concept of 'adaptability', particularly as it related to the Lifetime Homes design criteria. For example, in response to the question relating to the preferred level of accessibility for the downstairs toilet, a number of respondents suggested that a possible alternative to providing full wheelchair access would be to provide adaptable space for future conversion if required. The view was one of inclusion. For instance, the Scottish Federation of Housing Associations argued:

> "The proposal to amend the Building Standards provides an excellent opportunity to introduce completely new standards for housing built in the new millennium, in order that all new housing will be built in line with what most of the population want in their homes anyway."

One HA noted that, although associations are becoming increasingly cost conscious as "government subsidy has been reduced and the cost of providing homes has been supplemented by private sources", wide-ranging experience of 'successfully' building in Lifetime Homes features has resulted in an only marginal increase of overall cost. As the initial extra outlay is offset by the longer-term benefits, it was argued that private sector house-builders should follow the HAs' example:

> "It is the Association's view that over the average 20-year mortgage the additional costs will be insignificant and are not sufficiently high as to be taken as reasonable grounds not to introduce the proposals."

The long-term experience of meeting more stringent design criteria within a strict budget was a recurring theme. According to the National Wheelchair Housing Association Group:

> "The extension of Part M to residential buildings may be a daunting task for some house-builders. However, experience shared by many HAs currently building to Housing Corporation scheme development

> standards (1998) and to Lifetime Homes criteria, show that once builders have clear guidance, accessibility in design does not pose a problem for them – large or small. Some builders were so enlightened by the experience they reviewed their standard house type design."

Several HAs also noted that, contrary to the private house-building sector's overriding concern that increased regulation would result in 'uniform', 'bland' and 'institutional' designs, the challenge of creating more user-responsive housing design had resulted in some of the most innovative and interesting housing.

In conclusion, this group of respondents indicated strong commitment to incrementally upgrading the proposals to include the principle of Lifetime Homes design. It was suggested that adaptable features should be built in at the outset of the design process to respond to an individual's changing life stages, within mainstream housing provision.

Disability organisations and individuals

While there was a high level of pragmatism and an acknowledgement of the cost and difficulty of constructing all new homes to full wheelchair accessibility standards, a proportion of the larger pressure groups and private individuals stressed the need to drop the term 'visitability' and aim towards full 'independent living'. They argued that it is important to recognise that the standard of 'visitability' should be viewed as a staging post on the road towards achieving the greater objective. As one organisation pointed out:

> "For general housing this seems like a reasonable first step and a fair compromise given that to build every house to a 'wheelchair' standard would be extremely costly, pricing many individuals out of the home ownership market, and unrealistic. However, a proportion of the housing stock must be built to Lifetime Homes standard, that is, with built-in adaptability for changing circumstances and 'wheelchair' housing standards to cater for an ageing population."

However, it is clear from this statement that the Lifetime Homes standard should not be regarded as a substitute for, or misconceived as, fully wheelchair accessible or universal design – the two concepts are clearly differentiated. Another disability organisation added:

> "We feel this is only tinkering with the real problems of access faced by people with severe mobility problems, especially wheelchair users. It is welcomed that the improvements are being considered, but it appears to us that something more radical must be done, otherwise it is a meaningless exercise and does not meet the challenge, and in no way addresses any of the needs, far less the aspirations of people with a mobility problem."

Therefore, although the concept of lifetime homes is widely embraced, closer analysis of the specifications recommended by several leading disability pressure groups indicates that 'independent living' is variously defined as wheelchair accessible housing, the current Lifetime Homes standard or, as the following statement shows, an extended version of the latter:

> "The basic principle of 'visitability' is progress in terms of dwellings. However, this will not provide dwellings which increase the availability of accessible housing for disabled people. A higher level of accessible housing with at least one public room, one bedroom and an accessible WC/shower would increase the availability of accessible housing which is currently under-provided."

This point is exemplified by an individual respondent who vividly encapsulates many of the problems stemming from a 'starter home', albeit a home with provision of a downstairs toilet. She explains:

> "My daughter has just moved to a newly built home. Ok, it has a toilet downstairs – but it is so small – you sit on the toilet and wash your hands on the basin! If I or either of her two children had to be in a wheelchair – no way would there be room for it. When it comes to selling – who would want to buy it? Steep steps to front and rear doors. No space for a ramp as the front door leads straight onto the pavement. The doors are narrow; it's a job to get the baby (and the pram) together inside. My daughter takes out the baby and has to tip the pram or fold it, to get indoors. What would you do if the child was in a wheelchair? I wouldn't be able to stay with them if I couldn't manage here. Even if these small things were done in new houses, how much easier life would be and one could stay much longer at home, rather than going to an old people's home."

Although the above account offers support for the current regulations, it also illustrates the many benefits to be gained for the wider population, including wheelchair users, by designing over, rather than down to a minimum standard, whether at a 'visitability' or Lifetime Homes level.

These accounts indicate the need for increased clarification of the definition of 'independent living' and its relation to levels of accessibility outlined in Lifetime Homes standards and 'universal' design. Are we at present moving to a 'design for special needs', contrary to the underpinning principle of inclusion as opposed to exclusion?

The design professions

The responses from a number of architectural practices, as well as several large bodies representing the design professions, tended to offer conflicting views on whether or not to support the proposals, and to what extent. The Royal Institute for British Architects strongly favoured the proposals and argued against any exemptions on the grounds that:

> "The proposals should focus attention on how money is best spent causing a holistic approach to be taken on the use of space and the components that constitute built works. Taking a life cycle approach and making provision for easy subsequent designed adaptation is prudent. Intelligently designed products add value beyond their cost, for instance, the smaller two-bedroom house is very suitable for the elderly and would benefit from having a WC at entrance level. Additional costs are only likely to be significant at the lower end of the market."

This positive view was also shared by another smaller organisation, who argued that the proposals:

> "... enable property to be used by owners for longer periods, reducing the need to provide purpose-built 'special needs' housing. Such aims can be considered sustainable as they increase the potential for re-use of existing resources."

However, the main concern shared by a majority of those who did *not* support the proposals centred on the oft-used term 'prescriptive'. They argued that this overall lack of choice would lead to a lack of design flexibility, resulting in 'standardised' and 'uniform' design solutions, which may, as one respondent argued, lead to "an unusual site environment around dwellings designed to comply". It was also argued that a prescriptive approach, by failing to exempt individually designed 'one-off' or self-build houses, could remove a fundamental freedom of choice in terms of lifestyle, habitation and living environment:

> "Upside-down living accommodation, single-storey stilt houses, hanging terrace houses on exceptionally steep sites, for instance could all be precluded by these provisions."

Therefore, it was suggested that, not only might the proposals compromise innovative design solutions, but also that they might impede or even prevent development in certain areas – particularly urban sites – subject to considerable economic and space constraints. According to one respondent:

> "The prescriptive application of the regulations may therefore make some economic development land incapable of development, within the terms of planning and other requirements."

Another respondent added:

> "From the point of view of increasing urban capacity, urban windfall sites developed by small-scale builders, play a valuable part in re-using urban land. It is possible that additional constraints imposed on development of this type could deter or prohibit the development of 'tight' urban sites."

Due to these difficulties described, it was suggested that access may also have to be compromised if there are other competing priorities, and that it may not be reasonable in every instance for the provisions to take precedence over significant aesthetic, environmental or conservation concerns.

The dilemma

The conflicting, rather ambivalent, replies offered by the design representatives, reflect a key dilemma running through the responses to the proposals: how far can we legislate for accessible environments without compromising design flexibility and diversity? The main thrust of the argument adopted by the respondents, with the exception of the volume house-builders, was weighted in favour of the provision of the 'unassisted' access standard as a step towards reaching a future mandatory standard of 'adaptable' housing. However, this does not properly address the central aim of disabled people for 'independent living', nor does it address the severe housing shortage experienced by wheelchair users in particular. This begs such vexed questions as: Is there a need to extend building regulations to ensure that a proportion of buildings are designed to fully 'universal' or 'wheelchair' accessible standards? Would this mean that 'wheelchair accessible' housing could be labelled as 'design for special needs'? Should it be labelled as 'high quality' housing design meeting the widest range of user needs? As lifetime homes are described as 'adaptable', should 'universal design' be described as 'very adaptable'? The central paradox in the 'regulation versus deregulation' debate is, to what extent is it possible to legislate for good 'universal' design without compromising the degree of choice and flexibility necessary to achieve it?

Accessible housing: rethinking housing quality

The significant increase in regulation relating to housing quality and design reflects two trends: first, energy efficiency and sustainability and, second, 'inclusive', more flexible design to accommodate a wider range of people's needs – particularly older and disabled people (Goodchild and Karn, 1997; Karn and Nystrom, 1999; Sheridan, 1999). As with inclusivity, housing quality is multi-dimensional (Rapaport, 1977 and Lynch, 1989, as cited in Goodchild, 1977, pp 32-4) and can be viewed as "historically, culturally and geographically specific" (Lawrence, 1995):

> Because housing quality is content dependent and variable over time, there are no 'objective' static standards which enable us to comprehend it in a comprehensive way. Hence the presence of inadequate housing conditions should not only be considered as a technical problem, but also as an economic and political one. (Lawrence, 1995, p 1658)

Yet, how far can these ideals be brought into practice? The reorientation of access from 'bolt on extra' to integral component of housing quality criteria is reflected, not only within recent literature, but also as a principle element of the newly developed DETR Housing Quality Indicators (HQIs) (DETR, 1999). This is a complementary tool to strengthen The Housing Corporation's scheme development standards (The Housing

Corporation, 1998) which require minimal compliance in order to gain housing association funding for new-build social housing developments. The DETR recommend that the HQIs also have wider applicability for all housing as a "flexible measurement tool of housing quality to be used by consumers and developers alike in both the public and private sectors" (DETR, 1999, p 1).

Informed by research undertaken by the National Federation of Housing Associations in conjunction with the Joseph Rowntree Foundation (NFHA/JRF, 1998), this test of housing quality comprises 10 indicators, based on three categories: location, design and performance. Devised as a flexible mechanism for assessing an aggregate score for a range of levels and mix of quality criteria, the key indicators (as they relate to disabled and older people's needs) are expressed as: internal accessibility, safety, security, design and aesthetics, vehicle access and parking (Stungo, 1996). High scoring properties are intended to operate as a benchmark of high quality design for the consumer. However, we do not yet know how effective this index will be as a means of voluntary accreditation for use by the private housing market. The current accreditation scheme operated by the NHBC comprises a 10-year warranty for all new private homes. The HQIs, with indicators based on enhancing internal design flexibility, offers the public – particularly those who are more sensitive to design restrictions – the opportunity of also assessing housing quality and performance prior to renting or purchasing a property.

If Lawrence's (1995) perspective on the need for a more wide-ranging concept of housing quality is applied to the development of 'inclusive' design, it becomes clear that the discourse to date remains largely confined to regulatory frameworks. Indeed, examination of the current wider political debate indicates that, although the promotion of social inclusion was a central plank of the housing Green Paper (DETR, 2000) and other reports concerning regeneration (Urban Task Force, 1999), accessible design only considers the minimal access criteria of 'visitability' (DETR, 2000, pp 34, 123). As these regulations only apply to new housing, which comprises a small proportion of the total housing stock, there is a limit to the extent to which this measure will offset the severe shortage of accessible housing – particularly for wheelchair users – even in the long-term future (Goldsmith, 1997, p 340; Madigan and Milner, 1999). Although the Urban Task Force reports have generally recommended that good design can aid social inclusion, a study undertaken on its behalf to investigate public perceptions of the quality of modern housing design (URBED et al,

1999), yielded no direct reference to 'inclusive design' or its correlates, either within the literature review or in the main study.

Evaluation of the current trends suggests that, aside from the private house-building sector, the weight of support is for strengthening and extending the building regulations incrementally towards the inclusion of Lifetime Homes criteria (Caroll et al, 1999). Recent and ongoing research projects (for example, DETR, 2000) will inform the future development of mandatory access standards. The Housing Corporation now only awards HAG funding to RSLs who comply with the conditions set out in the 1998 scheme development standards, which embrace the Lifetime Homes principle of adaptability. This will be further strengthened by the required application of the DETR HQIs as a means of quality labelling to guide consumers.

Conclusions

This chapter has described the regulatory framework within which many of the considerations elsewhere in this book are located. We have shown that the practical design considerations necessary to make housing inclusive, although generally regarded in principle as a good thing, are far from simple to nurture in practice. While deregulation had a demonstrably negative effect on the quality of basic housing, reregulation has been controversial, and championed and resisted by different interest groups. Both social and private sector housing have become reregulated through access requirements – a form of minimal floor-space control – but this still does not meet the needs of wheelchair users for housing designed to 'universal' access standards, whether as 'special needs' or enforced standards. The planning and building regulations and the policy guidance must be re-examined with a view to addressing this need.

Those who criticise the existing access legislation argue that increased regulation brings with it increased design prescriptions which undermine design flexibility – the very basis of good 'universal' or 'inclusive' design. Perhaps it would be useful at this point, to return to Goodchild, who pointed out that:

> Flexibility in use is a prime criteria of quality, flexibility in use implies a flexible internal layout. Whereas the standards of equipment, fittings and finishes can be renewed, improved or added to from time to time, the size of a dwelling is limited by its structural shell and can only be altered at considerable expense. (Goodchild, 1997, p 34)

The drawback, as he later adds, is that flexibility in use is dependent on adequate floor-space, which is constrained by cost. It could therefore be argued that 'flexibility in use' equates with cost, but a cost that may be largely offset by the increased scope of the design to meet a wider range of needs. Thus, the argument that increased regulation, which requires increased space standards, can undermine design flexibility may be turned around; increased 'flexibility in use' is not possible without an increase in space standards – and standards need to be supported by regulation. Good 'universal' or 'inclusive' design, therefore, *can* be legislated for.

Notes

[1] In Scotland, the requirement for local authorities to build to Parker Morris standards was exercised under the Scottish Building Regulations. In 1981, they were amended to offer more scope for developers if they preferred to either meet the Parker Morris total floor area requirements, but incorporate fewer rooms and include storage, or provide more rooms that fall below the Parker Morris dimensional levels (Goodchild and Furbey, 1986). However, by 1985, pressure from the English volume house-builders persuaded the then Scottish Development Department to repeal the Parker Morris requirement of minimum room sizes, to allow English house-builders to trade and compete in a Scottish market (Karn and Nystrom, 1999).

[2] Housing association developments in both Scotland and Wales were less subject to a decline in floor-space standards. Scottish Homes, which funds and supervises Scottish HA developments, was not exposed to the same overall reductions in central government funding as England, and was hence more able to sustain higher levels of HAG funding; while Tai Cymru (now dissolved), operating in the same capacity as Scottish Homes for Wales, initiated the 'pattern book' approach, which sets out prescriptive space standards as well as design and layout features. Thus, although it is argued that this approach has served to maintain standards, they also act as the maximum allowed (Sim, 1993).

References

ACE (Access Committee for England) (1992) *Building homes for successive generations: Criteria for accessible housing*, London: ACE.

Barnes, C., Mercer, G. and Shakespeare, T. (1999) *Exploring disability: A sociological introduction*, Cambridge: Polity Press.

Caroll, C., Cowans, J. and Darton, D. (1999) *Meeting Part M and designing Lifetime Homes*, York: JRF.

CCPT (Central Coordinating Committee for the Promotion of Accessibility) (1990) *European manual for an accessible built environment*, Utrecht: CCPT.

Christie, I. and Mensah-Coker, G. (1999) *An inclusive future: Disability, social change and opportunities for greater inclusion by 2010*, London: Demos.

DETR (Department of the Environment, Transport and the Regions) (1998) *English House Condition Survey 1996: A summary*, London: The Stationery Office.

DETR (1999) *Housing Quality Indicators: Research report and indicators*, London: The Stationery Office.

DETR (2000) *Quality and choice: A decent home for all*, Housing Green Paper, London: The Stationery Office.

DoE (Department of the Environment) (1974) Housing Development Directorate, *Mobility housing*, HDD Occasional Papers 2/74, London: DoE.

DoE (1992) Design Bulletin 32 *Residential needs and footpaths: Layout considerations*, April, London: DoE.

Goldsmith, S. (1986) 'The gestation of x-housing', *Design for Special Needs*, no 39, January/April, pp 6-8.

Goldsmith, S. (1997) *Designing for the disabled: A new paradigm*, Oxford: Architectural Press.

Goodchild, B. (1997) *Housing and the urban environment: A guide to housing design, renewal and urban planning*, London: Blackwell Science.

Goodchild, B. and Furbey, R. (1986) 'Standards in house design: A review of the main changes since the Parker Morris Report (1961)', *Land Development Studies*, vol 3, pp 79-99.

Goodchild, B. and Karn, V. (1997) 'Standards, quality control and housing building in the UK', in P. Williams (ed) *Directions in housing policy*, London: Paul Chapman, pp 156-74.

Housing Corporation, The (1983) *Design and contract criteria for fair rent projects*, Issue 2/3, London: The Housing Corporation.

Housing Corporation, The (1998) *Scheme development standards* (3rd edn), London: The Housing Corporation.

Housing Market Report (1998) *Kerb appeal: New home design*, October, London: House Builders Federation.

Imrie, R. (1996) *Disability and the city: International perspectives*, London: Paul Chapman.

Imrie, R. and Hall, P. (1999) '*Property development and access for disabled people: Comparative evidence from Sweden and the United Kingdom*, ESRC Report, London: Economic and Social Research Council.

Karn, V. and Nystrom, L. (1999) 'The control and promotion of quality in new housing design: the context of European integration', in M. Kleinman, W. Matzutter and M. Stephens (eds) *European integration and housing policy*, London: Routledge, pp 125-54.

Karn, V. and Sheridan, L. (1994) *New homes in the 1990s: A study of design, space and amenity in housing association and private sector production*, Manchester/York: University of Manchester/JRF.

Langton-Lockton, S. (1998) 'Centre forward: extending Part M to new housing', *Access by Design*, no 75, January/April, p 72.

Lawrence, R.J. (1995) 'Housing quality: an agenda for research', *Urban Studies*, vol 32, no 10, p 1655-64.

Madigan, R. and Milner, J. (1999) 'Access for all: housing design and the Disability Discrimination Act 1995', *Critical Social Policy*, vol 19, no 3, pp 396-409.

Martin, F. (1992) *Every house you'll ever need: A design guide for barrier-free housing*, Edinburgh: Edinvar Housing Association.

MHLG (Ministry of Housing and Local Government) (1961) *Houses for today and tomorrow*, Report of the Parker Morris Committee, London: HMSO.

NFHA (National Federation of Housing Associations)/JRF (Joseph Rowntree Foundation) (1998) *Guide to standards and quality*, York: JRF.

Scottish Federation of Housing Associations (1995) *Design and construction standards*, Briefing Paper No 18, Edinburgh: Scottish Federation of Housing Associations.

Sheridan, L. (1999) *A comparative study of the control and promotion of housing quality in Europe*, London: DETR.

Sim, D. (1993) *British housing design*, Harlow: Longman.

Stungo, N. (1996) 'Space: the final front room', *RIBA Journal*, vol 104, no 3, March, pp 10-13.

University of Reading and DEGW (1996) *Quality of urban design: A study of the involvement of private property decision-makers in urban design*, London: Department of the Environment/Royal Institute for Chartered Surveyors.

Urban Task Force (1999) *Urban renaissance: Sharing the vision: Summary of responses to the Urban Task Force prospectus*, London: DETR.

URBED (Urban and Economic Development Group), MORI and School for Policy Studies at the University of Bristol (1999) *But would you live there? Shaping attitudes to urban living*, London: Urban Task Force/DETR.

Walentowics, P. (1992) *Housing standards after the Act: A survey of space and design standards on housing association projects in 1989/90*, Research Report No 15, York: NFHA in collaboration with JRF.

FIVE

The implications of smart home technologies

Malcolm J. Fisk

Introduction

There is no single accepted definition of a 'smart home'. At its broadest, a smart home is one where smart technologies are installed and where those technologies facilitate automatic or user-initiated *communication*, involving a range of appliances, sensors, actuators and switches – these are collectively referred to throughout this chapter as devices. In smart homes, communication takes place between devices in ways that can serve to empower people and, in so doing, improve their quality of life. There is, in other words, something to be gained by communication.

As noted in Chapter One, the context of smart homes in the UK is one in which older people live in a variety of different types of dwellings. Most 'ordinary' homes already have a range of devices which operate independently of each other and virtually all of these homes can host smart technologies insofar as links can be established between devices via radio, dedicated wiring or mains cabling. Dwellings that are already built according to 'design for all' principles can, in particular, employ smart technologies to benefit a much wider range of people regardless of their age or ability.

This chapter explores the significance of device communication and specifically relates it to the needs of older people and the empowerment that it offers. However, it also points to the danger of such technologies removing choice and control from the user through an over-reliance on automation, and the transfer, without proper consent, of personal information to third parties – a particular concern in what is known as lifestyle monitoring.

As a prelude to exploring smart homes and the significance of their capacity for communication, the point must be made that, while there is increasing discussion among service providers about the role of such technologies in supporting independent living for older people and others, little or no consideration has been given to their place within social theories of ageing. It could be argued that such an omission is appropriate insofar as the technologies can be considered as neutral and as of similar significance as the bricks and mortar from which our homes are constructed. This standpoint is, however, untenable. The technologies and the bricks and mortar that shape our homes create the social milieu of our lives. They, and their contents, are an integral part of our social identities. Their form – especially when the product of social rented sector provision – is in many ways a product of theoretical standpoints concerned with separation, integration, class, social justice or oppression.

Furthermore, smart technologies have a dramatic impact on personal communications whether relating to social or economic activity, such as contacts with family and friends, work, shopping, travel, and so on; and there are fears that their greater use may reduce the extent of social contact. More particularly, some commentators have expressed concern that smart technologies might be used to substitute more personal forms of care and support (see for instance, Harding, 1997). Yet, elsewhere, this author has argued that such technologies can "liberate people from ageist and oppressive regimes of the sort that have, for too long, characterised many housing and care services" (Fisk, 1999, p 26). The potential for liberation comes into clearer focus when the wider use of communications technologies within and outside the home is considered. Such technologies can give access to a rapidly widening array of services and information sources – many of particular benefit to older people. The same communications technologies can bring to our homes new medical and healthcare services that, hitherto, were confined to the hospital ward or the health centre.

The decentralisation of healthcare services from institutions to individual homes has led Valins and Salter (1996) to affirm that "perhaps the hospital was no more than an uninvited detour to satisfy a set of circumstances that may no longer apply" (p 4). It is considered that the process of such decentralisation is unstoppable (Fisk, 1997). The decentralisation carries with it, however, the danger that norms associated with medical models of ageing may be transported to the home, with approaches that emphasise patient compliance in relation to healthcare outcomes determined according to narrow clinical rather than holistic considerations.

Smart technologies are, therefore, of great importance to the position that individuals have in wider society, their interrelationship with others, their participation in economic and social life, and the extent of their oppression in the context of support and care frameworks. For older people the technologies could play a part in counterbalancing the forces of ageism, disempowerment and social exclusion. Furthermore, in helping to facilitate the decentralisation of services, elements of smart technologies may breach the boundaries between institutions and communities. And where the boundaries represent custody or exclusion, smart technologies have the potential to liberate by giving access to a range of advice and information services, employment and social opportunities that have traditionally been restricted or denied.

Smart technologies therefore demand careful consideration within social theory as endeavours are made to combat the structured dependency and oppression underpinning many current service frameworks (Braye and Preston-Shoot, 1995; Phillipson, 1998). This is particularly the case in view of their communications capacity, the development of which is expected to be the key feature of future generations of systems (Doughty et al, 1996; Tang and Venables, 2000). Consequently, smart homes take a rightful place alongside matters such as dwelling design, sheltered housing, residential care and different types of retirement community – all of which also have implications for social inclusion and empowerment.

The origins of smart homes

The origins of smart homes are to be found in intelligent, or smart, buildings. These began to appear in the 1970s and 1980s and were lauded as offering the potential means of improving energy efficiency, ventilation and the control of working environments. An intelligent building, according to Atkin (1988), contained a building automation system, an office automation system and advanced telecommunications via a central computer system. The working environment within the building would be automatically controlled and, it was considered, ensure the greater comfort of its occupants with potential gains in productivity.

Consideration of the potential for smart *homes* emerged in the 1980s as a consequence of the reducing costs of the technologies required and the dramatically increased power of micro-processors to receive, handle, analyse and distribute information around the systems concerned. It also reflected the growing awareness of the potential of such systems to incorporate a range of:

- *assistive technologies*, which were increasingly being used by people with mobility problems and/or sensory impairments; and
- *specialised communications technologies*, which were offering a way to obtain help in necessitous circumstances and of monitoring physiological well-being.

Assistive technology has been defined as "any item, piece of equipment or product system, whether acquired commercially off-the-shelf, modified or customized, that is used to increase, maintain or improve the functional capabilities of an individual with a disability" (Galvin, 1997, p 9). These have developed in range and number with some assistive devices becoming everyday items for all (such as the electronic can-opener and the television remote control).

One of the assistive technologies that we discuss in this chapter is social alarms. These include hard-wired systems normally provided for older people in grouped dwellings, such as are found in sheltered housing schemes, and dispersed alarm devices that can replace or operate with a conventional telephone. They are almost always active devices that need to be triggered by the user, but some passive monitoring systems have been in operation for a decade or more. For example, in the 1960s and 1970s, pressure pads were sometimes installed with hard-wired systems so that wardens in sheltered housing schemes could know whether or not residents were up and about every morning. Wardens' offices or hallways would feature large panels, reset every night, with lights for every dwelling in the scheme to signal resident activity. More recently, some housing service providers have installed passive infra-red sensors (PIRs), linking to hard-wired systems to both monitor for activity and provide a means of intruder detection (see Glasgow City Council, 1993; and Chapter Seven in this book).

The capability of both hard-wired systems and dispersed alarm devices has now dramatically increased and is associated with PIRs and other sensors that offer a means of passive and lifestyle monitoring. This means that we are several steps closer to technologies that are proactive in recognising abnormalities in behaviour that might indicate a problem, and immediately reactive to an event that could require intervention, such as a fall, seizure or heart attack. Such technologies could obviate the need for users to carry or wear the type of radio trigger device, normally worn as a pendant or on the wrist, that is currently associated with social alarm systems.

There are several early examples of smart technologies being developed in pilot projects in Europe, North America and Japan (see, for example, Hickling Corporation, 1991; Horelli and Leppo, 1994; Jeantet, 1994; Orsini and Stochino, 1993; Shobu, 1993; Vlaskamp et al, 1994). These initiatives tended to concentrate on home automation, but increasingly included features specifically relevant to older people, such as controlled or automatic lighting and a social alarm facility. However, much of the focus of these pilots was on grappling with problems concerned with signalling protocols and the incompatibility of devices used as part of smart systems. Some attention was given to the interface with users but ethical issues were rarely touched upon.

Moran (1993) was one of the first to pose crucial questions about the social impact of such technologies:

> The introduction of advanced technology into the home has the potential to change qualitative and quantitative aspects of relationships between household members, as well as the role and function of the home and its relationship with the wider environment. Such technologies consequently have important implications for our health and quality of life. (1993, p 1)

She noted that the early initiatives were "largely the result of technology push", with no "clear conceptual paradigm" (p 10) having emerged to underpin their development.

The impetus of that technological push was, however, mitigated by commercial constraints. Vlaskamp et al for instance, noted that:

> Integrated systems are only feasible when the manufacturers of system components agree upon a common standard. Standardisation is not only a technical problem but often also a marketing problem ... because many producers have already a company-owned standard for their own product range. (Vlaskamp et al, 1994, p 57)

The same difficulties were still being encountered more recently (Felbaum, 1999). They have been problematic for the initiatives in the UK supported by the Joseph Rowntree Foundation (JRF), with Gann et al lamenting that "attempts to develop standards have been painfully slow and generally resulted in cumbersome documents with little general agreement on the way forward" (1999, p 51).

However, there was evidence that at least some difficulties were being overcome and the opportunities relating to communication outside the dwelling were being explored. The extent of penetration of interactive cable networks in the UK and the rapidity by which users are gaining access to the Internet has given further impetus to this shift.

In aiding the conceptualisation of smart homes Gann et al (1999) have suggested that two forms are emerging: one more rooted in home automation, the other involving interactive communications within and outside the home. Vlaskamp et al (1994) have pointed to three technical environments for smart technologies, namely: the *direct environment* which transports, is worn or carried by the user; the *fixed environment* of the home itself; and the *distant environment* embracing "remote consultation partners" (see Figure 5.1). Smart technologies with the potential to benefit older people relate to all three. Communications are particularly relevant to the distant environment (even though, for someone with a physical or sensory impairment, that distance might be to an adjoining dwelling, a local shop or service provider).

Regardless of the extent to which particular smart systems relate to the three environments, fundamental questions must be posed regarding what, precisely, a smart home should do. Current and recent initiatives in the UK are beginning to provide some of the answers. They respond, not to technology push factors, but to a desire to test the merits of smart technologies in relation to the needs of particular users. These have increasingly focused on the communications aspect of smart homes and, importantly, some have given particular attention to the support needs of older people.

Figure 5.1: Environments for smart home technologies

Direct environment	Fixed environment	Distant environment
• Equipment worn or carried by the user	• Devices and sensors fixed within or close to the dwelling	• Networks operating in the wider community (using telephony and radio)
• Devices implanted within the user	• Cabling linking such devices	• Automated or personal services operating via such media
• Devices attached to prostheses of the user (including wheelchairs)	• Central processing and control unit	

Source: Based on Vlaskamp et al (1994)

What should a smart home do?

The lack of homes with installed smart technologies, the fact that they need to respond to the differing needs of residents and the lack of systematic evaluations of their impact means that there is some scepticism regarding their merits. This is healthy insofar as it helps to focus further development and application on ensuring progress towards relevant outcomes.

There is a danger, however, that while the credentials of organisations undertaking or promoting the smart home initiatives may be sound, technologies could be used in ways that underpin or consolidate ageist, disablist and oppressive service frameworks. Any failure to adequately consider the social context in which such technologies are placed might, therefore, result in the re-enforcement of medical models of older age and service provision. The decentralisation from institutions to the home of care or support services utilising such technologies might, therefore, be a long way from helping to achieve objectives concerned with individual empowerment and inclusion. Fortunately, the emphasis on communications with the distant environment helps to counter this.

An empowering and inclusive perspective – that of liberation technologies – is relevant here (Fisk, 1999), and offers a framework whereby technologies might be harnessed in ways that ensure that both they, and the services accessed through them, are within the user's control. Such a liberation perspective is considered as useful, if not essential, to underpin any smart system – especially where the needs and aspirations of older people are embraced. It is predicated on a belief that control should be vested in the user as the capacity of communications technologies is harnessed.

With regard to system functionality within smart homes, the possibilities are continually fluctuating and expanding. There is a welcome discussion of ideas such as the use of robots for lifting, guidance for wheelchair movement around the dwelling, and refrigerators which incorporate stock control facilities (see Gann et al, 1999). Another possibility relates to the monitoring of medicines and user compliance with prescribed courses of treatment (Hickling Corporation, 1991). However, Moran (1993) lamented that it would be a long time before smart technologies embraced areas of domestic work such as ironing, vacuum cleaning, bed-making and shoe-polishing!

A further idea is the smart or 'health' toilet. This may be the subject of some amusement among service providers and users alike, but it is considered to warrant serious attention insofar as there is a real and shorter-term possibility that such sanitary technology could play a significant role in healthcare monitoring. There is, after all, a substantial potential to monitor food consumption, a range of medical conditions and the success or otherwise of medical interventions, through the analysis of urine and faecal matter. The smart toilet can also be a means of checking body weight (Tamura et al, 1998).

With regard to generic smart systems there appears to be broad consensus on a core range of functions (see Figure 5.2). Not that the full range of functions, sensors and actuators would necessarily be present, active or used in all installations. Indeed, a basic, and now widely accepted, parameter for systems is that they should be modular, that is, with the ability to add functionality as needs arise or in the course of dwelling refurbishment. The latter point is particularly pertinent in that much of the UK's housing stock is both old and varied. It most certainly was not built with the later inclusion of smart technologies in mind. However, Doughty and Costa (1997) have affirmed, in the context of the decentralisation of healthcare and medical services, that every home could be made smart. They envisage homes being fitted with a variety of sensors for monitoring and with computer programs being able to build up activity profiles so that changes in the habits of occupants could be identified. The latter could be gradual changes or events relating to things such as accident or illness.

Whether or not the smart homes created would be newly built or refurbished, a range of core functions can be indicated (see Figure 5.2).

In view of the relatively limited experience of smart homes, there is an absence of user views about the relative merits of such functions. However,

Figure 5.2: Core functions of generic smart systems

- Control of system
- Emergency help
- Temperature monitoring
- Water and energy use monitoring
- Automatic lighting
- Door surveillance
- Cooker safety
- Water temperature control
- Window, blind and/or curtain control
- Property security
- Online links

Gann et al (1999, p 30) report that visitors to the JRF smart homes, described later, gave their highest rankings for those facilities concerned with gas detection, security alarm, social alarm and entry 'phones.

Detailed consideration of the operation of smart technologies in relation to each of the functions is outside the remit of this appraisal. These are, however, integral to the further development of system specifications discussed elsewhere (Hickling Corporation, 1991; Gann et al, 1999; Willems, 1999). Such work has sought to determine:

- the manner of control and operation of systems, for example, from fixed or portable devices and via remote telephones, and the provision of a central-locking security facility;
- the extent of discretion given to users to set or change timers and/or system operational parameters, determining the degree of user control over system operation and any personal information collected by the system;
- the feedback provided to the user via displays or other means, for example, in relation to the status of appliances, windows, doors, energy and water usage, visitors at the front door, and so on;
- the framework for the monitoring of individual lifestyles, for example, regarding the appropriate range of sensors and the manner in which data should be handled.

The range of potential online communication links to an assortment of services from the local library to home banking is explored elsewhere (see Fisk, 1996a; Cullen and Robinson, 1997).

In addition, and with a keener eye on the commercial potential of such systems, more attention is being given to the user interface for such systems. User interfaces are, of course, crucial to the acceptance and use of smart technologies (Vlaskamp et al, 1994; Karlsson, 1995; Cullen and Robinson, 1997; Fisk, 1998). Karlsson and Fisk also point to the importance of the perceived usefulness of the technologies in question as a prerequisite for their adoption.

Recent initiatives

There are now several smart home initiatives within the UK and other parts of the European Union (EU) (Bjørneby, 1997; Gann et al, 1999; Poulson and Nicolle, 1999). In addition, a small number of smart systems with limited functionality are being marketed. However, as yet, no system comes close to being able to offer the full range of core or additional functions noted above. Gann et al (1999) correctly summed up the current position:

> In Britain, smart home markets, technologies and supply industries are immature. Customers are ignorant or sceptical about potential benefits; technologies are difficult to integrate for interoperability; the industry is fragmented and there are no one-stop-shop suppliers providing a full range of bundled products and services. (Gann et al, 1999, p 88)

Notable within the UK are the JRF initiatives in York and in Edinburgh (with Edinvar Housing Association), developed partly with the specific needs of older people in mind (as outlined in Figure 5.3). In Edinburgh some consideration was also given to the needs of people with dementia. The JRF initiatives have been evaluated and technical details have been set out to help in determining future specifications for smart technologies (see Gann et al, 1999). Particularly relevant to this chapter, however, is the matter of lifestyle monitoring. Gann et al (1999) noted the possibility of "using smart home systems for continuous monitoring of people's health and well-being" and of "diagnosing changes in health status, automatically triggering an appropriate response" (p 30). Questions arise regarding how the communications capacity of such systems is used and the extent to which some responses are automated, that is, without information being sent to and mediated by a third party or central computerised facility. Such matters raise a number of ethical issues that are discussed below.

A further smart home initiative in the UK is that being undertaken by John Grooms Housing Association in collaboration with Portsmouth City Council and the University of Portsmouth; a sizeable part of the funding is through The Housing Corporation. This initiative focuses on the needs of people with severe disabilities and follows consultations with some 70 people who were members of disability groups in Hampshire.

Figure 5.3: Additional functions of smart systems associated with provision for older people

- Memory joggers and diary facility
- Lifestyle monitoring
- Medical monitoring
- Dementia care

It comprises installations in four out of six homes built to wheelchair and Lifetime Homes standards. A full evaluation, including attention to the user experience, is being undertaken with a view to outcomes being published at the end of 2001.

Several of the smart functions to be incorporated in the Portsmouth initiative depend on the successful integration of sensors into a multi-functional ceiling rose. It is envisaged that this will facilitate the monitoring of movement, room temperature, lighting levels, smoke and gas. Sensors elsewhere will monitor energy usage, water flow and external weather conditions. Attention is also being given to door and window automation, these responding to the particular needs of users. The sensors and other components of the system are to be linked through wired ducts and dado rails. Control of the system is planned via simple remote and/or wall mounted units.

Several other smart homes are known to be planned or under development in the UK. Conspicuous is the involvement of social sector housing providers, often in collaboration with other agencies. These include the 'Integer' (intelligent and green) home being developed with the Building Research Establishment and developments in Birmingham, Cheshire and Londonderry. Parallel smart home initiatives in Northampton, Gloucester and West Lothian consider the needs of older people with dementia and pay particular attention to monitoring in relation to the risks associated with wandering. They also offer automatic cut-offs when appliances are left on.

Looking more widely, in Europe there are a growing number of initiatives that are similarly characterised by increasing functionality and the use of communications technologies. As in the UK, some are focused on the needs of people with dementia, a well-known example being that of the BESTA flats in Tønsberg, Norway (Bjørneby, 1997). An initial evaluation of this development indicated cost savings over and above the additional £2,500 per dwelling spent on the technologies (Fisk, 1998).

The position in the UK is, therefore, echoed in other parts of the EU. The emphasis that all the initiatives place on communications sits well with design-for-all principles and, by virtue of relating to a wider market, may lead to the development of commercial products in the shorter term. It also facilitates the take-up of telecare (that is, the use of communications networks to support care services in people's own homes) within smart homes. Such telecare systems will supersede today's social alarms (see below), with smart homes and telecare being, according to Tang and Venables "natural companions" (2000, p 8).

In the broader context, however, and very important in relation to the use of smart technologies by older people, note must be taken of the growing range of online services that may be able to be accessed via such systems. These include the key functions of emergency help and lifestyle monitoring. Emergency help is best understood by reference to social alarms, that is, systems which, when activated by the user, automatically link them to a remote response and monitoring centre enabling assistance, if necessary, to be provided. Social alarm devices are used by over one million older people in the UK and have become relatively commonplace over a period in excess of 20 years (Fisk, 1996b). In contrast, lifestyle monitoring is a relatively new concept and entails the continuous or intermittent gathering and interpretation of data relating to the movement, activity and behaviour of people in their homes. Various EU-financed projects have helped promote technological developments in these areas and have been influential in increasing the focus on older and disabled people. These have been within design for all frameworks.

Two particular projects in the UK, neither of which benefited from European funding, are worthy of special consideration by virtue of their offering, or having offered, lifestyle monitoring. The first is the British Telecom/Anchor Trust initiative, which involved installation of prototype smart systems in 22 households in Newcastle upon Tyne, Ipswich, Knowsley and Nottingham (this initiative has been evaluated by Porteus and Brownsell, 2000). The second relates to installations of a prototype smart system and a range of smart sensors for local authorities in Durham (the latter are being evaluated by the University of Newcastle and, under the Better Government for Older People programme, the University of Warwick).

British Telecom/Anchor Trust initiative

The British Telecom/Anchor Trust initiative involved installation of 'lifestyle monitoring telecare systems'. The primary aim of the initiative was to "harness the application of new technology in a non-intrusive way to service the needs and wishes of older or vulnerable people, central to which is that of maintaining independence and choice" (Porteus and Brownsell, 2000, p 25). The system was developed by British Telecom but closely replicates another in France (Chan et al, 1998). It aimed to monitor the lifestyles of people "in their own home and look for deviations in their normal pattern of behaviour", and, by "detecting situations as they occur will enable people to be treated before the situation worsens and consequently we move from a reactive to a preventative system that should result in a reduction in healthcare costs per head" (Porteus and Brownsell, 2000, p 13).

The initiative involved recording the patterns of daily living of residents using PIRs in every room and magnetic switches on the entrance and refrigerator doors. Dwelling temperature was also monitored via a sensor in the main living room. The devices in question were linked in most cases by radio to the system control box and the information gathered was forwarded or collected, via the telephone network, to or by the British Telecom laboratories in Ipswich. People did not need to carry or wear any kind of device and, if they wished, they could turn off the system by dialling a designated telephone number.

Importantly this initiative gathered more than 5,000 days of lifestyle data and provided valuable pointers to their potential for identifying what were described as alert situations (that is, where there was significant deviation from the normal pattern). In all, 60 alert situations – one per household in every 80 monitored days – were identified. These generated automatic calls from the British Telecom laboratories to the dwelling so that the user could key in '1' to indicate that all was well. If the user keyed in '2' or did not respond to the call, nominated contacts would be then automatically telephoned in turn until one of them indicated that they could attend. While this was not part of the initiative, in the event of no nominated contact being available, a telephone link would be made to a social alarm service.

Examples of the ways in which alert calls would be generated include where the room temperature had dropped below normal levels; less activity was evident; there had been a change in the pattern of refrigerator use; or the user was still in bed after their normal time for getting up. Porteus and Brownsell acknowledged, however, that "finding the balance between detecting what is a deviation from the normal ... and what is not was particularly difficult to solve" (2000, p 35).

Focus groups involving those who used the system and their carers revealed that over three quarters (of both groups) were satisfied or very satisfied with the system. A total of 86% of users thought the new technology was "a good thing" (p 41), although it needs to be borne in mind that the initiative had "some difficulties in recruiting volunteers" (Porteus and Brownsell, 2000, p 36). A broader spectrum of users might, therefore, have been more sceptical. Carers were even more in favour with 93% considering the new technology a positive development.

The potential benefits were recognised by users as:

- reducing anxieties for them and their families;
- facilitating earlier discharges from hospital;
- in respect of temperature monitoring, providing a safeguard for people who might be frugal with heating (Porteus and Brownsell, 2000).

Also, 47% responded positively to the statement 'It helps me stay living at home', but this was quite strongly counterbalanced by the 36% who disagreed. Users expressed reservations about:

- potential loss of privacy and feelings of being watched;
- the potential for service providers to reduce personal care provision and/or warden services;
- possible predisposition of service providers to focus on the cost savings that might be brought about by use of the technologies rather than enhancing service levels.

While this evaluation is of undoubted interest, some of its eulogistic conclusions appear to be unsupported by the evidence. Examples of these are the affirmation that the "only disadvantages discovered centred on the possibility that technology could ultimately reduce or remove human contact" (Porteus and Brownsell, 2000, p 60), despite the range of concerns that have already been noted; and the claim that lifestyle monitoring is "proven" to be "an effective tool in automatically recognising alert conditions" (p 61). Furthermore, a claim that the Royal Commission on Long Term Care suggests a "requirement" to have some form of monitoring in the home (p 59), is considered spurious. However, the evaluation includes important discussion and there is a welcome call for longitudinal research into the effectiveness of such technologies in meeting some of the claims.

Durham initiative

Four prototype smart systems were installed in sheltered homes managed by different authorities in County Durham. The initiatives are being undertaken in collaboration with the county council and are seen as potentially underpinning the delivery of community support services. The systems were installed following a comprehensive review of technologies available in the UK (Durham County Council, 1999).

Doughty (2000) has affirmed the potential merits of such systems in the context of sheltered housing, and attested to their ability to operate with a wide range of sensors. Such sensors reflect the focus on older people's needs and herald the possibility, with the aid of smart technologies, of further steps being taken towards care in the community objectives and the decentralisation of healthcare. In Durham various sensors and devices are being tested in Teesdale, Easington and the City of Durham. These initially embrace:

- fall and collapse detectors;
- flood detectors;
- high and low temperature sensors;
- night time monitoring devices to identify when a user is out of bed for an extended period;
- night time monitoring devices to identify when a user goes out of the dwelling for an extended period;
- video systems to offer images of visitors at the front door;
- video recording to transmit facial images of visitors for storage, to a monitoring and response centre;
- remote front-door opening;
- monitoring of support service delivery by care staff;
- night time automatic lighting when a user gets out of bed.

The core functionality of the Durham systems has been detailed by Doughty et al (1999), and the study affirmed the objective of providing technologies that can "detect a wide range of emergencies but ... also include the monitoring of those parameters which can become indicators of future problems or decline" (p 2). In other words, both patterns of behaviour that deviate from the norm (as in the British Telecom/Anchor Trust initiative) and longer-term changes, perhaps over many months, can be identified. The latter, they surmised, could help in the identification of deteriorating mobility and things such as longer-term changes in patterns of sleeping, eating, bathing, and so on. Also of interest is the suggestion that predictive indices could be developed, based on lifestyles, that might help signal the risk of falls and identify behaviour consistent with the early stages of dementia. Already, the Durham initiatives have identified, through recording video images of visitors, the fact that some users have very few or no visitors and thus appear to be very socially isolated.

Symptomatic of the potential for use of such systems in health or medical care is the experimentation (in Durham and elsewhere) with fall and collapse detectors carried or worn by the user; bed movement detectors to determine the need for turning in order to guard against bedsores; and incontinence detectors to effect action in the event of beds being wet or soiled. Crucially, however, it is not only reactive interventions that are facilitated which can 'put things right' or obtain assistance after the event, but the planning of proactive interventions. To illustrate the point in the three cases indicated, the respective responses might be as set out in Figure 5.4.

Both the JRF and Durham initiatives point to the possibility of facilitating proactive interventions, with envisaged health gains, through monitoring some aspects of people's daily and nocturnal routines. There is also a substantial potential for cost savings through the use of lifestyle monitoring as opposed to conventional social alarms, with research in Birmingham suggesting a £5 million saving over 10 years for every 10,000 people, or £58 million a year in total for the UK (noted by Porteus and Brownsell, 2000).

Figure 5.4: Reactive and proactive interventions

Nature of event	Reactive intervention	Proactive intervention
Occasional or regular falls	Check for injury	Reduce danger of falling due to external causes
	Obtain medical assistance if appropriate	Promote personal exercise regime to improve strength
	Arrange for hospital visit, X-rays, etc	Check personal health and for any adverse effects of medication
Regular bed-wetting or soiling at nighttime	Wash person	Check personal health
	Provide clean nightclothes	Promote exercises to improve control of body functions
	Change bedding as necessary	Arrange for toileting at appropriate intervals before likely times of bed-wetting or soiling
Problem of bedsores due to long periods of immobility when sleeping	Treat bedsores Apply dressings	Arrange for turning at appropriate intervals and/or within maximum period of immobility deemed advisable
	Provide special mattress	Reduce sedative effects of medication

User acceptance and ethical issues

In considering the extent to which older people are willing to accept smart technologies, a range of factors need to be considered. First, however, it is necessary to lay to rest any notion that older people are reluctant to accept technologies or are somehow unable to cope with them. The contrary has been proven repeatedly in a host of different contexts both within the UK and further afield. For instance, Cullen and Robinson (1997), in appraising the opportunities of new technologies for older and disabled people throughout the EU, identify an immense range of actual and potential technology applications being utilised. And, more specifically for England and Wales, Appleton (1999) concluded from a telephone survey of 500 people aged over 55 years old (for the Technology for Living Forum) that older people are using and value a wide range of technology.

The results of the Technology for Living Forum survey provide the most up-to-date picture. They found that, for six items of technology (seven if you add the telephone itself), a majority of older people used them (Figure 5.5). Particularly interesting, perhaps, is the fact that personal computers were used by a third of respondents. This was mainly for word processing but a quarter of them used email. While men constituted exactly half the sample, few gender differences were evident. Nearly two thirds of the sample (63.4%) were aged 65 or over, the remainder being aged between 55 and 64.

With regard to smart home technologies, however, less than one in five respondents felt they could find a use for devices that controlled lighting

Figure 5.5: Technology used by older people

- Television (98.6%)
- Radio (98.6%)
- Washing machine (95.2%)
- Video recorder (85.4%)
- Microwave oven (84.2%)
- CD player (61.4%)
- Dishwasher (39.6%)
- Mobile telephone (38.8%)
- Computer (35.2%)
- Satellite or cable television (30.6%)

Source: From Appleton (1999)

(17.2%), heating (16.0%), opened and closed curtains (14.6%) and doors (10.6%).

Appleton's (1999) findings add to the evidence that older people are avid users of, and readily adapt to, technologies. They are, however, wary of new technologies in the sense that they need to see clear benefits before making decisions about their acquisition. A lower take-up by older people would, in any case, be expected for several reasons, including the fact that many of the technologies are marketed specifically at younger people with older people either being unaware of them or not recognising their wider applicability; and older people's generally lower disposable incomes.

With regard to telecare services, there is a range of other factors affecting user acceptance that relate to their intrusiveness. These include the user's prior experience of the technologies, the attitudes of others and the extent of control the user has over the equipment (Fisk, 1996b). Telecare services, as noted earlier, are increasingly part of smart systems and have especial relevance to older people. Fisk concluded that, in order to maximise user acceptance, the intrusiveness of the technologies and associated services should be minimised. He affirmed that:

> ... the minimisation of intrusiveness requires that both the technology and associated services recognise the rights of users and that the restrictive and potentially dis-empowering aspects of medical care for patients are reduced as services are moved from institutional settings to the home. (1996b, p 54)

The issue of intrusiveness raises a number of ethical issues. These essentially relate to the functionality of smart technologies and the ways in which they operate; and the configuration of, or changes made to, service frameworks in order to use such technologies. Both can dramatically impact on the extent to which users are empowered.

Consideration of functionality raises questions about the extent to which smart systems should incorporate the capacity for lifestyle monitoring and the extent of intrusiveness that is appropriate and/or necessary. A second question concerns the extent to which it is appropriate to rely on computers to make automated decisions, despite the fact that they might only do so in accordance with parameters and operational frameworks determined by service providers and/or users.

With regard to how lifestyle monitoring is done, it must be reaffirmed at the outset that information about any person, their health, habits, movement, social, sexual and economic activity belongs to that person alone unless they choose to share it with others. Therefore, no smart technology should operate and no information should be communicated to others without the full consent of the person whom it is intended to benefit. By the same token any service user must have access to an on/off switch that controls any aspect of the lifestyle monitoring or broader aspects of smart systems that they consider intrusive.

Particular concerns relate to the use of closed-circuit television cameras within users' homes. These are considered to be potentially highly intrusive, although have been found acceptable at fixed locations, as part of videophones for people receiving nursing care at home (Schoone et al, 1998). Furthermore, videophone technology is likely to become a common feature of homes in coming years and is, of course, capable of being controlled by the user.

Linked with such concerns is the requirement for smart systems that incorporate lifestyle monitoring to be configured in a manner determined by or in partnership with the user. In other words, the user should determine when, how often and in what quantities any lifestyle information should be sent to a third party. And, regardless of the agreed parameters, further safeguards need to be put in place regarding how that information is stored, responded to or, in certain circumstances, passed to others by that third party. Establishing such parameters or the use of an on/off switch mean that aspects of a person's activity would remain unmonitored. This respects the need for user privacy and would not, it is considered, compromise the objectives of lifestyle monitoring. Arguably it would increase the likelihood of such technologies being accepted. In any case, a significant objective of lifestyle monitoring relates to longer-term issues whereby gradual changes can be identified.

Benefits of smart homes

Overall, it is considered that smart homes can bring a range of benefits to older people and improve their quality of life. This is particularly the case now that the technologies are characterised by increasing communications capacity and are being applied in design for all contexts. The benefits can be measured in terms of the extent to which people are able to live more independently and, importantly, the extent to which they may be empowered and socially included through the availability and use of such technologies. However, some empowerment derives, not from the smart technologies themselves, but from the fact that older people can have access to a wide range of online services, including those that provide information directly relating to their needs.

Several difficulties, however, must be overcome in order to achieve such objectives. The barrier to technological advances because of the lack of agreement in signalling protocols has already been noted. The technology push has, as a result, been less effective than might have otherwise been the case. Also, as briefly mentioned, is the fact that many older people have limited disposable incomes and would not be able to afford such technologies (Fisk, 1999; Pieper, 1999). The promotion of smart technologies by statutory agencies would be, therefore, an essential prerequisite to the empowerment and social inclusion of many older people who are already disadvantaged by virtue of physical or sensory impairment, their limited wealth and their marginalisation in economic, tenural and geographical terms (see Fisk, 1999).

A further and fundamental barrier to the development of smart homes relates to the absence of ethical frameworks to underpin them. This is especially the case as lifestyle monitoring becomes possible, but where there are real dangers that the associated technologies may be promoted according to medical models of older age and service provision. Users might, in other words, be regarded as patients rather than users; and, while there might be benefits in terms of their compliance with regimes of treatment, there might be fewer gains in terms of empowerment, social inclusion and, therefore, overall well-being.

The potential for cost savings through the use of lifestyle monitoring poses a particular threat in that powerful arguments might be placed to promote their usage without appropriate ethical safeguards being put into place. Furthermore, there is a worry that the power given to service providers to monitor older people might also be afforded to relatives and/or informal carers without proper cognisance being given to the user and their wishes. In this context, the need for the user to have control over the technology must be strongly reaffirmed, with such control only being exercised by a third party in the event of substantial disability or dementia, and then only in accordance with agreed protocols (see Chapter Six of this book). It should also be noted that the grounds for such a transfer of control have been well explored in the context of electronic tagging (see Bewley, 1998).

The fears of reductions in personal contact through the use of smart technologies are considered, in large part, misguided. Indeed, an exciting element of them is the potential to liberate users from inappropriate and oppressive frameworks of support and care. In so doing there is the possibility of developing new service frameworks that afford greater control to users and are based on more equal partnerships between them and service providers.

Smart technologies also have implications for dwelling designs. Through their communication capacity they offer the prospect of more people of all ages working from home and/or being active virtual participants in economic, social and family networks. Such activity would be likely to require additional workspace in at least one room and the need for equipment in one or more other locations. With the increase in online activity comes the likelihood of more people shopping remotely – a phenomenon that Durham County Council (1999) noted would reduce pressures on support workers. A design implication noted by Moran (1993) and Gann et al (1999) is the need for hatches or boxes to permit the delivery and temporary safe storage of goods as people increasingly use home-shopping services. In addition, the association of smart homes with the support of people with severe physical or sensory impairments and, increasingly, a wide range of medical conditions, points to the need for larger dwellings. As well as conforming to design-for-all or Lifetime Homes standards, these might usefully incorporate a spare bedroom for accommodating a spouse, partner or carer.

It can be concluded that it is the potential gains in terms of user empowerment and inclusion in economic and social life that makes smart homes so relevant to debates about the needs of older people. Smart homes may, through home automation, have promised increased physical independence, but now, by harnessing their communication capacity, they can deliver so much more.

References

Appleton, N. (1999) 'Technophobe or technofan survey: findings of Technology for Living survey', Technology for Living Forum Launch Conference, London, 10 November.

Atkin, B.L. (1988) 'Progress towards intelligent buildings', in B.L. Atkin (ed) *Intelligent buildings: Applications of IT and building automation to high technology construction projects*, London: Kogan Page, pp 1-7.

Bewley, C. (1998) *Tagging: A technology for care services?*, London: Values into Action.

Bjørneby, S. (1997) *The BESTA flats in Tønsberg*, Oslo: Human Factors Solutions.

Braye, S. and Preston-Shoot, M. (1995) *Empowering practice in social care*, Buckingham: Open University Press.

Chan, M., Bocquet, H., Campo, E., Val, T., Extève, D. and Pous, J. (1998) 'Multisensor system and artificial intelligence in housing for the elderly', in J. Graffmans, V. Taipale and N. Charness (eds) *Gerontechnology: A sustainable investment in the future*, Amsterdam: IOS Press, pp 145-9.

Cullen, K. and Robinson, S. (1997) *Telecommunications for older people and disabled people in Europe: Preparing for the information society*, Assistive Technology Research Series, Amsterdam: IOS Press.

Doughty, K. (2000) 'Super MIDAS: an advanced telecare system for sheltered housing', Paper presented at the Monitoring of Residents in Sheltered Housing Symposium, City University, London, 3 February.

Doughty, K. and Costa, J. (1997) 'Continuous automated care of the elderly', *Journal of Telemedicine and Telecare*, vol 3, Supplement 1 to vol 1, pp 23-5.

Doughty, K., Cameron, K. and Garner, P. (1996) 'Three generations of telecare of the elderly', *Journal of Telemedicine and Telecare*, vol 2, no 1, pp 71-80.

Doughty, K., King, P.J., Smith, P.C. and Williams, G. (1999) 'MIDAS – Modular Intelligent Domiciliary Alarm System – a practical application of telecare', Paper presented at the Institute of Electrical and Electronics Engineers Conference on Engineering in Medicine and Biology, Atlanta, GA, 2 November.

Durham County Council (1999) *People at home and in touch: The use of technology to support older people in their own homes*, Durham: Durham County Council.

Felbaum, K. (1999) 'State of the art on technology for smart homes', Paper presented at the International Conference on Smart Homes and Telematics, Eindhoven, 22-23 February.

Fisk, M.J. (1996a) 'Elderly people and independent living: the implications of smart house technologies', Paper presented at the British Society of Gerontology Annual Conference, Liverpool, 20-22 September.

Fisk, M.J. (1996b) 'Telecare equipment in the home: issues of intrusiveness and control, *Journal of Telemedicine and Telecare*, vol 3, supplement 1, pp 30-2.

Fisk, M.J. (1997) 'Telemedicine, new technologies and care management', *International Journal of Geriatric Psychiatry*, vol 12, no 11, pp 1057-9.

Fisk, M.J. (1998) 'Telecare at home: factors influencing technology choices and user acceptance', *Journal of Telemedicine and Telecare*, vol 4, no 2, pp 80-3.

Fisk, M.J. (1999) *Our future home: Housing and the inclusion of older people in 2025*, London: Help the Aged.

Galvin, J.C. (1997) 'Assistive technology: federal policy and practise since 1982', *Technology and Disability*, vol 6, no 1.2, pp 3-15.

Gann, D., Barlow, J. and Venables, T. (1999) *Digital futures: Making homes smarter*, Coventry: Chartered Institute of Housing.

Glasgow City Council (1993) *Housing and elderly people in North West Glasgow: Results of a survey of housing alarm users and sheltered housing applicants*, Glasgow: Glasgow City Council Housing Department.

Harding, T. (1997) *A life worth living: The independence and inclusion of older people*, London: Help the Aged.

Hickling Corporation (1991) *Applications of building automation for elderly and disabled persons*, Montreal: Canadian Automated Buildings Association.

Horelli, L. and Leppo, A. (1994) 'Experiences with the assessment of smart home technology for the elderly and disabled in Finland', in C. Wild and A. Kirschner (eds) *Safety-alarm systems, technical aids and smart homes*, Akon Series Vol 8, Knegsel: Akontes Publishing.

Jeantet, B. (1994) 'Home automation in France', Paper presented at the BESTA International Conference, Lillehammer, 8-9 June.

Karlsson, M. (1995) 'Elderly and new technology: on the introduction of new technology in everyday life', in I. Placencia Porrero and R. Puig de la Bellcasa (eds) *The European context for assistive technology*, Amsterdam: IOS Press, pp 78-81.

Moran, R. (1993) *The electronic home: Social and spatial aspects*, Dublin: European Foundation for the Improvement of Living and Working Conditions.

Orsini, V. and Stochino, G. (1993) 'Intelligent home in Italy: Arision experiences and actual trend', in A. Morini (ed) *Information technologies for buildings in a changing society*, Milan: CNR-ICITE, BE-MA Editrice.

Phillipson, C. (1998) *Reconstructing old age: New agendas in social theory and practice*, London: Sage Publications.

Pieper, R. (1999) 'The societal aspects of smart homes and telematics', Paper presented at the International Conference on Smart Homes and Telematics, Eindhoven, 22-23 February.

Porteus, J. and Brownsell, A. (2000) *Using telecare: Exploring technologies for independent living for older people*, Oxford: Anchor Trust.

Poulson, D. and Nicolle, C. (1999) 'From CASA to DISCUS – using new technology in the provision of care services', Paper presented at the International Conference on Smart Homes and Telematics, Eindhoven, 22-23 February.

Schoone, M., Bos, W. and Piël, S.A. (1998) *Monitoring thuiszorg*, Leiden: TNO Preventie en Gezondheid.

Shobu, K. (1993) 'Tron House: innovative ideas of intelligent houses', in A. Morini (ed) *Information technologies for buildings in a changing society*, Milan: CNR-ICITE, BE-MA Editrice.

Tamura, T., Togawa, T., Ogawa, M. and Yamakoshi, K. (1998) 'Fully automated health monitoring at home', in J. Graffmans, V. Taipale and N. Charness (eds) *Gerontechnology: A sustainable investment in the future*, Amsterdam: IOS Press, pp 280-4.

Tang, P. and Venables, P. (2000) 'Smart homes and telecare for independent living', *Journal of Telemedicine and Telecare*, vol 6, pp 8-14.

Valins, M.S. and Salter, D. (1996) 'Looking back', in M.S. Valins and D. Salter (eds) *Futurecare: New directions in planning health and care environments*, Oxford: Blackwell Science, pp 1-5.

Vlaskamp, F.J.M., van Dort, W.J. and Quaedackers, J.E.W. (1994) 'Integrated systems: towards modular and flexible control and communications systems for disabled persons', in A. Davies, H.M. Felix and H.A. Kamphuis (eds) *Research development knowledge-transfer in the field of rehabilitation and handicap*, Hoensbroek: Institute for Rehabilitation Research, pp 55-68.

Willems, C. (1999) 'Independent living and care provision for people with special needs in a smart home environment', Paper presented at the International Conference on Smart Homes and Telematics, Eindhoven, 22-23 February.

SIX

Dementia and technology

Mary Marshall

Technology in the future

> People constantly look to modern technology to improve their lifestyles. This includes for example, personal computers, the use of the Internet, technology used in hospitals, the telephone and the television and devices such as washing machines and vacuum cleaners. One of the ways in which life could improve for older people is in the harnessing of new technology in new, imaginative and profitable ways. (Royal Commission on Long Term Care, 1999, p 2)

This optimistic section of the Royal Commission report does not specifically mention people with dementia. It refers to "technological aids which will enable people to live safely in their homes" (p 2), and stresses that the design of new housing should encompass technology to facilitate communication and tasks of everyday living. It also refers to the life-enhancing potential of technology. All of these aspirations can and should apply to technology for people with dementia. This chapter will consider how this can happen in practical terms as well as considering approaches to ethical concerns that can arise in the use of technology for a group of people who will not usually understand it. People with dementia make up the largest group in long-stay institutional care and, whether within institutions or living in the community, they are extremely vulnerable to forms of social exclusion. General communication is difficult, with misunderstandings and problems for many social groups in accepting people with dementia. While technological developments can be no replacement for a broader approach to inclusion in policy and practice terms, they can offer enabling support and assistance to people with dementia and their carers.

Dementia and negative attitudes

People with dementia struggle to be seen as people behind a frightening label. People who work with them are usually a long way from seeing dementia as 'just another disability' – to quote the City of Glasgow slogan (see below, page 128). This must be, in part, because of the stigma of any mental illness – especially one which is both very common (about 600,000 people in the UK have a diagnosis of dementia) and one which can strike anybody. The risk of dementia increases exponentially with age from about one in twenty at age 60 to about one in five at age 80, so our attitudes to it are related to attitudes to ageing. Indeed, the fear of dementia colours many people's personal attitude to ageing. People who work with people with dementia are not exempt from these feelings of dread about ageing and the disease.

Fear of dementia is compounded by the dominance of the medical model in dementia care. This is a deeply pessimistic model since there is very little that conventional medicine can do for dementia. Cholinesterase inhibitors, the exciting new drugs now available, are still only effective in about a quarter of people with Alzheimer's disease. Further, only about half of people with dementia have Alzheimer's disease; most of the rest have either vascular or Lewy Body dementia.

Most training for staff in the field of dementia will start with definitions like this one:

> Dementia is a group of progressive diseases of the brain that slowly affect all functions of the mind and lead to a deterioration in a person's ability to concentrate, remember and reason. It can affect every area of human thinking, feeling and behaviour. (Murphy, 1986, p 12)

The danger of such a definition is that it implies that all of the disabilities are inevitable and associated with the progressive deterioration of the brain. The reality is that, as with any disability, some people are more disabled by the condition than others. Also, other factors are at work – many associated with the built environment. However, this disability perspective is not usually presented to staff in the field to balance up the medical model, and people with dementia are usually confronted with staff who, if they have any training at all, will have received training that emphasised brain damage and the powerlessness of any intervention. Small wonder then that people with dementia make up the majority of the population in long-stay institutional care, since staff feel there is very little that can be done to preserve or even improve their capacity for independent living. Sylvia Cox, in her useful book about housing and support for people with dementia, says:

> People with dementia may sustain many of their strengths and abilities, as well as their independence, if they have the right kind of physical environment, the right kind of social support and a daily pattern of living which supports their preferred lifestyle and maximises their potential. Even the positive aspects of remaining at home may not be realised if a routine, standardised approach is taken to providing care and support. (Cox, 1998, p 10)

It may be European policy (Warner et al, 1998) to keep older people with dementia at home wherever possible, but this policy tends to be viewed in terms of support for carers rather than assisting the person with dementia to remain as independent as possible. The current preoccupation with risk in social services (Waterson, 1999) is rarely translated into risk management for people with dementia. It is much more likely to be risk assessment and removal to what is seen as 'a safer place'.

Staff cannot be blamed for all of this. There is often considerable relative and neighbour pressure to remove people with dementia who are perceived as being at risk of hurting themselves or others. The dangers are usually around what is often called 'wandering' (a very misleading term for an activity that is usually purposeful, even if the purpose is not clear to those observing it). People with dementia sometimes go out at unsuitable times, such as the middle of the night, or inadequately clad. Other risky situations relate to fire and flood, and include people who put on the gas but do not light it, or who put pans on the stove with nothing in them, or turn on water taps and forget to turn them off. The most common response to all of these is removal from home following a risk assessment.

Dementia as a disability

The last 10 years have seen a radical reappraisal of dementia care and our expectations of what can be achieved. Perhaps the most influential writer has been the late Tom Kitwood who charted the development of his thinking in his last book (Kitwood, 1997). He lucidly expounded the concept of a malignant social psychology experienced by people with dementia, which is characterised by very low expectations, a blame culture – where everything is blamed on brain damage and dementia – and a failure to see the person behind the diagnosis. He identified the poor quality of the built environment in which many people with dementia live as a problem with which they have to contend.

In almost every aspect of dementia care there have been huge strides in our understanding of how to reduce the disabilities associated with it. Most relevant here is the work on the design of buildings for people with dementia, led initially from the US, with work on design generally (see for example Calkins, 1988; Shroyer et al, 1989; Cohen and Weisman, 1991; Hiatt, 1995) or as part of work on specialist dementia units (see for example Coons, 1991; Peppard, 1991). There is now also useful European and Australian literature (Annerstedt et al, 1993; Netten, 1993; Judd et al, 1997) and developments into cultural sensitivity in dementia design (Bennett, 1997).

Our understanding of therapeutic design for people with dementia is slowly finding its way into design guides for buildings for disabled and older people. The most recent guide produced by the Centre for Accessible Environments (CAE, 1998) addresses design needs for people with dementia in marked contrast to very reputable design guides for older people, such as the one by Valins (1988) only a decade before. Two recent Scottish design guides produced by Scottish Homes (Pickles, 1998, 1999) both consider the disabilities arising from dementia. However, designing for people with dementia has yet to be fully incorporated into the guides for 'Lifetime Homes', in spite of the fact that the pioneering Edinvar Housing Association drew attention to the need to consider this in their influential guide to barrier-free design (Martin, 1992).

Design for people with dementia

In 1999 Glasgow was the UK City of Architecture and Design, and dementia was chosen as the disability for special attention under the slogan 'just another disability, making design dementia friendly'. The intention of this initiative was to extend and promote the understanding of design for people with dementia within everyday design, for example for hospital wards, general residential and nursing homes and, perhaps most importantly, in the design of ordinary housing. A set of publications about this important initiative are yet to appear, so far only the proceedings of a European conference are available (Stewart and Page, 2000).

Few of these publications about design include technology, although this has been attempted in some academic textbooks (Marshall, 1997a). Nevertheless, the Glasgow customised council flat is also a 'smart' flat in the sense of incorporating a computer cable which links items of equipment (Gann et al, 1999), making the home a great deal more responsive. For example, if a smoke alarm is activated, the equipment can be programmed to switch off the stove, switch on the extractor fan, alert the response centre or a neighbour and unlock the front door. In Norway there are several examples of smart flats for people with dementia (Clatworthy and Bjørneby, 1997), but they are only recently emerging in the UK, and still only as demonstration flats rather than part of ordinary provision.

Design for people with dementia follows on from an understanding of the disabilities most commonly experienced by people with dementia. These almost always include:

- impaired memory;
- impaired learning;
- impaired reasoning;
- increasing dependence on the senses;
- high levels of stress.

The built environment can compensate for all of these to a greater or lesser degree. A domestic house, for example, should be familiar in terms of best memories, which is likely to be the best brain function retained. Thus, it should have fixtures and fittings that make sense for people whose most vivid memories are of about 50 years previously. It should not rely on new learning, for example, about the location of the toilet. High levels of visibility and plenty of light can be very helpful so that the person does not have to learn; they can see. Cupboard doors that can be removed could be very helpful for some people. It should not be necessary to apply reason. This may mean that the heating system should be able to adjust itself to the routine of the person; the oven should be a familiar one or have very simple controls, and so on. Dependence on the senses may mean that a familiar touch sensation such as the fabric of a chair cover is very important to aid recognition. Being able to hear, see, smell and touch food while it is being prepared can be important to aid mealtime behaviour and eating. High levels of stress are a predictable result of coping with life with a mental impairment; if we can provide a familiar, safe home that enables as much independence as possible, we can reduce the stress levels. This is not, of course, confined only to the person with dementia – relatives can experience very high levels of stress and exhaustion, so anything design can do to help them is clearly also important.

The following principles of design for dementia are emerging as an international consensus, although they have been developed mainly for group care rather than the domestic home:

- design should compensate for disability;
- design should maximise independence;
- design should enhance self-esteem and confidence;
- design should demonstrate care for staff (relatives in this context);
- design should be orienting and understandable;
- design should reinforce personal identity;
- design should welcome relatives and the local community;
- design should allow control of stimuli (Judd et al, 1997).

Technology can usefully be seen as an extension of such thinking about design.

Technology for people with dementia

Technology in the homes of people with dementia is generally called assistive technology in the sense that it assists the person to live as normal a life as possible (see also Chapter Five, pp 104-6). It would be possible to have a lengthy debate about the term 'technology' itself since it appears to only be used when the device is new and unfamiliar: few of us think of our telephones or our vacuum cleaners as 'technology'; we just accept them as part of our lives. The equipment described in this chapter is unfamiliar in its application and is therefore generally called technology. It could be argued that the most useful technology for both carers and people with dementia is the telephone, and although this is not mentioned as such here, the alarm systems discussed are based on the telephone and a device to assist the use of the telephone is mentioned. A very useful introduction to the use of technology with older people and community care is provided by Cullen and Moran (1992).

Assistive technology can have many purposes. They are perhaps most easily clustered into three groups (Marshall, 1999b) although this is rather arbitrary since the purposes overlap:

1. those which improve the safety of individuals and others;
2. those concerned with monitoring and maintaining health;
3. those which enhance the quality of life.

The first cluster would include devices that switch off cookers when they get too hot or those which alert helpers if someone goes out in the middle of the night. Extra large clocks can be in this category for people who have lost their sense of time and their ability to read a normal-sized clock. A device can link a movement detector to a light switch in order to automatically switch on the light when a person gets out of bed – particularly useful if they sometimes forget how to get to the toilet. If the device is a weight detector under the foot of the bed it can also be programmed to switch the light off again after a certain length of time, when the person is back in bed. A much-needed device, which does not yet exist, is one that switches off the water taps in a bath or sink when there is danger of an overflow. Devices do exist which can monitor excess wetness on the bathroom floor and then alert a helper, but it would be useful to be able to pre-empt this happening.

The second cluster would include devices that assist in the taking of medication or which monitor an individual's temperature and blood pressure. It might also include devices that monitor a person's behaviour, to see if there has been any change that might require an alteration to the care package. Thus, for example, if someone started to get up five or six times in the night to go to the toilet rather than once, then some investigation might be helpful.

The third, and usually most neglected cluster of technologies, are those which help a person to remain active, involved and obtaining as much enjoyment from life as possible. These would include reminder devices, such as those which let a person know, on leaving their house or flat, that they have left a window open or the cooker on. Another such device would be a photo-box to help a person to use the telephone when they can no longer remember telephone numbers nor how to look them up. These technologies might also include devices which are purely about enjoyment such as personalised videos or songs accessed via a touch screen (Maki, 1994).

Characteristics of technology

One key characteristic of this set of technologies is that many of them are passive. They do not require the person with dementia to remember what they are for or how to use them. The safety devices, for example, are programmed to alert helpers when they are activated by an event such as smoke, heat or a door opening. Other devices have a very obvious application such as the photo-box. The person with dementia simply presses the photograph and the phone automatically dials the number. The touch screens are similarly very direct; the screen displays a set of photographs of singers and the person with dementia presses the photograph of the person whose songs they want to hear. No memory, reasoning or learning is required, although even this degree of action may be beyond many people with dementia.

The passive nature of many of these devices implies that there is a back-up service. The UK is uniquely well served by community alarm services for alert older and disabled people to be able to call for help at the press of a button or the pull of a chord. These alarm services are also ideal for passive alarms since the call centre will be able to have action instructions immediately on their screens, which can be tailored to each individual. The computer at the call centre can also be used to monitor the times at which the system is alerted in order to gauge changes in behaviour patterns.

Another characteristic of technology for people with dementia is that choosing the technology for a person with dementia is crucially part of an assessment and care planning process (Marshall, 1999a). The assessment should reveal needs which can be met by technology, along with those that could be met by help from individuals or modification of their accommodation. The process of need assessment is no different in relation to technology; it merely extends the repertoire of available responses.

The invaluable *Technology, ethics and dementia* guide to the use of technology (Bjørneby et al, 1999) provides a list of desired characteristics for technology which are both very obvious and yet easy to neglect:

> When taking these aspects into consideration, a product should have the following characteristics:
>
> - The product must provide the user with an experience of success.
> - Possibilities of using the product wrongly must be minimised. Making a mistake must not result in punishment/negative feedback, but, eg, in some humorous comments.
> - The product should not contain information that was unknown 30-40 years ago.

- The product should not look like it has been designed for a special group. It should have the look of a high-quality product that has been designed for adults.
- The product should not require demanding intellectual performance from the user.
- The use of the product should demand the use of at least two senses. This stimulates several abilities and supports his/her ability to perform the task.

In addition, good products and technical solutions have the following characteristics:

- They give a feeling of independence to the person.
- They support the skills maintained and do not emphasise lost skills.
- They do not treat the user as a person with disabilities, but supports the self-image of being a person with abilities.
- They remind of solutions that existed before.
- The use of the product is possible by the information visibly/available at all times. (Bjorneby et al, 1999, pp 60-1)

The availability of technology

Technology for people with dementia usually has one of three origins. First, there is technology which is specially designed to meet the specific needs of people with dementia, such as the photo-box for telephoning, or an oven which is designed to switch off when there is nothing in a saucepan. The second is generally available technology which has been adapted or combined to suit people with dementia. An example of this would be movement detectors (passive infra-red) which are plugged into the back of a community alarm. Finally, there is technology designed for a purpose other than helping people with dementia, but, when seen to have application for them, may be purchased off the shelf. For example, devices that remind you to shut the windows when you open the front door are generally available, as are large-faced clocks, but they can be especially useful for people with dementia.

But, how widespread are these technologies? The Astrid project was a European Union project charged with producing a guide to assist front-line staff to understand the potential and appropriate use of technology (Astrid Group, 2000). The project looked at the availability of technology for people with dementia in four European countries and found that it was not generally available in any country, not even in Norway where its use is the most widespread. The reasons for this are complex. In the UK it is salutary to look at one successful technology project and to speculate about the reasons why it has not been replicated.

The Mobile Emergency Care Service (MECS) was started as a general community alarm scheme for Central Regional Council in Scotland. Ten years ago a small extension was pioneered for people with dementia, in which passive technologies replaced or supplemented the push-button pendants. Smoke detectors, thermostats, carbon monoxide detectors and door magnets could be wired into the back of Tunstall telephone alarm equipment in whatever combination was appropriate, and the equipment was linked to a response centre. When the devices were activated the response centre computer displayed the person-specific instructions, which were usually to inform a neighbour or relative. If the contact was not available a warden from the response service would go out. As part of a package of care, this service was helping about 30 people with dementia remain at home when they would have otherwise been in institutional care. In 1996 the service was described in some detail to a large audience at a Council and Care lecture and the paper was then published (Marshall, 1997b). The whole service was also described in a publication of the Dementia Services Development Centre (Macnaughton, 1997).

A year or so after the Scottish reorganisation of local government, the MECS service was split into three. Falkirk is one of the three councils running the service where, at present, 60 people with dementia, who would otherwise be in institutional care, are helped to remain at home. Yet no other local authorities have replicated this successful initiative. Possible explanations include:

1. Low expectations of the capacity of people with dementia, and lack of concern that they are not able to benefit from the community alarm service available to people with other disabilities.
2. Lack of knowledge about the potential of this technology for people with dementia, although many local authorities are aware of it.
3. A lack of confidence that risks could really be diminished by the service, despite the fact that this was demonstrably the case in the MECS scheme.
4. A fear that jobs would be lost as technology replaced human services – although this is plainly not the case in Falkirk where it is supplementary to the domiciliary care service.
5. A failure to really address the unmet needs of people with dementia who want to live at home.

6. A fear of cost implications, although the items linked to the Tunstall equipment in Falkirk are all cheap and simple – not one costs more than £100.
7. An inability to provide the complex mixture of staff or the key professional required to make the services work. It is this last that has been identified in the Astrid project as a major obstacle to progress.

The integration gap

To make technology work for people with dementia living in their own homes requires a combination of skills and expertise: working directly with people with dementia and their carers with regards to communication, needs assessment and care planning; understanding technology in the mechanical sense; and, crucially, linking the two. The linking role is the one which connects the technology to the back-up service, ensures that the whole system is operating properly, monitors equipment failure and ensures that action is taken, ensures that there are reviews of the equipment and so on. In Falkirk this is undertaken by a small team including the homecare team manager, a specialist dementia care social worker or community practice nurse and an electrician with very good communication skills and a great deal of empathy. They meet regularly and regularly review all the clients with dementia.

The Astrid project took the view that their guide to technology would whet the appetite of enthusiastic staff in dementia care but that the service would not develop without this role of facilitator/*animateur*. There has been an attempt to provide this role through a 'care and repair' service in Wales, but it has been slow to develop. Until this gap is filled, it is unlikely that many people with dementia will be able to benefit from technology.

A professional with the right background could achieve the linking role. Occupational therapy would seem to be the ideal background but occupational therapists (OTs) have not played a significant role in the UK. This is curious given that the technology can be seen as an extension of the equipment and adaptation service that OTs offer in most localities. The practice guide for OTs by Carr et al (1998) includes a section on technology. Cox (1998) points out that carrying out repairs, adaptations, and the installation of new technology can have an impact on the stress levels and anxiety of the person with dementia. Most available technology requires little in the way of disruption but her point about the importance of training the people actually doing the installation is well made.

Ethical practice

Ethical issues are raised much more often at training sessions about technology than at those about neuroleptics or locked doors. While it is entirely appropriate that they should be raised, it is nevertheless striking that the connections are not made – all three can be considered to put constraints on people with dementia against their will. Possible reasons for resisting the use of technology are discussed above and ethical concerns may be yet another reason. However, there are useful ways of addressing ethical concerns so that the work can proceed. These do not offer answers but they clarify the issues and assist in making decisions. Inevitably a balance must be found to ensure that the best possible outcome for all concerned is achieved.

Tony Hope and Caroline Oppenheimer (Hope and Oppenheimer, 1997) provide a very useful trilogy of approaches that have been distilled in the Astrid guide and elsewhere (Marshall, 1998; Astrid Group, 2000) as the three 'p's: *perspectives*, *principles* and *paradigms*. Not all the approaches will be useful in all situations, but they are an improvement on previous guidance on ethical practice, which tended to focus on the principles alone whereas people struggling with ethical dilemmas often naturally use approaches which resemble perspectives or paradigms.

Perspectives involve the process of looking at the views of all concerned. Clearly the most important person is the person with dementia but sometimes he or she is not able to communicate a view clearly. However, conventional understanding about the extent to which they are able to communicate are now being radically changed (Allan, 2001). Research projects such as that by Mozely et al (1999) found that people with dementia who had an MMSE[1] score as low as 10, were able to voice opinions about the building in which they lived. The issue of the ability of people with dementia to give consent is also being revisited (see for example Dimond, 1999). Goldsmith's (1996) book pulled together attitudes and research on communication with people with dementia and is seen as a landmark text. A great many projects and changes in attitudes have resulted.

Currently, with ever-earlier diagnosis, there is a great deal of interest in advance directives, which may include wishes about aspects of care. There are clearly problems as to whether an advance directive made in one frame of mind still applies in another, but we will increasingly have this perspective of the person with dementia to weigh in the balance. Until recently proxy consent was considered appropriate. There are three potential ways of achieving proxy consent: asking the relative, inferring current views from past views about similar issues and inferring views from actions. Increasingly this is seen as inappropriate and is now illegal in the UK. However, this is not to say that it is not good practice to consult relatives and to know the history of the person. Other perspectives would include the views of relatives, friends, neighbours, involved staff such as the GP, community nurses, home helps, social workers and so on.

With regard to ***principles***, three are usually presented. *Autonomy* is a major principle, which seems to be of increasing significance in today's society. In the recent past *fairness/justice* were considered the most important but are less so now, except perhaps in Scandinavian countries. The importance of a person having all the necessary information and being able to make their own decision is seen as the most ethical approach by many people. *Beneficence* (doing ones best for the patient) and *avoiding maleficence* (not causing harm) are traditionally very important and often used to justify decisions. Justice/fairness can be raised, especially in resource allocation dilemmas where it can be very helpful. Murna Downs (1997) points out that ethical principles may conflict with one another in real life applications and it is the resolution of these conflicts which is central to ethical practice.

Paradigms are similar situations in which ethical issues appear to be more straightforward, which can usefully be compared to the situation causing the concern in order to illuminate what is different and make a judgement possible. Quite often the difference is age. What is not acceptable for a younger person with cognitive impairment is often considered acceptable for an older person.

A case study may help to show how these three approaches work in practice:

Mrs McFee is 84 and lives alone in a council flat on the ground floor, in a small industrial town. She is very disabled by her dementia being unable to cook for herself, clean the house or dress herself. She has little sense of time. She has a lot of help during the day. A homecare assistant comes in to get her up at 8.00, another comes in to clean mid-morning and stays to cook her lunch and eat with her. Another homecare assistant comes in to give her an evening meal and a district nurse puts her to bed. At weekends her daughter who lives about two miles away, provides the meal in the middle of the day and leaves a snack for the evening. Mrs McFee has lived in the flat for 30 years and is well known and liked locally. She has good neighbours, also older people, who pop in to visit in the afternoons.

Mrs McFee occasionally gets up in the middle of the night and goes out in her nightclothes. Sometimes she puts a coat on. This causes great consternation to her daughter and her friends. Mrs McFee was offered a passive alarm service, which she refused. Assuming that she did not understand the request the social work department went ahead and installed Tunstall community alarm equipment wired to two magnets: one on the front door and the other on the frame. They also attached a timer to activate the system between the hours of 10.00pm and 7.00am. If Mrs McFee went out of the front door, breaking the contact between the magnets, the alarm would be raised at the response centre. The computer was programmed to suggest a list of people to be alerted, the warden only being called out if no one else was available. It was considered that Mrs McFee would not take kindly to a stranger telling her to go back home.

Mrs McFee would not tolerate the equipment. She threw it out of the front door. The suggestion was made that it could be reinstalled but hidden from her. This was clearly against her wishes.

Perspectives approach

Mrs McFee has expressed her views on the equipment both verbally and in her behaviour. She has indicated that she does not want the equipment. Her daughter and neighbour want it to be installed. They feel that they could sleep more easily knowing that they would be alerted should she go out at night. The social worker feels that the alternative will have to be an admission to residential care since Mrs McFee puts herself at great risk going out in the middle of the night. The homecare assistants and the district nurse are very keen that that there is some cover at night because they feel anxious that she is on her own for such a length of time. The GP thinks she should probably be in residential care since she should not be on her own at all.

Principles approach

The principle of *autonomy* would advocate that Mrs McFee is given all the information available and then make up her own mind. If she is incapable of such a decision then she should be the subject of a legal order. *Benificence* would suggest that as long as staff are basing their decision on her best interests and not doing her harm (maleficence), it is ethical to install hidden equipment. *Justice* is less helpful – the key question is whether or not she is receiving the same care and attention as anybody else.

Paradigm approach

A comparable situation in which the ethical issues are clearer would be that of a younger person with a severe learning disability. A woman of 25 with severe cognitive impairment, for example, would be unlikely to have her clearly expressed wishes overruled.

Result

In Mrs McFee's case, the decision was made to install the equipment and hide it under the hall-stand. In this, and other similar decisions where the wishes of the person are clearly overruled, an *ethical protocol* should be used. This is a written and signed sheet, outlining the problem, the action taken and how monitoring and review will be undertaken (Astrid Group, 2000).

Conclusions

Can housing be inclusive if it excludes people with dementia? In terms of human rights it is clear that dementia should not debar people from the right to enjoy social contact and the comfort of familiar and supportive environments. Some people with dementia can be helped to remain at home with technology – if their house is 'dementia friendly' in terms of design it can be a great asset, and technology can extend the capacity of the built environment to support rather than undermine routines and confidence. There are obstacles to widespread use of technology – especially the lack of a link person or team to ensure that the technology operates effectively – and inclusive housing would need to address these aspects. Ethical concerns can be approached constructively using a set of approaches to illuminate the issues, which can then be considered and addressed. Technology is a developing area which can improve the lifestyles of those disabled by dementia, help their carers and support conditions which will allow many more people with dementia to remain in or re-engage with social groups.

Note

[1] MMSE, the Mini-Mental State Examination, is used to measure a person's basic cognitive skills, including short- and long-term memory, orientation, writing and language.

References

Allan, K. (2001) *Communication and consultation: Exploring ways for staff to involve people with dementia in developing services*, Bristol/York: The Policy Press/JRF.

Annerstedt, L., Fournier, K., Gustafson, L., Hallen, U., Malmkvist, I., Salo, S., Schultz, J., Stjernfeldt, G., Ahlund, O. and Tennek, J. (1993) *Group living for people with dementia*, Stirling: Dementia Services Development Centre, University of Stirling.

Astrid Group (2000) *A guide to using technology within dementia care*, London: Hawker Publications.

Bennett, S. (1997) 'Cultural issues in designing for people with dementia', in M. Marshall (ed) *State of the art in dementia care*, London: Centre for Policy on Ageing.

Bjørneby, S., Topo, P. and Holthe, T. (1999) *Technology, ethics and dementia – A guidebook on how to apply technology in dementia care*, Sem: Norwegian Centre for Dementia Research.

CAE (Centre for Accessible Environments) (1998) *The design of residential care and nursing homes for the older people*, London: CAE.

Calkins, M.P. (1988) *Design for dementia planning: Environments for the elderly and the confused*, Marylands, MD: National Health Publishing.

Carr, J. , Garton, C. and Munroe, H. (1998) *Dementia: A practice guide for occupational therapy staff*, Stirling: Dementia Services Development Centre, University of Stirling.

Clatworthy, S. and Bjørneby, S. (1997) 'Smart house installations in Tønsberg', in S. Bjørneby and A. van Berlo (eds) *Ethical issues in use of technology for dementia care*, Knegsel: Akontes Publishing, pp 67-72.

Cohen, U. and Weisman, G.D. (1991) *Holding on to home: Designing environments for people with dementia*, Baltimore, Maryland, MD: Johns Hopkins University Press.

Coons, D.H. (1991) *Specialised dementia units*, Baltimore, MD/London: Johns Hopkins University Press.

Cox, S. (1998) *Home solutions: Housing & support for people with dementia*, London: Housing Associations Charitable Trust.

Cullen, K. and Moran, R. (1992) *Technology and the elderly*, Luxembourg: Commission of the European Communities.

Dimond, B. (1999) 'Consent, competence and the elderly patient and the law', *Psige Newsletter*, vol 70, pp 9-10.

Downs, M. (1997) 'Assessing ethical issues in the use of technology for people with dementia', in S. Bjørneby and A. van Berlo (eds) *Ethical issues in use of technology for dementia care*, Knegsel: Akontes Publishing, pp 57-66.

Gann, D., Barlow, J. and Venables, T. (1999) *Digital futures: Making homes smarter*, Coventry: Chartered Institute of Housing.

Goldsmith, M. (1996) *Hearing the voice of people with dementia: Opportunities and obstacles*, London: Jessica Kingsley.

Hiatt, L.G. (1995) 'Understanding the physical environment', *Pride Institute Journal of Long Term Care*, vol 4, no 2, pp 12-22.

Hope, T. and Oppenheimer, C. (1997) 'Ethics and psychiatry in old age', in R. Jacoby and C. Oppenheimer (eds) *Psychiatry in the elderly*, 2nd edn, Oxford: Oxford University Press, pp 709-35.

Judd, S., Marshall, M. and Phippen, P. (1997) *Design for dementia*, London: Hawker Publications Limited.

Kitwood, T. (1997) *Dementia reconsidered: The person comes first*, Buckingham: Open University Press.

Macnaughton, D. (1997) *The role of technology in the care of people with dementia in the community*, Stirling: Dementia Services Development Centre, University of Stirling.

Maki, O. (1994) *Multimedia and the stimulation of demented old people*, Tampere, Finland: School of Public Health, Tampere University.

Marshall, M. (1997a) 'Design and technology for people with dementia', in R. Jacoby and C. Oppenheimer (eds) *Psychiatry in the elderly*, 2nd edn, Oxford: Oxford University Press, pp 424-35.

Marshall, M. (1997b) *Dementia and technology*, London: Council and Care.

Marshall, M. (1998) 'Keeping in touch: ethical dimensions', in Swiss Alzheimer Association, *Alzheimer 8th European Meeting*, Lucerne: Swiss Alzheimer Association, pp 285-90.

Marshall, M. (1999a) 'Person centred technology?', *Signpost*, vol 3, no 4, pp 4-5.

Marshall, M. (1999b) 'Technology to help people with dementia remain in their own homes', *Generations*, vol 23, no 3, pp 85-7.

Martin, F. (1992) *Every house you'll ever need: a design guide for barrier free housing*, Edinburgh: Edinvar Housing Association.

Mozley, C.G., Huxley, P., Sutcliffe, C., Bagley, H., Burns, A., Challis, D. and Cordingley, L. (1999) '"Not knowing where I am doesn't mean I don't know what I like": cognitive impairment and quality of life responses in elderly people', *International Journal of Geriatric Psychiatry*, vol 14, no 9, pp 776-83.

Murphy, E. (1986) *Dementia and mental illness in the old*, London: Papermac.

Netten, A. (1993) *A positive environment*, Aldershot: Ashgate Publishing.

Peppard, N.R. (1991) *Special needs dementia units: Design, development and operations*, New York, NY: Springer.

Pickles, J. (1998) *Housing for varying needs: Part 1: Houses and flats*, Edinburgh: Scottish Homes.

Pickles, J. (1999) *Housing for varying needs: A design guide: Part 2: Housing with integral support*, Edinburgh: Stationery Office.

Royal Commission on Long Term Care (1999) *With respect to old age*, Edinburgh: Stationery Office.

Shroyer J.L., Hutton, H., Gentry, M.A., Dobbs, M.N. and Elias, J.W. (1989) 'Alzheimer's disease: strategies for designing interiors', *The ASID Report*, vol 15, no 2, pp C4-C7.

Stewart, S. and Page, A. (eds) (2000) *Just another disability: Making design dementia friendly, conference proceedings of the European Conference, 1-2 October 1999*, Glasgow: Just Another Disability.

Valins, M. (1988) *Housing for elderly people: A guide for architects and clients*, London: Architectural Press.

Warner, M., Furnish, S., Lawler, B., Longley, M., Sime, L. and Kellaher, M. (1998) *European Transnational Alzheimer's Study (ETAS): European analysis of public health policy developments for Alzheimer's disease and associated disorders of older people and their carers*, Pontypridd: Welsh Institute for Health and Social Care.

Waterson, J. (1999) 'Redefining community care social work: needs or risk led?', *Health and Social Care in the Community*, vol 7, no 4, pp 276-9.

Part Two
New lives for old?

So far, we have described some positive moves in the future development of ordinary housing, which could be inclusive enough to meet the needs of people of all ages. But what of the present situation? While the majority of older people live in mainstream housing, as outlined in Chapter One, until now our ageing society has largely dealt with older people's needs for support through the development of age-related housing and associated care services. By bringing people to places, the solution to individual needs has been in degrees of collective living. The next section of this text analyses a number of developments in age-related housing, from adapted tower blocks to retirement communities. The authors take a different look at inclusivity by considering a range of places in which older people currently live their everyday lives.

SEVEN

Integrated segregation? Issues from a range of housing/care environments

Brian McGrail, John Percival and Kate Foster with commentary by Caroline Holland and Sheila M. Peace

Introduction

In this chapter, we consider three environments that cross the age-related–mainstream housing divide, exploring ways in which structured technological and social interventions might enhance the domestic life of older people. We draw on recent empirical work, conducted separately by the authors, at locations in Scotland and in London. Brian McGrail examines the development of adapted high-rise housing in Edinburgh and Glasgow; John Percival looks at traditional sheltered housing in an inner London borough; and Kate Foster considers shared housing for people with dementia in Scotland. Further discussion of the issues raised by the individual studies, along with more detail on the settings themselves and illustrations from interviews, are available[1]. Here the three studies have been merged to offer insights into variation.

The three types of housing provision discussed in this chapter represent different stages in the evolution of policy on housing the general population and those defined as 'vulnerable'. High-rise housing (defined variously as over four or five storeys) had been a planning solution to urban density for some time in parts of Europe and in Scotland before most English high-rise schemes were developed in the 1960s and 1970s. As a consequence proportionately more older people live in high-rise housing in Scotland than in England, and Scotland has the stronger tradition of flat dwelling on the whole. The schemes investigated by

Brian McGrail in this chapter are 'tower blocks' with many more than four or five storeys, and date from the 1960s.

In contrast, most sheltered housing schemes date from the late 1970s and 1980s, as public subsidies for housing were largely diverted from general social housing to 'special needs' and other specific purposes. Initially, sheltered schemes were provided by local authorities, but by the 1980s most were being developed by housing associations and trusts, with a smaller number being developed for sale. By 1997 there were 451,114 units of sheltered housing in the UK (DETR, unpublished data). In the early 1990s it became evident that the balance of provision was not entirely compatible with demand (McCafferty, 1994) and since then there has been more concentration on sheltered housing with extra care and the diversification of particular schemes in some areas.

Until the development of extra-care sheltered housing, and arguably since then, the situation of people as they cope with increasing frailty in sheltered housing has been precarious. In this chapter John Percival outlines some of the characteristics of daily life in sheltered housing which work for and against the integration of vulnerable people for whom matters of self may increasingly dominate.

From the 1970s onwards, as forms of senile dementia came to be defined and managed, providers have increasingly aimed to produce specialised environments that can protect and support people suffering from Alzheimer's and related conditions. It has been estimated that 20% of people aged over 80 may have some degree of dementia and, in Scotland, a majority of people with dementia are cared for at home (Alzheimer's Scotland, 1997). But this is not always possible or desirable and in this chapter Kate Foster looks at some small-scale specialist schemes developed in the 1990s.

What then are the themes to be explored across these settings? Three are apparent from the outset – technology and social organisation; finance; and quality of life – and they are used to form the focus of the discussion developing from these empirical studies. But first, we turn to the research.

High-rise housing

Tower block communities have always included a number of older people, but they are more likely to have been regarded as 'residualised' communities than as environments of choice. Here we consider the tower blocks' renewed potential for quality housing in later life through applications of new and expanded electronic technologies.

Management rethinking of high-rises in and through electronic technologies slowly evolved through the 1990s (McGrail, 1999). Starting from basic, manually-controlled closed-circuit televisions (CCTV) and tenant-controlled door-entry systems in the late 1980s, when the focus was on common areas and security (Coleman, 1985; SNU, 1988), management systems have become increasingly reliant on telecommunication networks, desk-top computers and databases (all utilised by ever more remote concierge stations). These developments have encompassed individualised smart keys, intruder and vulnerable tenant inactivity alarms, online smoke detectors, automatic doors and windows (opened remotely in the event of fire), tank and pipe leak monitors, and lift operation sensors linked by mobile telephone to a 24-hour repair service. Here four case studies are described in which some of these technologies have been used to improve the quality of life of older tower block residents.

Almost sheltered?

Citadel Court and Persevere Court in Edinburgh are both 20-storey tower blocks with 78 maisonette flats located in the harbour of Leith. In 1989 tenants were decanted and the blocks were completely refurbished with double-glazing and recladding, door-entry systems, built reception areas in each block, and the introduction of 18-hour concierge cover utilising four cameras in each block. The blocks were 'designated' for people aged over 35 with no children and are therefore to some degree age-integrated while not family oriented.

Concierges can now contact tenants via the door-intercom, but not vice versa. Although not 'wardens', as in sheltered housing, the concierges perform similar roles (Clapham et al, 1990, p 178). They often undertake numerous 'handyperson' jobs, such as fitting light bulbs or shifting heavy furniture. Their role includes most of the tasks which are important to sheltered housing tenants (Clapham and Munro, 1988), including "having someone friendly around to talk to", "to keep an eye on residents", "to offer advice" and "prevent vandalism and crime", but they provide these services for a broad age group – from the forties to the high eighties. As in other estates, these tasks are not part of the job description but evolve in situ. The physical proximity of staff between 6am and 12am means that little is required in the way of high-tech communication and surveillance equipment. The presence of staff is also important since tenant-to-tenant relationships are not generally crucial – the blocks being described as "quiet and pleasant" *without* a strong sense of community.

With their mature population and concierges, these two blocks fall between existing concepts of sheltered housing and 'normal' flats. The existing services, with the addition of dispersed alarms (provided by other agencies), mean that many tenants will 'stay put' until "I go down the lift in a box". But one clear reason for wanting to stay is the human mediators of the block – the concierges – rather than any particular renovation or technological adaptation.

Flexible wiring

The second case study, Hutchesontown, Glasgow, consists of four blocks of 138 flats each within the Gorbals Comprehensive Development Area. In 1994 inadequate door-entry systems were replaced by a control room for daytime use (dispersed concierge), and reception rooms (with security guards and CCTV monitors) at the foot of each block for nighttime. Four cameras were located in each foyer, eleven externally, and one in each of eight lifts – which were also renewed. These were complemented by automated glass doors on all eight entrances, concierge–tenant intercoms, individualised fob-keys, and the fitting of double-bar security doors on every flat.

Security measures were integrated with other efforts to enhance the quality of life in the flats by improving the heating and the appearance of the blocks, and by giving some people more living space (for example, some balconies were enclosed to make conservatories). The final phase entailed upgrading interiors and exteriors with new roofs, cladding, redesigning of balconies and windows, as well as further 'wiring', including attaching smoke alarms to the system. Significantly, a communal district gas-boiler is now used to heat water which is pumped round the buildings for both radiators and washing for about £4-5 a week per tenant.

These blocks are not age restricted. Although intended for a broad range of tenants, many features of the redesign have considered the needs of older people and other special needs tenants. In addition, two blocks on Caledonia Road have 30 converted flats in each block linked by alarms to resident wardens, with communal kitchen and meeting areas on the ground floors. The physical shape of high-rise flats (single floors, with lift access) made them an obvious choice for such conversions, but, from the outside, there is no way of identifying these particular flats as 'special'. The potential to wire every flat in the blocks to the concierge system created the opportunity to take the idea of sheltered conversions one step further.

In future any of the 552 flats could be connected to one of the warden call systems, and disconnected, as and when necessary. Meanwhile, the latest concierge systems use an electronic-mail-type interface to indicate which flat is calling. The computer can be programmed to prioritise a disabled or ill tenant, putting them to the top of the list for response. In this way several flexible layers of support can be offered, from (active) inactivity alarms, 'good morning' calls and wardens, through to (passive) emergency alarms.

Interestingly, tenants preferred the single-block-focused guards to the more remote day concierges. This is not necessarily just about physical contact. One respondent (a single pensioner) daily holds her first conversation over the elevator address system with her block guard – typically discussing the morning papers. Rather, it is about having a *personalised* service, a face and name with which to identify.

"Ideal for pensioners"

The strategy at Moredun, Edinburgh, was to house people of any age or family size, but at the same time promote the high-rise flats to what were regarded suitable tenants – mature and older single-person households. Six multi-storey blocks (554 flats) were fitted in 1994 with a concierge system very similar to the one in Hutchesontown, but with a site office rather than reception areas. One outcome of this is a much heavier reliance on CCTV – where you do not have a person standing by, you need several cameras linked back to a control room. The blocks were reclad (to a very high standard), with double-glazing and new central heating fitted in every flat. One ground floor flat was given over as a community flat where lunch clubs are held once or twice a week. Every flat is wired to a system that can be expanded to include inactivity, intruder and online smoke detectors. The system allows the fob-key usage of particular tenants to be monitored. However, due to financial limitations, only the intercoms are currently fitted (with extra handsets in flats where it is felt necessary, for example, to be reachable from a wheelchair).

Together, these developments make the blocks as warm and secure as any sheltered scheme but with greater internal space. The main differences are height (15 storeys) and living with other age groups. As at Hutchesontown, managers see one clear role of the surveillance systems as quickly and effectively dealing with problems of internal or external noise, litter, graffiti, and so on. In so far as there are no internal stairs to climb, the flats can be classified as amenity housing, with the extra facility of concierges holding names of relatives, home-helps and doctors on computer. The block manager stated that several older tenants had demonstrated the system's value by staying in their flats rather than moving to sheltered housing, adding that the new services made the flats "ideal for pensioners". This vision is not always shared by other public sector and health and welfare professionals, especially given past images of high-rise housing.

"Tailored, very much, to our own needs"

Balgrayhill in north Glasgow consists of four 24-storey blocks. Unlike the three previous case studies, it had never suffered severely from crime and vandalism, much of the original population had grown old in the flats, and the estate had been run by a Tenant Management Cooperative (TMC) for the previous 10 years. There were also five daytime (8 'til 8) caretakers who carried out traditional manual tasks and had no extra electronic equipment in their office.

The radical approach here was to retain a manual caretaking presence while passing most of the surveillance and support services over to an even more remote housing alarm centre. Although there are only 11 cameras (three on car parks; four front-entrance; four back-door), every single flat has an intruder alarm which doubles as an inactivity alarm. Hence, responses to emergencies (medical or otherwise) must come direct from the ambulance, police and fire services, entailing a centralised coordination of these and their response times. So emergencies are covered, but what about the social aspects of concierges – their physical or nearby presence? The system has many additional, even compensatory, communication features:

> "There's the telephone-based system which is linked [to every flat]. There's a number of BT lines and cable lines which link up to the Hamish Allan Centre [housing alarm centre, three miles to the south] and the flats, in two-way communication. All 392 houses have got a [specially adapted] telephone.... Also, they can answer the 'phone from the bedroom and do various other things with it. There's the smoke alarm and the intruder detector – the movement sensor [an inactivity sensor].

> The controlled door entry system – if somebody buzzes at the front door, they [the tenant] can turn their television to channel 6 and see a picture of the person at the door, and can let them in by using the telephone. All tenants here can talk free of charge to their neighbours in the flats on this telephone system. And because there's a number of lines coming in with this system, anyone in the world can 'phone in [as with] an ordinary telephone. Therefore an elderly person can have a telephone in their house free of charge and receive in-coming calls at no cost to the tenant....
>
> The idea was that it was going to be expanded, not only in order to talk to our office and the caretaker's office, but they can talk to the benefits section, or the library department, or the hospitals with this system, but the network in Glasgow's not set up for that. That's a futuristic ideal. That's the global view of it." (Estate Manager)

In addition to these services, the system has a digital voicemail service that allows tenants to leave messages for each other or memos for themselves. Other facilities were discussed when the system was installed and may be possible in the not too distant future. The system could deal with outgoing calls, although the TMC does not want to get into the business of charging tenants for calls. There are also a number of inexpensive upgrades, for example a 'call-minder' facility, or if someone wanted to be woken in the morning or reminded to take medication, the telephone could alert them.

In this model the conventional free link to concierges has been replaced by numerous links to a number of diverse agencies but also, very importantly, to other tenants in the buildings. From tenants' perspectives, the main current advantage of this system is that (for the first time) all the inactivity, intruder and other alarms have been afforded, while the additional service of leaving and receiving messages makes the organisation of social events, meetings and outings much easier for less mobile tenants.

Sheltered housing

But what do people feel about moving to an age-related environment rather than staying put and coping with adaptations? John Percival used individual interviews, focus-group sessions, informal discussions and observation in three sheltered housing schemes in inner London, to concentrate on ways in which tenants' self-esteem affects, and is affected by, their interactions. The three schemes were about the same size (25-28 residents) and, on average, tenants had been living there for six years. Within these fairly standard sheltered housing schemes – based on the premise that many older people prefer to live independently but with formal support, and in their own homes but within similar-age communities – the study explored how tenants maintained their self-esteem in the face of the challenges of ageing.

Adjusting to age-segregated housing

> "If I'd known I'd live this long, I'd have taken better care of myself." (Mr Snow)

The research showed that tenants in the three schemes identified specific ways in which sharing their domestic environments with others underpinned their self-esteem; 'creative compensatory behaviour'; 'self-appreciation and self-respect', and 'the maintenance of valued interactions'. Compensatory behaviour included strategies to redress the deficits of old age, the use of humour and a commitment to helpful work in the wider community. Self-appreciation could centre on the accentuation of present personal attributes and abilities, whereas self-value was reinforced by shared reminiscences.

Some tenants also valued the social interactions that they had established within the schemes as correctives to loneliness and introspection, and to provide structure to their days:

> "When you're left on your own it is nice to be able to get in with someone else.... You can pick up with a couple of friends, and that is what you want." (Mrs Carlow)

Developing social relationships with fellow tenants was important in order to continue to maintain an aspect of their lifestyle, particularly if previous life circumstances involved regular patterns of new interactions. In this context former employment situations could be significant for re-establishing meaningful contacts within the scheme. The loneliness which can result from loss of a spouse was given by some people as the reason for their interest in forming social ties with fellow tenants, and the need for 'company' was often expressed as a corollary of widowhood.

Yet, if a person was feeling in a bad mood, had experienced a death in the family, or was feeling depressed, closing their front door was one way in which they might try to deal with their problems. Important aspects of socially appropriate behaviour, such as respect for privacy, appeared to be interpreted and enacted according to subjective rather than objective criteria, in ways that suited the person rather than social norms.

The study also showed ways in which the age-segregated nature of sheltered housing could exacerbate certain negative experiences, attitudes and behaviours. The experience of bereavement, which can be an increasing feature of old age, was keenly felt in the sheltered housing environment, and people spoke of their sadness at having got to know fellow tenants who subsequently died. Tenants generally valued the quiet atmosphere that was said to be a positive feature of living with other older people – but it could also be experienced as oppressively quiet, especially at weekends and in under-used communal lounges.

> "Sometimes you can get very depressed if you're just sitting down here ... you're not wanted any more ... you're finished now ... it does make you more aware of your age." (Mrs Morrissey)

Words such as 'cemetery' and 'morgue' were invoked to describe an environment perceived as too quiet or lifeless, the embodiment of mortality. Of course, older people living alone in their own homes in the wider community may also feel that the immediate home environment is too quiet. For tenants in sheltered housing, however, this perception may be exacerbated by the lack of incidental sounds which emanate from a more mixed age group and also, perhaps, because of the knowledge that a few feet away on the other side of a wall, is another older person feeling alone.

Community, inclusion and exclusion

Fennell (1986, p 75) referred to sheltered housing tenants' negative feelings towards others who are more disabled, describing these as 'segregationist impulses'. Such impulses appeared to be operating in all these schemes, and account for talk and behaviour that suggested a tendency to exclude others whose presence could undermine self-esteem.

It was a commonly expressed view that tenants who lacked sufficient independence and had care needs which required extra attention from the warden or the provision of nurses or intensive home-help were better suited to a care establishment, such as a residential care or nursing home.

Implicit was the belief that people living in sheltered housing should not be health or social care clients, but people capable of taking responsibility for a tenancy and their own well-being. Tenants viewed their environment as socially oriented rather than care oriented and that, in spite of an awareness that deteriorating health could affect any individual, living alongside others with frailty could upset this community ideal and be a potential threat to positive self-evaluation.

As with the 'disheartening' experience of being confronted by a frail tenant whose appearance offends, fitter tenants could also suffer lowering of morale if the frailty of fellow tenants resulted in less social activity in the scheme. It was certainly the case that some older people were experiencing debilitating health problems, which prevented them from engaging socially with others. However, their number was small in each of the schemes and this was probably one of several reasons for limitations on social engagement, emphasising the interrelationship between the demands of the age-segregated environment and self-esteem. The effort and resolve needed to find ways to maintain individual self-esteem were acknowledged as sometimes difficult to harness in the social setting of sheltered housing. For these reasons people often accepted, albeit begrudgingly, that a decrease in, or withdrawal from, social interaction, was an inevitable consequence of old age. Resurrecting social life was said to be difficult in such circumstances.

There was also some opinion that those tenants with dementia were particularly unsuitable for sheltered housing. One warden admitted that goodwill had to be built up if people were to accept new tenants who were frail, and this was certainly the case with regard to those with dementia. Indeed, it was noticeable how those tenants whose personality was known prior to the onset of dementia were more likely to receive sympathy, and have allowances made for their behaviour, than those who were new and unknown. Such an observation had been expected, given the results of Petre's work in this field (see Kitwood et al, 1995). However, it was interesting to learn that wardens and professionals often shared tenants' perception that new applications for sheltered housing, on behalf of those with dementia, were not appropriate.

In contrast, people often referred to the cleanliness and tidiness of those frail tenants who they were more sympathetic towards: who perhaps were more socially acceptable because they were seen to be making an effort, and whose lack of obvious decline confirmed a greater sense of self-esteem in the onlooker. Conversely, those who were dirty or dishevelled, unable or unwilling to make the required effort were 'disheartening' to the onlooker and more likely to lower morale.

Within the range of housing options available to older people, sheltered housing has perhaps had a prominence greater than its statistical significance. Although most older people live in other forms of accommodation, sheltered housing has had a significant role as a model of age-related, quasi-communal accommodation, with varying degrees of orientation to security and safety. It has been an aspiration of some, but – largely because of the social environment – something that other older people have wished to avoid.

Care housing for people with dementia

The tensions that lie within the collective setting which offers personalised support has been seen in accommodation for people with dementia. Kate Foster studied three dementia care houses which opened in the early 1990s: two offering support to eight people with 'mild to moderate dementia' and the third accommodating twelve people with 'moderate to severe dementia'. The aims of these schemes were in line with contemporary ideas of good practice (Marshall and Archibald, 1998) and offered home-like settings intended to combine the privacy of single apartments with the security of 24-hour staff support.

Familiar household chores provided activities for residents and staff served as role models to engage them. The aims were to preserve residents' individual patterns; promote their independence and choice; enable families and friends to share residents' daily lives as they wished; and facilitate participation in community life. Each house operated within a local catchment area and the intention was to provide a 'home for life'.

These houses became showcases for a model of care regarded as innovative, and were a rare product of interagency collaboration. They were challenging a medicalised model of care, with one that optimistically emphasised the potential of environment to make a difference to people with dementia. Area-based and specialist housing associations worked with health and social services to find ways of dividing responsibility for 'health', 'social' and 'housing' costs – at least for capital funding. The onus was on the housing and support agencies to demonstrate that providing basic accommodation was beneficial to people with dementia, and that it was 'cost-effective' in relation to institutional alternatives.

Technically, the care houses were registered as providing residential care; occupants were not offered tenancies and access was limited to those needing 24-hour support. All the same, respondents described these as 'home' for the residents, rather than 'a home'. 'Home' was defined as, ideally, a comfortable place in which you can live to the end of your life, where you can choose who you live with, which is, by definition, private and where you can please yourself. But for the occupants of care housing, the previous reality of living at home had latterly fallen below the ideal and, for several, it had been an isolated and lonely experience.

Other options had sometimes been tried: sheltered housing had not been able to provide the support needed, and sometimes other residents were intolerant. Sheltered housing was, however, acceptable in a way that hospital and nursing homes were not and, according to respondents, residential care had no advantages to offer over care housing. Stereotypes of institutional care framed these comparisons and respondents had very limited experience of other housing options or community support. Relatives were convinced that care houses were the best places available – many said that they hoped that there would be a place like it for them when they needed it.

Most of the residents had lived on their own, becoming increasingly isolated and dependent on relatives' visits and community services for support and contact. They may have been alone for large parts of the day and at night, and informal support could not be relied on, even where people with dementia had enjoyed good relations with neighbours and friends. Relatives portrayed the residents in these circumstances as, on one hand, becoming more anxious and, on the other hand, finding it difficult to recognise their own needs for support, and apparently not having any insight into the degree of strain that their relatives were under.

From the outset those providing care houses stated they could not provide regular nursing care and recognised that residents would need to be able to live with others in a group. The staff were torn between their commitment to provide a home for life, and their accumulating experience that it was difficult for people who were very different from each other to live together. Working within an ethos that rejected medicalised care, staff were reluctant to cast suitability for residence in clinical terms, but referred to people's previous experience of care as well as their personal characteristics and preferences. Annerstedt et al (1993) linked the quality of care in (Swedish) specialist group-living projects, at least in part, to the selection of a well-diagnosed, clinically homogeneous group of residents. Marshall and Archibald (1998) placed this issue in international context, while noting that, in the UK, we tend to be particularly committed to the idea of a home for life (p 338).

A move for life

The central question was how to cope with progressive disability arising from dementia and physical frailty. Staff were satisfied if they had supported someone until they died. Unanimously, relatives believed that residents were already in the right place and hoped that there would be no need for another move. However, early on there were signs that this model of care could not provide a home for life for all residents[2]. It appeared that experience made staff and managers less assertive in claiming that care houses should always be a home for life. The following account was given of someone who had become increasingly dependent over a period of some months, and was making substantial demands on staff time:

> "She couldn't manage her meals and cutlery. The other tenants were cruel, we ended up taking her to the staff table to protect her. At the end she was neither getting anything out of, nor contributing to, the care house." (staff interview, see Foster, 1997, p 161)

By not "getting anything out of" the care house, this respondent implied that its special characteristic of involving people in household activities was being wasted on a resident who essentially needed nursing care.

Residents who needed longer-term medical or nursing care, and who developed behaviour experienced by others as disruptive, were very likely to move on. Factors that may have affected whether someone moved included how long-term the problem seemed and whether staff were prepared to use any form of restraint. The ability of management to provide intensive additional support from staff appeared to be important and, hypothetically, staff may have been more willing to sustain greatest levels of support to residents they were particularly attached to. The facilities provided by the house (especially whether it had single rooms and good facilities for people with disability) and the availability of community and specialist services such as Macmillan nurses could have been influential; also important, perhaps, was whether relatives were able to provide intensive support.

Moving because of behavioural problems was most common in the house with most male residents. Here rooms were shared with limited communal space and staff had not always been successful in controlling who moved into the house. Care staff had little or no professional training to work with aggressive behaviour and could feel vulnerable and out of their depth when it was experienced. It is paradoxical that in a specialist house for people with dementia such as this, behavioural problems particularly challenged the limits of care housing.

Living in the care houses

The qualitative assessment of responses from staff and relatives was that, for some residents at least, the move to care housing was followed by an improvement in physical health and the mental well-being of residents. This showed in their general appearance, improved communication, ability to care for themselves and participation in household activities. Respondents ascribed these positive changes to residents becoming more confident in a setting in which they had company and lived according to a normal daily pattern. The staff celebrated 'success stories', including people moving in both from institutions and from community housing. These reports echoed the notion of 'rementia' (Kitwood and Bredin, 1992), that is, positive effects or stabilisation that may result from someone with dementia moving to an improved environment. The potential of a positive approach to bring mental health benefits has also been discussed by Holden and Woods (1995). Of course, both relatives and staff wanted to think the best of care housing and they did not refer to any negative effects of the move. But, according to informants, the beneficial changes levelled over time. This has also been recorded in other studies (see Annerstedt, 1995; Dean et al, 1993; Ritchie et al, 1992).

Feeling at home

From time to time, residents were restless and had a sense of being misplaced and betrayed, although feeling unsettled and insecure about where they lived may well have predated the move to care housing. The disorientation brought about by dementia made it hard for people to link their past to their present and it became progressively more difficult to recognise where they stayed as where they should be or as 'home'. Collectively, residents could sometimes reinforce to each other the idea that they were trapped and should leave. People varied from day to day. Staff had the task of reinforcing the idea that the care home was where residents lived and sometimes they had to ensure that the residents stayed there. Access to a private room helped to reinforce the idea for residents that they were where they should be, as this room contained their own possessions. For residents who settled in well, demands to go 'home' became less frequent.

Some staff thought they should not insist that care housing was home, nor attempt to replace home, but preferred to respect residents' views on this. The difficulty of accepting care housing as home was not just related to dementia. Feeling at home depended in part on personal biography and relationships, but was undermined by living alongside strangers (coresidents, staff and other visitors) whose presence and behaviour were at times hard to explain. Furthermore, in practice residents were restricted in how they could use the house and depended on staff to structure daily patterns. How residents interpreted their surroundings depended, at least in part, on what they saw around them. Sometimes they thought of care housing as a hotel, at other times as a nursing home. Those who had moved from hospital sometimes thought of staff as nurses.

Engagement

In each house care staff and domestics did most of the work, and all of the heavy domestic work. They initiated essential household jobs, such as cleaning, laundry, shopping and cooking, and had the responsibility of involving residents in ways that offered choice and maintained as much independence as possible. Taking part in these daily household activities required considerable support and encouragement from staff, who in turn required support and supervision to sustain their therapeutic optimism. Residents could be skilled in their refusal to join in, perhaps making a joke or politely declining, saying that they could not manage something, or sometimes simply not responding to suggestions staff made.

Living in groups

The nature of relationships between residents was hard to define, partly because they fluctuated, but also because their living arrangements were unusual. Residents could adjust to each other, but it was a matter of opinion as to how deep their relationship and concern for each other was. Friendships and helpfulness occurred, but relationships were complicated by changes in individuals and in the composition of the group. Residents appeared to observe each other closely, and sometimes critically. Dementia could complicate disputes, for example if residents misidentified each other and their settings, or mislaid possessions.

It became clear that circumstances of social background, gender and personality, as well as the presence of dementia, influenced the way that people got on with each other. Strikingly, residents could be intolerant of those who were most affected by dementia. It also appeared that staff tended to see most readily the viewpoint of those least affected, in that they gave more examples of how people with advanced dementia could disturb those less afflicted. Dementia was not in itself a leveller, and at times staff had to actively smooth out relationships. Staff thought there were fewer tensions between residents who were similarly advanced in their dementia. They believed it was necessary to screen potential new residents carefully for the sake of social relationships with other residents and to maintain the household model of care.

Given the experience of residents and staff in these care homes which were designated and staffed for people with dementia, it perhaps comes as no surprise that their position in standard sheltered housing is much more precarious. In sheltered housing their own quality of life, and that of residents who are not suffering from dementia, is compromised by lower staffing levels and poorer understandings of dementia, and by the necessity for a social orientation based on maintaining independence.

Discussion: segregation, integration, and the organisation of housing for groups of older people

The three studies in this chapter provide differing views of how accommodation and support may be offered in the future and raise questions regarding the interface between people and places. Given that the three types of setting under consideration differ in terms of purpose, scale, age, design and proportionate use by older people, what do they tell us about technological and social management systems?

Technological solutions and funding

The tower blocks which McGrail discusses, while innovative in architectural terms at the time they were built, predate modern communications technology and were designed with minimal intervention and maximum household privacy in mind. The well-documented problems which came to be associated with high-rise dwellings led to a number of improvement projects, as well as the demolition of some blocks, and, in 1992, the Department of the Environment commissioned the Safe Neighbourhoods Unit (SNU) to evaluate various improvement schemes in terms of their impact on crime, letability and repair performance, and resident satisfaction (Farr and Osborn, 1997).

These improvements included 'technology-based', 'intensive concierge' and 'dispersed concierge' schemes in which personnel used CCTV. The relatively expensive concierge schemes, in conjunction with improved management procedures, tended to be most effective in improving the situation in problematic blocks and Brian McGrail describes how these types of improvements impact on the options for older residents. As a consequence of increasing limitations on finance, a development of his final case study (at Balgrayhill) is the likely future of 'intelligent' high-rise buildings in Glasgow and possibly other cities. Furthermore, similar models of technology-based communications systems could be used in conventional sheltered housing and dispersed housing for older people within specific geographical areas. There is a growing role for communication and intelligent technologies in extending the possibilities of supportive care for people with dementia (see Chapter Six).

Given the ageing of the British housing stock (DETR, 1998), an estimated shortfall of accommodation units nationwide (Holmans, 1996) and the anticipated growth of small pensioner households (Hall et al, 1999), coming years will see an urgent need for upgrading, replacement and additions to the current stock of housing that can support older people. The reinvention of existing spaces through electronic technologies has many potential outcomes. By enabling our existing environment to cope with social change, greater choice or variety in the living environments could be available to ageing populations – even if this choice is short term. Electronically adapting existing buildings may be one of the few options available under certain historic conditions as we make a longer-term demographic transition. Within the context of current thinking and legislation – on human rights, citizenship, accessibility, inclusion and sustainability – the cost of accommodation must be assessed to include material and social costs to the community and the individual. As technological inputs become increasingly ubiquitous and cheaper to install, but the cost of back-up staff increases, we might expect to see continuing experimentation with the design of systems. Brian McGrail discusses a range of installations and staffing solutions in high-rises that require differing levels of capitalisation and running costs. These need to be explored in relation to other forms of age-related housing.

These developments on high-rise estates show that we cannot really consider living environments for older people in separation from the rest of our ageing society. But such technological change does raise questions regarding the ability to 'stay put' and interactions between people.

Continuing quality of life

What can these three environments contribute to the quality of life of older residents? In each case the physical standards of housing and amenities provided are intended to be good, barrier free or at least minimally problematic for physical ageing, and offering some level of collective security against crime and disorder.

Tower blocks and other high-rise developments have long since been discounted as the solution to general housing needs and, in particular, have been dismissed as unsuitable for families with young children. They are seen as more suitable for young adults and for mature residents. Not every older tenant wants to move to purpose-built sheltered housing; many do not want to live in a specially segregated place; and not everyone wants a house with a garden. There *are* also certain perceived advantages to flats, including greater safety from break-ins (above ground level) and 'cosiness'. High-rise flats are relatively unproblematic in terms of internal space, being larger than sheltered flats (they often have two bedrooms). Tenants feel they can do more with them and they are not specifically identified with old age. But the refurbishment of blocks is crucial, since tenants no longer simply want security and clean common areas (although these remain high priorities) but 'the full package' – making the buildings not only habitable but attractive and comfortable, with good central heating and double-glazing. Perhaps most of all, however, tower blocks described here benefit enormously from the new kinds of technological upgrades not (yet) found in other types of housing, although the role of the concierge and the ways in which residents communicate with each other through technology needs further study.

High-rise is, however, an essentially urban housing form that does not exist in many non-urban areas. Sheltered housing, although numerically much less significant than mainstream housing, has been developed with a much wider geographical spread. It has also been the yardstick for age-specific independent housing for some time, and for many people has served the function of extending the quality of their later life by combining good accommodation with the possibility of companionship and security.

Here we have considered the situation of older people in some age-related settings. The people who live in these schemes share with others in the wider community both positive and negative perceptions of themselves as older people. In bringing accommodation and support together, the interaction of people and places from familial to non-familial settings is highlighted.

John Percival describes the crucial importance of the social life of sheltered housing in individuals' experiences of living in such schemes, underlining the role of social organisation in a quasi-communal setting. He has indicated the importance of maintaining self-esteem in the face of certain challenges and has discussed how older people, as tenants of sheltered housing, benefit from an environment in which their strategies for maintaining self-esteem are shared and strengthened. Social interactions with fellow tenants may be valued as opportunities for continuation of lifestyle, as a way to lessen feelings of loss and isolation and as replacements for important past relationships. However, he has also shown that the age-segregated setting may exacerbate feelings of loss, loneliness and alienation, emphasise tendencies to exclude others and limit availability of, or desire for, social interaction with fellow tenants. Most importantly, his analysis showed that tenants experienced the age-segregated setting in both positive *and* negative ways – and that this has consequences for social motivation and inclusion. Here we can see that inclusion depends on internal organisation and attitudes to dependency, and on the mix of people living together. The cohesion of sheltered housing communities is challenged by advancing frailties and especially by dementia.

Kitwood et al (1995) suggested that, for people with dementia, living in sheltered housing appears to work best for those who are in sound physical health, sociable by disposition and well-supported by friends and family within and outside the sheltered housing community. Those still living with their spouse fare best of all. Kate Foster looked at the extent to which one model of residential care home could provide people with 'mild to moderate' dementia a degree of social involvement within communities which supported and stimulated them. However, the care houses in her study found that two of their aims could be in conflict with each other: should the priority be to provide a home for life, or was it was more important to maintain shared domestic living? The tension between individualism and collectivism was potentially resolved if reciprocity and interdependence could develop. In the circumstances this was difficult, not least because the residents did not choose to live together and there were quite frequent changes in membership. Staff shared an assumption made in the dementia literature that small groups are preferable, but the optimum size of these groups remains an open question. It was not clear that scale alone made a difference to the quality of care (see also Stokes and Bowler, 1996); the creative organisation of time and space and staff ethos could also have contributed.

In practice, the care houses were set up in such a way that shared living took priority; the cost was that people who needed nursing care or whose behaviour stretched the tolerance and skills of staff and coresidents had to move out. The accumulating experience of the staff was that a homogeneous group was preferable, but their loyalty to a social model of care made them couch this in personal rather than clinical terms. More often than not, the houses did not provide lifetime support. This was unsatisfactory, not only in that residents had to move from a place that may have in some sense become their home, but also because they moved to settings that all respondents believed provided inferior care. If the future of long-stay care for people with dementia best lies in diversity, then the quality of services depends on whether the challenge is met of caring for those people who are the most difficult to support.

Exploring the lives of older people brings the everyday experience to the world of policy makers, designers, architects and carers. These empirical studies show how different forms of living – from familial to non-familial, living alone to collectivity, age-integrated to age-segregated – engages people and places in different ways. In some cases place may remain fixed and adapted through technology, in other cases places change. The impact on the quality of life of older people is felt in how they are able to maintain their selfhood. This is a key factor in exploring further how people can live in other age-related and non-age-related settings.

Acknowledgements

The authors would like to acknowledge and thank all the people and organisations who took part in their respective projects, and the organisations that funded their research. Full details of the research can be found in endnote 1.

Notes

[1] Case study and evaluative material is drawn from the three principal authors' respective research as follows:

Brian McGrail: The research project, 'The virtual remake of high rise housing: electronic technology and social space' (No. L132251037), received generous funding from the UK's Economic and Social Research Council (ESRC) under their 'Virtual society? The social science of electronic technologies' programme (see McGrail, 1999).

John Percival: Material is drawn from doctoral research (Percival, 1998).

Kate Foster: Material is drawn from a multi-method evaluation funded by Scottish Homes as a research studentship between 1991 and 1994 (Foster, 1997).

[2] By October 1994, over 60% (40) of the 65 former residents of the seven specialist Scottish care houses had had to move out. Seven had moved following an assessment period within the house (within four to eight weeks); 27 had moved to hospitals where it can be assumed that they stayed until they died; four had moved to nursing-home care and two (who had not fully met the entry criteria) to community housing.

References

Alzheimers Scotland (1997) *Response to the Scottish Executive Care Development Group*, Edinburgh: Alzheimers Scotland.

Annerstedt, L. (1995) *On group-living care for the demented elderly: Experiences from the Malmö model*, Lund, Sweden: Lund University.

Annerstedt, L., Gustafson, L. and Nilsson, K. (1993) 'Medical outcome of psychosocial intervention in demented patients: one-year clinical follow-up after relocation into group living units', *International Journal of Geriatric Psychiatry*, vol 8, pp 833-41.

Clapham, D. and Munro, M. (1988) *The cost-effectiveness of sheltered and amenity housing for older people*, Edinburgh: Central Research Unit, Scottish Development Department.

Clapham, D., Kemp, P. and Smith, S. (1990) *Housing and social policy*, Studies in Social Policy, London: Macmillan.

Coleman, A. (1985) *Utopia on trial: Vision and reality in planned housing*, London: Hilary Shipman.

Dean, R., Briggs, K. and Lindesay, J. (1993) 'The domus philosophy: a prospective evaluation of two residential units for the elderly mentally ill', *International Journal of Geriatric Psychiatry,* vol 8, pp 819-26.

DETR (Department of Environment, Transport and the Regions) (1998) *English Housing Conditions Survey, 1996*, London: DETR.

Farr, J. and Osborn, S. (1997) *High hopes: Concierge, controlled entry and similar schemes for high rise blocks*, London: The Stationery Office.

Fennell, G. (1986) *Anchor's older people: What do they think?: a survey among tenants living in sheltered housing*, Oxford: Anchor Housing Association.

Foster, C.V. (1997) 'Care housing for people with dementia: towards an evaluation', unpublished PhD thesis, Stirling: University of Stirling.

Hall, R., Ogden, P. and Hills, C. (1990) 'Living alone: evidence from England and Wales and France for the last two decades', in S. McRae (ed) *Changing Britain: Families and households in the 1990s*, Oxford: Oxford University Press.

Holden, U. and Woods, R. (1995) *Positive approaches to dementia care* (3rd edn), Edinburgh: Churchill Livingstone.

Holmans, A. (1996) *Housing demand and need in England 1991-2011*, York: JRF.

Kitwood, T. and Bredin, K. (1992) 'Towards a theory of dementia care: personhood and well-being', *Ageing & Society*, vol 12, Part 3, pp 269-87.

Kitwood, T., Buckland, S. and Petre, T. (1995) *Brighter futures: A report on research into provision for persons with dementia in residential homes, nursing homes and sheltered housing*, Oxford: Anchor Housing Association.

McCafferty, P. (1994) *Living independently: A study of the housing needs of elderly and disabled people*, London: HMSO.

McGrail, B. (1999) 'Communication technology and local knowledges: the case of peripheralised high-rise housing estates', *Urban Geography*, vol 20, no 4, pp 303-33.

Marshall, M. and Archibald, C. (1998) 'Long-stay care for people with dementia: recent innovations', *Clinical Gerontology*, vol 8, pp 331-43.

Percival, J.F. (1998) 'Balancing lives: an ethnographic study of older people's social interactions in sheltered housing', unpublished Phd thesis, Milton Keynes: The Open University.

Ritchie, K., Colvez, A., Ankri, J., Ledesert, B., Gardent, H. and Fontaine, A. (1992) 'The evaluation of long-term care for the dementing elderly: a comparative study of hospital and collective non-medical care in France', *International Journal of Geriatric Psychiatry*, vol 7, pp 549-57.

SNU (Safe Neighbourhoods Unit) (1985) *After entryphones: Improving management and security in multi-storey blocks*, London: HMSO.

Stokes, G. and Bowler, M. (1996) 'Small isn't necessarily beautiful', *Health Services Journal*, p 21.

EIGHT

Older people's CoHousing Communities

Maria Brenton

What is CoHousing?

A way of living as a group where individuals each have their own private space but share some communal facilities and activities.

An environment where all women have equal voice and are valued equally irrespective of age, ethnicity, class, political persuasion and sexual preference.

A community of women aged 50 or over, in which their skills and talents are valued, shared and developed.

A living group where health and well-being are enhanced through cooperation, companionship and mutual support.

A community that is self-sustaining and self-managed by its residents.

The Older Women's CoHousing Project London, 2000

Introduction

A familiar development among older people in the Netherlands, Denmark (BiC, 1994) and Germany (Jones, 1997), the CoHousing Community is relatively unknown in the housing sector in Britain. It is, however, a way of living that has attracted the interest of a number of small groups of individuals of all ages in this country and one which is being pioneered by a group of older women in London. This chapter sets out the main characteristics of an older persons' CoHousing Community as it has been developed in the Netherlands, examines its feasibility in the context of housing policy in Britain and describes the efforts that are being made to introduce CoHousing in this country as an option for older people. Much of the material on the Netherlands is drawn from a study carried out for the British Housing Corporation (Brenton, 1998), and material on the Older Women's CoHousing Project in London is drawn from the author's own role in assisting it, funded by the Joseph Rowntree Foundation (JRF).

The CoHousing Community

A CoHousing Community is a way of life which offers people privacy, independence and their own front door as members of a group who share some common space and choose to be with each other. It can be intergenerational or it can be for older people only. A bumper sticker produced by the American CoHousing Community movement reads: 'Creating an old-fashioned neighbourhood in a new way'. The Netherlands CoHousing study (Brenton, 1998) shows that, for older people who have lived in streets or blocks where they knew none of their neighbours or where they have felt vulnerable because everyone else was out at work during the day, the CoHousing Community represents the re-creation of a small-scale familiar neighbourhood plus an extra element of group solidarity, mutuality and optional common activities. Above all, it gives its members a sense of control over their own lives. It is a development set up and organised by the group itself and it is a means of staying socially active, sharing interests and offering mutual support. It is within this context that CoHousing is considered here as a model of housing with social inclusion at its heart.

The need for a familiar neighbourhood

Being able to stay in their own home and not feel isolated or lonely is a desire that most people anticipating old age would state as their preference. Taking steps to secure their own continuing autonomy and social connectedness while they still have the energy and capacity to make choices – in other words, planning ahead for old age – is not an activity that comes easily to fit people in their mid-fifties and early sixties, who do not yet feel old. However, some 6,000 people (VROM, 1998) in this age group and older in the Netherlands have left and are planning to leave homes they may have lived in for years in order to enrich their old age and be part of a congenial group. Over the past 20 years in the Netherlands, some 200 CoHousing Communities of older people have been or are in the process of being developed (VROM, 1998).

The development of CoHousing Communities

CoHousing Communities arose in Denmark in 1972 when a group of 27 families who felt isolated by modern urban living got together to form cooperative housing enterprises where space, resources and activities could be shared (Fromm, 1991; McCamant and Durrett, 1994). CoHousing Communities are mostly intergenerational and family-based and are now a well-established feature of the Danish housing sector. A study by McCamant and Durrett (1994), two American architects, gives a full and beautifully illustrated account of the movement in Denmark and it is they who have given currency to the term 'CoHousing' for English speakers. A flourishing CoHousing movement in the US followed McCamant and Durrett's creation of the CoHousing Company and its CoHousing network has a website and a journal[1]. Developments in the US have been initiated by intergenerational groups of families and single people financing themselves through the private housing market. An intergenerational model of CoHousing also took hold in the Netherlands, but it is on the Dutch development of age-specific (55+ years) CoHousing Communities or 'living groups' for older people that this chapter focuses. Similar communities of older people are to be found in Denmark and some in Germany. All vary in size and design but share the following features characterised by Fromm (1991) as:

- common facilities;
- private dwellings;
- resident-structured routines;
- resident management;
- design for social contact;
- resident participation in the development process;
- pragmatic social objectives.

Initiated and controlled by the residents, acting as a corporate group, the Dutch CoHousing Communities of older people make a commitment to the mutual support of their members. Nearly 200 groups have developed since 1981 and they range in size from very small (around six apartments) to very large (around 70 apartments). Their average and ideal size is 24 units (VROM, 1998). This is felt to be an ideal size because, involving between 30 and 40 people, it is neither so small that it cannot take the strain of group living nor is it so large that life in the group becomes anonymous and impersonal. The majority of groups have men and women members but, as their average age is 70 years, the ratio of women to men is 3:1. A small number of women-only groups are to be found around Amsterdam (see Brenton, 1998). The CoHousing Communities are mostly found in the rented social housing sector. This sector is far larger in the Netherlands than in Britain and, because it has a broader social mix, it does not suffer the same stigma as in Britain. Housing association landlords borrow capital at very low rates of interest and work with each group to find a site and develop a building. There are generally management agreements with the housing association for the physical maintenance of the building and service charges reflect this. Seen from a British perspective, rents are relatively low and rent subsidy is available on an individual basis for those who have insufficient incomes. In the late 1990s, as the social housing sector has been pushed by government policy to become more market oriented, cost-pressures have increased. This has led to more ownership-based schemes and a mix of rental and ownership tenure in some developments.

Infrastructure of the Dutch CoHousing Communities movement

Older people's CoHousing Communities in the Netherlands have not developed in a vacuum. They have been assisted actively by central and local governments keen to encourage self-help and independence among older people. It is felt that continued social involvement and interaction will help keep people happier and healthier, and that mutual support will ease demand on health and social services. The Dutch legal system also facilitates CoHousing – groups form legally recognised associations and mutual ownership with binding contracts between residents is possible – while it would be much more difficult under British housing law (although the promised development of a commonhold form of tenure may ease this; DETR, 2000, s 4.17).

While only a small minority of Dutch older people opt for CoHousing, it does add to the range of options available to older people in the Netherlands which have been developed since the early 1980s to reduce a historical tendency towards over-institutionalisation (see Brenton, 1998). Local authorities – particularly in the larger conurbations – may fund part-time development workers in the voluntary sector to assist local groups and some give subsidies for the group preparatory process. They may take a flexible approach to planning controls and will sometimes make a piece of land or building available at less than the market price.

Dutch housing associations are cooperative players in the infrastructure of support for CoHousing Communities. They have gradually come to accept and facilitate the autonomy of their tenants, to whom they cede the landlord's right to allocate new tenancies. Hedged by provisions such as limits to the length of time that an apartment may be left vacant before its cost must be met by the group, such concessions reinforce the solidarity and togetherness of the CoHousing group. Housing associations sometimes take the initiative in bringing large numbers of older people together to introduce them to the concept of CoHousing and it is not unknown for them to give favourable financial terms to older people's CoHousing groups in order to encourage their development. The associations will also help occasionally with rehousing individuals who have proved incompatible with group living.

How groups get started in the Netherlands

The Dutch CoHousing study shows that new groups come together in a variety of ways (Brenton, 1998). The group may begin with a nucleus of friends and neighbours who then advertise for others to join them, they may evolve from a meeting called by a local authority or a housing association, or they may spin off from a voluntary agency active in older people's welfare or the welfare of a particular ethnic community. There is, for example, a CoHousing Community of Chinese older people in Rotterdam whose apartments cluster around a Chinese cultural centre and community restaurant; there is also a Surinam group in Rotterdam who were supported through the development process by a local immigrant welfare agency. In Amersfoort, members of a CoHousing Community which moved into a building in 1999 are partly drawn from a group of local citizens and partly from members of one family from Rotterdam who have been travelling regularly to planning meetings for several years. Another project is under development where the extended families of a migrant group are to be enabled to live together as a CoHousing group, with elderly parents housed in accessible senior flats alongside their younger families' accommodation. 'Flexibility' is the key word and CoHousing developments in the Dutch social housing sector are frequently focused around affinity groups such as friends and neighbours or families or communities of interest. Indeed, one group of 44 owners and renters near Amersfoort came together because they were keen on gardening and growing their own produce. An interesting development in the late 1990s is the encouragement of existing older residents of blocks of ordinary flats to form a CoHousing Community from among their own numbers.

Initiating groups are generally motivated and propelled by fit and independent people in their sixties; it is important for people to plan and take action early, particularly as the process is a lengthy one. The groups must organise themselves, find out people's preferences, put together a list of requirements and find a housing association and local authority to support them. Groups learn from each other, visit existing groups to talk about their experience and get advice from the national association. Finding a site in the Netherlands is a problem because the country is so densely populated, and the preparatory process takes an average of four years before a building is ready. The group uses this period, often with the help of a development worker, to build group solidarity and go through a process of community development. Many groups use the time to attend courses in group living and conflict management, and they learn many new skills simply through participating in and taking responsibility for meetings and planning. They have regular meetings, go on trips together and get to know each other fairly well. The group often loses a fair number of members during this time, so it needs to be initially larger than the eventual membership. It also needs to ensure an age range that is future-proof – if all members are in their sixties when they move in, they will all age together and there will be little chance of a process of natural renewal, with older members dying and younger ones coming in. Groups with top-heavy age structures do find that they become less attractive to new, younger members and they can struggle to retain vitality and mutual support. Of a group established in Nijmegen in 1997, 20 were aged between 50 and 59 years; 15 were aged between 60 and 69 years and 13 were aged over 70 years. These proportions were intended to establish a good age-balance for the group.

CoHousing and design

As noted earlier, the distinguishing feature of CoHousing Communities of older people in the Netherlands is tenant control. This extends to participation in the process of the design of their building but will vary with the competence and willingness of individual architects and the constraints of social housing space requirements. Most of the Communities are new-build but some are imaginative adaptations of existing buildings such as small schools or large barns or farms. Some of the new-build CoHousing Communities in the Netherlands have been designed to maximise casual social interaction with front doors that face each other from deck access, internal or external galleries, sometimes with an internal plaza or atrium and a lobby where everyone collects their mail. This common circulation space is probably more important than a common room to the nurturing of everyday neighbourly contact and it is one of the design ideas that could translate to other forms of grouped housing in which older people live.

Other common aspects of CoHousing design specifications indicate how standards for older people and others in Britain could be raised. Of necessity in the densely populated Netherlands, virtually all the developments are in blocks of one- and two-person apartments, sometimes with a common garden. The clearest way in which this social housing accommodation differs from its equivalent in Britain is in its space allocations. Projects built in the early 1990s tend to be around $70m^2$ but new apartments are starting to increase in size to $80m^2$ and $90m^2$, with recognition by the government that older people will no longer tolerate having only one bedroom (VROM, 1997). Residents in the smaller $70m^2$ apartments often complain of feeling cramped, but these space allocations are vastly more generous than British social housing allowances of around $50m^2$. A common room with kitchen facilities can be supplemented by a hobby room, a laundry or a library, depending on the housing association. Frequently the common room consists of one or two apartments with internal walls removed so that, should the group fail or dissolve, space can be converted back for rent. Group members pay for their common facilities through a service charge. They may raise the funds for furnishing and equipping their common spaces either through appeal to a national charity or sometimes by taking a long-term loan from their landlord. Individual flats generally have large windows and their own small balconies and may have some internal flexibility in that walls can be removed to allow alternative use of space.

The conversion of older buildings where possible to make them more accessible to older people and to conform to an official benchmark of accessibility has been stimulated by government cash incentives (ten Brinke and Eikelboom, 1999). New-build dwellings for people aged 55 and over must conform to the official standards, with lifts, wide doorways, level access and bathrooms that open into the main bedroom as well as having doorways into the hall. Those that aim to achieve a higher benchmark (the *Seniorenlabel*) are planned to also take account of factors such as public transport routes, local shopping areas and facilities such as post office and doctors' surgeries. Most buildings will have secure intercom-based door-entry systems, but individual apartments are not wired up with alarm systems as a matter of course, as there is no warden. Individuals may buy into community alarm systems if they choose.

Life in an older persons' CoHousing Community

Typically an older person's group will include people who are relatively fit and self-reliant, aged from their mid-fifties to late seventies, and a mix of couples and people who are divorced, widowed or single. Depending on the area and the group, members may be retired tradespeople, shopworkers, skilled workers such as electricians or plumbers, with a sprinkling of professional people, or they may be more clearly from a blue-collar background – factory workers or farming people. Some groups have a more professional and white-collar composition, but generally not particularly high incomes. How and where they were gathered together as a group will determine the social mix, and prior to moving in there will have been a degree of self-selection in and out of the group, reflecting how much the cultural and other interests are shared (Brenton, 1998).

There is usually a number of small subcommittees that take responsibility for aspects of the group's life, such as social activities, membership, cleaning the common areas, communications and so on. As a CoHousing Community, the entire group will have regular formal meetings, make its own day-to-day household rules for peaceful coexistence in the building and decide together how much common activity its members might want. Early groups used to have regular communal meals but this is more the exception nowadays. Many groups have morning coffee in the common room and a regular 'happy hour' but gatherings are otherwise more occasional celebrations. In some groups, there are small supper clubs – usually of single people – who meet, maybe once or twice a week, to cook and eat a meal. What is valued highly is the fact that 'there is always someone to do things with'. Activities are often ad hoc – a trip or a concert for which members are invited to sign up – but some groups also have regular singing clubs, art groups, keep-fit clubs and so on.

The value of a CoHousing Community

What are the benefits that most members of an older persons' CoHousing Community feel they have gained as a result of their decision to help form a group or join an existing one? Research enquiries (ten Brinke and Stegink, 1987; Brenton 1998; VROM, 1998) have shown that the dominant motivation has been to ensure the continuance of social activities and to avoid loneliness. There is a higher proportion of divorced and widowed people in the groups than in the general population (VROM, 1998) and, for them, the organised and casual social interaction possible in the CoHousing Community is particularly helpful. Also, couples are sometimes consciously planning for the eventuality that one of them might be left alone. A number of respondents in the CoHousing study (Brenton, 1998) voiced a concern about maintaining their independence and autonomy, citing their parents' experiences of life in residential homes as an example to avoid.

Besides social interaction and the desire for autonomy, the knowledge that your neighbours would quickly notice if you failed to appear one morning is a major source of security. Many groups have developed simple systems to signal whether a member has got up in the morning, as well as 'buddy' arrangements for when people need basic help in short episodes of illness. Larger groups may have morning telephone circles for some of their older members. If suffering from a serious and long-term illness, it is expected that group members will utilise the local home help, meals on wheels and nursing services. Members have more or less the same likelihood of eventually moving out to hospital or a nursing home as they would if they had stayed in their former homes, but they avoid the move to residential care that was once so prevalent in the Netherlands and have less need of any form of sheltered housing.

The CoHousing Community should be seen as a cluster of friends and neighbours in their own homes, loosely associated with each other for a common purpose, rather than as a closed-in institution and in this respect it is a more inclusive model than that of sheltered housing. Privacy and personal space are valued and individual members lead their own lives. "Someone who wants to live happily in a CoHousing Community must also be able to live alone" (ten Brinke and Eikelboom, 1999, p 61). Some members may still be working; those who have retired often have outside interests and activities and their own networks of friends and family (usually readily accessible in a country as small as the Netherlands). Most groups also make an effort to connect with the surrounding neighbourhood, often through the loan or hire of their community rooms to small local groups, through open days or through individual members joining activities in the area.

It was noted earlier that the CoHousing Community aims to re-create a small neighbourhood in which everyone will know each other and feel some sense of shared responsibility. The research (Brenton, 1998) found that these positive benefits may be counterbalanced by the drawbacks of small-scale intimacy – 'everyone knowing your business' – and the opportunity for inevitable personality and other conflicts to proliferate. 'Nowhere is perfect' is a common refrain. Where care and support in illness is needed, groups have learned to set limits on over-visiting, for example, and to organise clear rotas or 'buddy' arrangements. Groups have resolved conflicts in various ways – through small mediation committees, through having an independent person from the locality to chair the board, by bringing in an outside facilitator, or, by mutual agreement, a member or members seceding from the group but continuing to live in the building. In some cases, small groups have ceased to function as a group where one of their members has proved an insoluble problem. This contrasts with sheltered housing, where similar conflicts would typically involve the intervention of a warden or manager, or the housing authority.

The CoHousing Community and policies for old age

In the Netherlands CoHousing Communities for older people have been officially encouraged at all levels and form part of a range of housing options for old age. This must be set against a background of cultural readiness to adopt innovative and flexible approaches and to encourage self-determination and mutuality among older people. In turn, the older population has an effective voice in the Netherlands, articulated through many non-profit organisations and membership-based associations which act as advocates for them. There is a robust network of local old age 'unions', for example, which make a clear impact on government policies relating to old age and a significant proportion of the older population belongs to them. Joining a CoHousing group can represent a challenge – particularly for older women who may not have ventured much out of a domestic setting or participated in the employed workforce – but it is a move encouraged by a wider climate which values participation and citizenship.

Challenges in the British context

How might a development that has flourished in a different culture take hold in Britain? It has much to recommend it, but will older people in Britain see the CoHousing Community as a desirable alternative to staying in their own homes or opting for sheltered housing; and, if they do, will they get any help?

It has already been suggested that CoHousing is a way of living more likely to appeal to and be initiated by people in their sixties, rather than those in their eighties. Today's British population approaching sixty is the postwar baby-boomers. They have had different life experiences from those of their parents – higher standards of living, more freedom of movement, more exposure to different cultures, greater labour market participation, fewer children, more divorce and so on. Women in this age group, in particular, are more likely than their parents to find themselves living alone at the end of their lives and they know this. They also have the personal resources and collaborative skills necessary for community building, which is the most important aspect of CoHousing. The following sections follow the premise that radically different models of provision for old age are required to meet the aspirations of a new, 21st-century generation of older people in Britain, and that traditional models are no longer adequate. It is argued that, as a new model, CoHousing is likely to appeal to the soon-to-be-old more than it would have appealed to their parents. Whether the CoHousing concept can really take root as an option for a more communal approach to old age in Britain will be determined by a number of factors that are briefly explored.

An unrecognised need

The need for community building among older people has not been widely recognised or understood in Britain by policy makers or housing providers or by older people themselves. The increasing numbers of people aged over 50 and 60 in the next decades are acknowledged and vast numbers of new houses have been projected as necessary to meet the rapid growth in single households in Britain (DoE, 1996). Yet little thought has been given to the growing isolation of single living, especially among older women. There is also little evidence of attention to designing neighbourhoods and housing complexes in a way that fosters the creation of any kind of community life. British culture and social policies are not inherently favourable to the development of CoHousing Communities, yet there is a real need for them among older people.

It might be suggested, however, that among people aged over 50 in Britain there is recognition and indeed demand for some of the constituent values inherent in the CoHousing concept, even though there is a general lack of awareness that the CoHousing model exists. The 'soon-to-be-old' generation will not, once they themselves know what it is to be old, continue to be quiescent in the face of institutional ageism and the low value society gives to older people. They are also more likely to have more disposable capital than their parents and fewer children to pass it on to. Some of them are likely to demonstrate a cultural shift in favour of a new model of collaborative living – one that will meet their assumption of continued autonomy and independence.

Confusion with sheltered housing

In Britain, CoHousing tends to be confused with sheltered housing – a model based on a third party providing and managing accommodation *for* older people who are essentially strangers to each other, in the hope that a sense of community will emerge from people being put together as neighbours. There is no reason why sheltered housing could not become a CoHousing Community, but it would need to start from a very different point – identifying its end users and engaging them in equal partnership from the very beginning, working with them to form a sustainable community, ceding control and management of the enterprise to them and either dispensing with wardens or placing them in the direct employ of the residents: "Sheltered housing must change. More flexible frameworks of service provision must be put in place with traditional ageist and disempowering services and service frameworks dismantled" (Fisk, 1999, p 38). Indeed, some housing associations are beginning to question whether a top-down, essentially paternalistic model of housing provision is appropriate as the main option available to older people for what is expected to be an increasingly articulate older population of consumers in the 21st century.

Rising aspirations and buildings fit to age in

One of the attributes of CoHousing in the Netherlands which has helped motivate older people to leave familiar homes for new housing is that these environments are generally attractive and reasonably spacious. One older Dutch woman commented: "Yes, it was a wrench to leave but once I saw what I was coming to, there was no contest" (personal communication with the author). However, if CoHousing were to develop in Britain along the ungenerous lines that other provisions for older people have developed, the allure might not be so great.

Lack of an infrastructure of support

There is no equivalent in Britain to the infrastructure of support provided to CoHousing in the Netherlands. Britain's culture fosters individualism rather than collective enterprise and our social and financial institutions are not geared to facilitating group mortgages, mutual ownership and group autonomy. The dominance of homeownership reduces flexibility and the rental sector is small compared to that in the Netherlands. This has contributed to segregation by housing tenure and social exclusion of the poorest people in undesirable and low quality environments in which social and economic problems are concentrated and compounded. A CoHousing Community is based, by definition, on resident choice, empowerment and sustainable community. It could also valuably contribute to breaking down the separation of tenures. The following account of an innovative project in progress in London will illustrate some of the challenges and difficulties associated with this.

A case study – the pilot CoHousing project

The CoHousing pilot group in London formed to plan CoHousing after being introduced to the concept at a JRF-sponsored workshop on CoHousing in 1998. Its members were drawn from older women's informal networks and from a number of existing formal networks, particularly the Older Feminist Network, the Growing Old Disgracefully Network and the Older Lesbian Network. The JRF has supported the group by providing a paid consultant for a pilot project designed to test the feasibility of such a development in Britain and its replicability by other older people. In June 2000, a study of the financial and legal implications of a CoHousing development in the social housing sector, related to the needs of the pilot project, was initiated under the auspices of The Housing Corporation, following its earlier sponsorship of a study of Dutch CoHousing Communities (Brenton, 1998). Two broad challenges have faced the project group in realising their hoped-for CoHousing Community: one is developing a sense of group solidarity and community in preparation for living together (and to sustain this over a lengthy timeframe); the other, to find a site and the necessary finance to develop or renovate a building.

The community development process

Beginning in mid-1998, the project group met regularly and steadily acquired new members, aiming at a total membership of around 35 women over the age of 50, in order to achieve a desired total of 24 members of a CoHousing Community. Membership of the group tended to fluctuate, but in early 2000, it had achieved a membership of 20 women ranging in age from their early fifties to early seventies – two thirds of them over 60 – who were currently living alone in different parts of London and outside London. Most had retired and, as most had worked in public service and welfare professions, the average income of the group was relatively low. From the outset the group decided to restrict its membership to women, feeling that this arrangement would secure them the kind of cooperativeness and companionship they were seeking and enable them to remain non-competitive and non-hierarchical in the management of the group. A recruitment drive has been aimed at women aged 50 and over who are living alone and are relatively fit and independent. The group's main strengths are that it is entirely self-energising and self-motivating and that among its members there are to be found a range of skills and experience drawn from the diverse backgrounds represented within the group.

During their first 18 months, the women developed agreed procedures to get to know each other better outside of the formal meetings and to generate mutually supportive links between individuals. The eventual CoHousing Community should embody mixed tenure arrangements whereby some women would own their accommodation, others would have a form of shared ownership and the rest would be tenants. This means that, while some group members would have sufficient equity to buy into a Cohousing development, additional finance would be required to render shared ownership and rental affordable, especially in the context of London house and land prices. The group is keen to participate in the design of any new-build or property renovation and it has a development partner in *Housing for Women* – a small housing association which has subscribed fully to the CoHousing philosophy and has undertaken to delegate the letting of the rented apartments to the group.

Advantages

The pilot group has a number of advantages in its favour and these are:

- It is addressing the challenge of an ageing society in promoting continued independence, an active life and mutual support by means of a self-help formula which should reduce demands made on local services.
- It is pioneering a new concept in Britain for the future housing and support of older people – one which aims to meet the changing aspirations of those who are approaching old age at the beginning of the 21st century.
- It represents a sustainable, socially inclusive alternative to existing mono-tenure policies and the 'zoning of the poor' which have been much criticised in relation to the disbursement of Social Housing Grant over the past two decades.

Housing policy

An important objective of the pilot project has been to develop a wider understanding of CoHousing and its potential benefits for older people. Compared to tenures in the Netherlands, the dominance of owner-occupation in this country is a very important factor to take into account, particularly among people aged over 50. Reflecting on the growth of homeownership and paid-up equity among successive cohorts of older people, Forrest and Leather wrote: "The generation of home owners which is nearing retirement and which will reach this stage in the next two decades is the one which will probably have experienced 'the golden age' of home ownership" (1998, p 38). They point out that there is evidence to suggest that "there is substantial unmet demand to move amongst older home owners" (p 58), and that demand for purpose-built accommodation that is manageable and accessible is likely to grow:

> Most are likely to seek dwellings without the housing and care services which private sheltered housing schemes provide, but perhaps with high standards of accessibility, security, and services to deal with repair and maintenance. (p 58)

Forrest and Leather also speculate about the future "emergence of innovative designs to convert the typical suburban semi into two flats with both providing a high standard of privacy and accessibility" (p 59). This type of development has also been adopted in the Netherlands, but as one of a range of options which includes the more communal design of a CoHousing Community that offers not just privacy and accessibility but also social activity, companionship and security.

Older people's confidence levels

Promulgation of the CoHousing model also needs to address the confidence factor. Older people need to know that CoHousing is achievable. They need to understand that CoHousing can offer them attractive, modern, Lifetime Homes-standard accommodation, in which they would enjoy social activity and support as part of a group but still feel at home in their own space. Although it is likely that most of those who will embrace the idea of CoHousing and seek to initiate it will be at the younger end of the age spectrum, it also requires the participation of people in their seventies or older, and it is this group that may have the most difficulty in coming to terms with the model. Some of the few existing family-based CoHousing Communities in Britain might inspire confidence more generally as they become better known.

The need for public subsidy

Older people with sufficient capital need the type of support described above. People who are homeowners with insufficient capital may well need a public subsidy to facilitate CoHousing. As a mixed-tenure development for a relatively low-income group, the London project would need to draw on a source of capital over and above its existing equity and any loans taken out on its behalf in order to finance a proportion of its dwellings on a shared ownership and rental basis. Although one possibility would be to try to raise charitable funding, it is important to the group and for the project that the development of a CoHousing Community should be replicable by other groups of older people in similar situations. This means staying within mainstream routes to housing finance if possible.

Lack of recognition of social as well as housing needs

Because of the way that Social Housing Grant is currently administered, it is difficult to see how it could foster the development of a CoHousing enterprise for a mixed-tenure group without an imaginative leap and some flexibility on the part of a local authority. The grant for general social housing is usually allocated by a local authority on the basis of individual priority *housing* need, rather than on a person's need for support and companionship, nor necessarily even for accessible accommodation. It is not universally strictly applied except in areas of housing pressure, but where it is strictly applied this contributes to the 'tenure of last resort' problems and lack of a balanced community in social housing as alluded to earlier. The system has been criticised by Young and Lemos (1997) for not also allowing for a wider concept of social need in which factors such as friendship ties or a need for, or ability to give, support might be taken into account. It is also customary for the local authority to retain nomination rights for 50% or more of tenancies. This renders it impossible for the group itself to self-select members on the basis of support of the group ethos and broadly shared interests – elements that are essential ingredients for building an integrated community.

The experience of housing cooperatives is that they may be permitted to make a selection of new tenants from the housing register and may occasionally manage to negotiate on the basis of a person's perceived willingness to participate in the cooperative. In an older persons' CoHousing Community, where people live together more interdependently than in most cooperatives, the need for a new tenant to actively subscribe to the life of the group and its philosophy of mutual support make it all the more essential that the group should have the freedom to select on that basis.

Equal opportunities and communities of interest

A standard reaction in the housing world to the notion of selection of new tenants by a CoHousing Community is that this would run counter to the principles of equal opportunity. It is suggested that people might favour their friends and relations and exclude others. The norm is for professionals to make objective allocations, even if the net result is (as it is all too often) a dysfunctional and far from sustainable community. Nomination rights for the local authority or any other body are not compatible with successful CoHousing Community building and self-managing groups will have to be trusted. Clearly, an older persons' CoHousing Community needs to show, in policy and practice, that it does not discriminate against applicants on any grounds *but* the capacity and willingness to participate fully in the life of the group. The London project group's literature states that women from any background or culture are welcome as long as they are prepared to commit themselves to the group's values and to be active participants.

To work well, the building of a CoHousing Community draws on existing bonds and networks. If these bonds do not already exist at the start of the process, they have to be developed consciously as time goes on. CoHousing extends the real value of social links that are already forged among older people and this should be seen, as it is in the Netherlands, as a form of *social investment* and *a means of prevention* that can be allowed to supersede administrative boundaries and lead to flexible interpretation of regulations.

Conclusion – innovation in Britain?

The aim of the London project is to produce a 'how to' training guide that is accessible to older people. However, there is also a need for a central point to which people can go to obtain introductory information, as well as reassuring advice and support about the way forward. The small but growing network of intergenerational CoHousing Community groups around the country are evolving a system of information exchange, enabling each one to learn from the other's experience, particularly in legal and financial matters. The CoHousing Communities Network[2] (of which the pilot project is a member) and the CoHousing Communities Foundation[3] are at the hub of this exchange.

It is also important that the most effective support to groups of older people interested in developing CoHousing Communities is a local resource. Local authority strategies for older people and 'Best Value' reviews of services need to demonstrate a shift away from traditional forms of service provision to anticipate a new generation's different expectations. Ideally, a development capacity dedicated to facilitating the self-generation of community groups among older people could become part of the arsenal of forward-looking and innovative housing associations.

The older people's CoHousing Community offers an innovative model that will be attractive to some, although not all, older people in Britain. It will appeal particularly to those who place a high premium on staying in control of their own lives and who will also enjoy the experience of combining a private life with living as part of a group (Brenton, 1990). CoHousing is a model of living which requires members to consider the issues of ageing alongside others and the nature of inclusion and exclusion in bounded communities. As one of a range of choices open to older people it could set a benchmark for change away from the more traditional approaches to old age to which our society has clung for too long.

Notes

[1] The CoHousing Network website in the US may be found on www.cohousing.org and the Network's quarterly journal is *CoHousing: contemporary approaches to housing ourselves.*

[2] The British CoHousing Communities Network website may be found on www.cohousing.co.uk.

[3] The CoHousing Communities Foundation website may be found on www.liv.ac.uk/~arch/coho.

References

BiC (Boligtrevsel I Centrum) (1994) *Co-housing for senior citizens in Europe*, Report from EU Conference 'Growing grey in a happier way', Copenhagen, Copenhagen: BiC.

Brenton, M. (1998) *'We're in charge': CoHousing Communities of older people in the Netherlands: Lessons for Britain?*, Bristol: The Policy Press.

Brenton, M. (1990) *Choice, autonomy and mutual support: Older women's collaborative living arrangements*, York: York Publishing Services/Joseph Rowntree Foundation.

DETR (Department of Environment, Transport and the Regions) (2000) *Quality and choice: A decent home for all*, London. DETR.

DoE (Department of the Environment) (1996) *Projections of households in England to 2016*, London: HMSO.

Fisk, M. (1999) *Our future home: Housing and the inclusion of older people in 2025*, London: Help the Aged.

Forrest, R. and Leather, P. (1998) 'The ageing of the property owning democracy', *Ageing & Society*, vol 18, Part 1, pp 35-63.

Fromm, D. (1991) *Collaborative communities: Cohousing, central living and other forms of new housing with shared facilities*, New York, NY: Van Nostrand Reinhold.

Jones, C. (1997) *The empowerment of older people: Examples of good practice from European countries*, Coventry: Community Education Development Centre.

McCamant, K. and Durrett, C. (1994) *CoHousing: A contemporary approach to housing ourselves* (2nd edn), Berkley, CA: Ten Speed Press.

ten Brinke van Hengstum, A. and Stegink, M. (1987) *Het bouwen aan een woongemeenschap van ouderen*, Wageningen: Landbouwuniversiteit Wageningen.

ten Brinke van Hengstum, A. and Eikelboom, L.(1999) *Een leven lang wonen huisvesting en zorg*, Amsterdam: Boom.

VROM (Ministerie van Volkshuisvesting, Ruimtelijke Ordening en Milieubeheer) (1997) *Huisvesting van ouderen op het breukvlak van twee eeuwen*, Zoetermeer: VROM.

VROM (1998) *Van idealisme naar realisme*, Zoetermeer: VROM.

Young, M. and Lemos, G. (1997) *The communities we have lost and can regain*, London: Lemos and Crane.

NINE

Retirement communities in Britain: a 'third way' for the third age?

Judith Phillips, Miriam Bernard, Simon Biggs and Paul Kingston

Introduction

This chapter addresses a form of community living that has been proposed as an antidote to many of the problems of traditional residence for older people while maintaining the advantages of community living. Retirement communities have been associated with active lifestyles in later life, non-discriminatory practice in relation to ageing, participation in day-to-day decision making, and have been credited with improvements in health status and well-being. In many ways a growing interest in retirement communities can be seen as complementary to social-democratic social policies, such as the 'third way' in British politics at the turn of the millennium. It is, of course, also a third way in a more particular sense: as a third position between living in the community or in a residential or nursing home.

Historically, housing and care services have been provided within a framework that has been ageist and has fostered dependency. Increasingly, more flexible approaches are being encouraged, which empower, provide choice and promote the autonomy of older people. Emerging perspectives focus on standards of building on community and participation, on what people can do, and on active involvement of consumers and citizens (Riseborough, 1998). Such positive approaches are being promoted through what has been described as 'new ways of living', where individuals can prescribe their futures and identities. Retirement communities are seen as one such positive alternative approach to combining housing and support for older people. In Britain, the supportive housing field and retirement communities in particular are a relatively recent phenomenon. In the US and other parts of Europe, most notably the Netherlands, Germany and Denmark, such communities have matured, both in terms of their development and in the profile of their residents.

This chapter summarises the historical growth of retirement communities in the US and Europe, looks at the literature on the logic and critique of such provision and discusses whether such communities do herald the development of new lifestyles or whether they are simply a further form of institutional care. This sets the scene for a discussion of some of the empirical studies currently being conducted in Britain; these include a study of the health impact of age-specific living and an ongoing evaluation of a new purpose-built retirement village.

What is a retirement community?

Webber and Osterbind (1961) defined a retirement community as "a small community relatively independent segregated by age and geography and non-institutional, whose residents are mainly older people ... free of the regimen imposed by common food, common rules, common quarters and common authority" (pp 1-2).

Forty years later, in a British context, retirement communities appear to us to include the following definitional characteristics:

- *A retirement element* consisting of residents who are no longer in full-time employment, which affects the use of time and space.
- *A community element*, which includes an age-specific population, living in the same bounded geographic area.
- *A degree of collectivity* with which people identify and which may include shared activities, interests and facilities.
- *A sense of autonomy with security.*

Retirement communities grew rapidly in the US following the Second World War, and evolved in three main ways: first, through in-migration of retirees, usually drawn by environmental amenities; second, by the ageing of the local population; and third, by the out-migration of younger people leaving behind a disproportionately high number of older adults (Howe et al, 1994). The latter two of these can be described as naturally occurring retirement communities (NORCs), which take place through evolution of 'ageing in place' and are not through formal planning. In contrast, there are what we call here, formally organised retirement communities (FORCs), which have been specifically constructed to meet the needs of older residents. Such FORCs became associated with affluent middle classes, physically separated from the surrounding neighbourhood, often 'gated' communities with an emphasis on security, surveillance and social similarity of residents.

Retirement communities have also been categorised by whether they were planned or unplanned, according to size, the age and health status of residents, whether they are subsidised or not and what types of services they provide. Marans et al (1984) used such features to identify five types of retirement communities: new towns, villages, subdivisions, residences and continuing care centres. More recently, Stallman and Jones (1995) have delineated types of retirement communities by the features that attract retirees, the types of retirees attracted, the promotional campaigns used, the economic considerations involved and the potential problems faced by each type of community. They also identified five types, which they label resource amenity, planned, continuing care, old home town and regional centre. By contrast, Health Care Investment Analysts Inc (1997) identify four categories: assisted living (shelter with various personal support services), congregate care (private living quarters with centralised dining services, shared living space, and access to social and recreational activities), independent living (houses, condominiums, apartments and mobile homes) and continuing care retirement communities (CCRCs) (facilities that provide contracted services ranging from skilled nursing care to housekeeping, usually for the remainder of the resident's life). There are a variety of possibilities therefore in a definition of 'retirement community' and the traditional model of sheltered housing in Britain, a type of independent living, is one of them.

The above literature summarises our knowledge of retirement communities in the US. Retirement communities in the US are very diverse but are usually built with shops, activity centres, a church, gym and bars on site, and schemes can vary between a few units to tens of thousands of units. The most successful villages are those operated by and for people with a common interest such as membership of a particular church or a shared pastime. Communities such as Sun City are also geared to an affluent middle-class and active senior population. Spatial as well as social segregation is emphasised – walkways are within the complex rather than connecting the community to the outside world.

Several European models stand in contrast to the US experience, with a focus on 'community' rather than other lifestyle aspects (Baars and

Thomese, 1994). CCRCs have been a common option for housing and care for older people in Germany since the 1950s, with around 600 such communities in existence in the early 1980s (Hearnden, 1983). In this context, CCRCs comprise small village-like settlements with independent housing units and a central community building that provides respite, residential and nursing care facilities. Such care can be provided on an 'outreach' basis to older people within their own homes or within the centre.

Since the 1980s communal living in CoHousing communities has also become popular in the Netherlands (see Chapter Nine in this book). Cooperative housing models have also developed in Denmark, where the growing need for community interaction has also led to the development of '*Bofellesskab*' communities, again, offering individual privacy while at the same time providing communal space for interaction (Rodabough, 1994). Cooperative housing is becoming increasingly popular in Scandinavia, for example at Anderslov and Klippan in southern Sweden, based on Lifetime Homes principles in which concepts of security, participation and fellowship at both individual and community levels are key (Ahlund et al, 1998).

The above summary highlights the diverse nature, terminology and definitions of retirement communities. Key features, however, are that they are age segregated, catering primarily for people over the age of 55, have a philosophy that encourages active participation within a community, promote independent lifestyles and rely on peer support rather than paid staff to create a climate of independence. Cultural assumptions, which underpin such communities, focus on enjoyment and involvement, viewing frailty as a challenge and promoting themselves as 'one big team' with an emphasis on empowerment.

British experience

Large-scale seasonal migration of older people to retirement communities from one part of Britain to another is not as common a phenomenon as it is in the US. Although there is movement to seaside resorts in the UK, retirement communities are not necessarily concentrated in these areas. Most retirement communities tend to accommodate people who have decided to move permanently to such facilities.

In Britain, 'assisted living' has been used in the literature (Laing & Buisson, 1998) to describe a variety of such communities. Retirement communities were traditionally provided by enlightened employers or occupational groups such as the Licensed Victuallers and the Linen Drapers (Laing & Buisson, 1998). The first CCRC was set up by the Joseph Rowntree Housing Trust in 1998 following protracted planning negotiations (Rugg, 1999). Based on a single-site campus style design, with spaciousness being a key feature, these developments are designed to be attractive to middle-class retirees. The cluster of bungalows, built to Lifetime Homes standards and close to the care centre, allows continual monitoring of residents' care needs.

Benefits of retirement community living

Studies, such as those of Lucksinger (1994), assume that as alternative, communal forms of housing, retirement communities are directed at giving meaning to older people's lives through engendering a sense of community. Such findings are supported by work in the Netherlands, where a national survey found a high degree of contentment with CoHousing (VROM, 1998).

In their classic study comparing older people in both age-segregated and age-integrated communities, Bultena and Wood (1969) found that the retirement community population scored much higher in terms of life satisfaction. Higher incomes, better educational levels and health status, the features of the age-segregated community and the homogeneity of the population all contributed to satisfaction in comparison to those living in age-integrated communities. Others have suggested that such communities can help combat loneliness and isolation, improve morale and engender a sense of belonging and social integration (Longino and McLelland, 1978; Osgood, 1982; Lucksinger, 1994).

Further research has focused on the activity levels of residents. Madigan et al (1996) examined the relationship between purposeful activity and life satisfaction of older men in five different locations: adult day care centres, retirement communities, adult homes, nursing homes and senior centres. Results indicate a significant difference in activity levels, with participants in the senior centres showing the highest level of activity and residents of the nursing homes showing the lowest, while men residing in retirement communities were the most satisfied of all the groups. Kahana et al's (1996) ongoing US research stresses the relationship between healthier lifestyles and retirement communities in the US. From a study of 1,000 residents the authors develop a model of 'successful ageing'. Residents of retirement communities walk, play golf and so on, and maintain active lifestyles well into their eighties. Of those who reported severe, limiting arthritis, 33% also reported regular physical exercise. Cross-sectional analysis revealed a consistently high correlation between lack of exercise and disability. Newcomer (1994) found that CCRC residents are more likely to use a nursing unit after a hospital stay or outpatients' surgery than are community residents. On the other hand they have a lower rate of hospital admission and higher rate of outpatient surgery. However, it is unclear whether people entering retirement communities are similar, with particular histories and social status, or whether the social space of the community is effecting a healthier lifestyle.

Security is a further motivating factor for joining such a community as well as meeting the need to move to a setting which is physically designed for decreasing mobility, without routine garden and house maintenance.

On a broader level, another area of research has investigated the cost of retirement community living compared with other living arrangements. On this basis, Schwenck (1993) considers retirement communities as viable alternatives to costly nursing homes and intensive home-based personal healthcare. However, it is difficult to assess the cost benefits of retirement communities, particularly in terms of how they can relieve pressure on the family to provide care. In looking at cost, the cost to families, the local community and a comparison to other forms of care, needs to be made.

Research in Florida, found that the older population was most often perceived as an economic and cultural asset in the communities studied (Howe et al, 1994). Visitors to retirement communities in the US are also a source of income for local areas, without making the same long-term care demands as permanent settlers. Such findings have implications for the physical design of shopping malls, waterfront features and recreation areas in these areas.

Retirement communities also possess the ability to become effective pressure groups and watchdogs of older people in general, which is a demonstration of 'grey power' with a say over local politics (Howe et al, 1994). In their study of various types of retirement communities, Hunt et al (1984) found that in one area (Leisure World, California) residents gave continual support to local public schools; residents at another community in Florida blocked construction of a large manufacturing plant nearby.

Critique of retirement communities

Research has begun to question some of these findings, reinforcing Maggie Kuhn's earlier critiques of such 'unnatural environments' or, as they are described, 'playpens for the elderly' and 'geriatric ghettos'. Criticisms from the UK come, for example, from Forrest and Leather (1998) who address the issue of social exclusion. They argue that such selective communities are both age and class segregated, and can exclude a major section of older people. Hoonard and Kestin (1994) examined the relationships between widowed and married members of a US retirement community, revealing the existence of a stigma associated with widowhood, resulting in lower social status than married people. Such findings, however, may not be particular to retirement communities. Sherwood et al's (1997) longitudinal study of CCRC residents indicate that they predominantly serve white, well-educated middle- to upper-class people, mainly women over the age of 75, and can exclude groups outside of this description.

Netting and Wilson (1991) also find that, although resident participation is a key feature, residents do not always agree on how environments should be structured, while other studies have shown that residents do not always include their coresidents who have developed disabilities.

Retirement communities have also been criticised for their leisure, as opposed to their care, orientation. Metsch (1996), for example, argues that they are more about helping older adults to meet the challenges of adapting to retirement status, rather than providing continuing care into old age. Glenda Laws (1995, 1997) has stressed the need to look more at the psychological aspects of space and at how such communities help in the creation and maintenance of identity in old age. She suggests that more attention needs to be paid to the social and spatial 'props' that retirement communities provide. In her study of retirees living in Sun City developments, she shows how they are specially designed to bolster age-based identification, but with the disadvantage that ageing and disability are subject to denial and manipulation. Such exclusivity can lead to exclusion of those who become disabled and ill. Exclusivity has also been criticised by Kastenbaum (1993). He suggests that retirement communities can become reactionary enclaves, which constitute an attempt to exclude contemporary social problems such as those perceived as arising from multicultural and urban environments.

Further, the structure of retirement communities can deny residents certain elements of freedom and choice due to the expectation and pressure to conform to the appropriate norms. At the beginning of a continuing debate since the 1950s, Mumford (1956) argues that older people should not be segregated or regarded as a separate group because the narrowing of interests could have psychological consequences. In communities which are gated or walled it is difficult to access the outside community unless residents can drive. Walking to local facilities is not possible due to the lack of sidewalks and the construction of retirement communities alongside major expressways (for example, Seven Lakes, Florida) can lead to isolation within the community, particularly for older women who do not drive.

Although retirement communities may contain positive features they are neither instant nor static communities: new schemes can be built but 'communities' cannot be created 'off the peg' within them. This requires the collaboration of residents and adaptation to constant evolution and change. Little longitudinal work has produced results in favour or against retirement communities in general, and it is far too early to evaluate the UK examples. However, there are concerns about the ability of such communities to sustain people into late old age when the potential for physical disability and dementia increases. The increasing age profile of these communities will lead to increasing and concentrated demand on local health and welfare services (Rugg, 1999). Why people enter and exit such communities could be an interesting area for further research.

Similarly, there are potential problems in the level of contact across the boundary, with family, former neighbours and local services. Even if retirement communities did cater for people with severe disabilities and mental health needs, there is also a question about the willingness of older people to accept a move from their individual unit to a central communal residence that provides nursing care. Evidence also shows that people do not use the 'communal care spaces'. In age-segregated communities, people also miss out on intergenerational community life.

Researching health, identity and well-being in retirement communities

In Britain, some local authorities have, in recent years, taken policy decisions not to put more resources into traditional forms of institutional care, but instead to actively support the development of purpose-built retirement housing. This trend is broadly in line with wider UK and European policy agendas regarding old age (Bernard and Phillips, 1998; BGOP, 2000) which are emphasising the deinstitutionalisation of care and the shift of responsibility for health and personal support onto individuals and their families. They also focus on independence rather than dependence, and on the importance of new lifestyles for a healthy old age. The development of retirement communities in Britain appears well suited to such a policy agenda, resonating strongly with desires to increase autonomy and inclusive practices for those in later life.

It also appears that the number of British retirement communities is growing apace. There are, however, no nationally collated statistics to confirm the extent of this trend. Moreover, despite the emergence of environments ostensibly designed to meet the requirements of retired people, we in fact know comparatively little of what it is actually like to live in such communities in Britain. While North American and European experiences may have relevance to the British context, there are historical, cultural and policy differences which mean that this cannot be taken as a given. Unfortunately, most British developments have been undertaken with a strong measure of faith rather than being grounded in solid research-based evidence, since little was known about what types of people in Britain choose to live in such communities. This paucity of British research led us, in 1996, to begin to explore new retirement community initiatives being developed in the West Midlands. It is to these initiatives and our associated research that we now turn.

The health impact of age-specific housing

The Keele team[1] secured independent funding from the NHS Executive (West Midlands), for a two-year project entitled 'Assessing the health impact of age-specific housing'. The project was largely designed with a primary focus on health and compared the health status of a retirement community population with a population of older people living in the same locality. The purpose-built retirement community housing 48 tenants was sited in the middle of a public housing estate and deliberately drew on the surrounding working-class community for the majority of its tenants. In collaboration with the social services department, we were also able to secure a community sample of older people residing in the same locality (n=98).

The project set out to evaluate both populations cross-sectionally at two specific points, one year apart, and to begin to explore something of what it was like to live in a British retirement community. The methodology also allowed analysis of change over time for both cohorts over one year.

The aims of the project were:

1. To consider the health implications of retirement community living.
2. To compare the health status of the retirement community sample with a comparable community sample.
3. To explore the impact of retirement community living on tenants in terms of social functioning and participation.
4. To assess the views of local health professionals on retirement community living in terms of its implications for physical and mental health service provision.

We adopted a 'multi-strategy' research design (Layder, 1993, p 108) using both quantitative and qualitative approaches to data gathering[2]. We concentrate our discussion of some of the findings on two areas: first, on a comparison of the health status of tenants with older people living in the locality and, second, on what it is actually like to live in such an age-segregated environment.

Longer life, better health?

While the two samples of older people (in the retirement community and in the local area) were broadly comparable in terms of features such as gender and social class backgrounds, the people living in the retirement community were, on average, nearly four years older: 80.1 years old compared with 76.4 years old. Despite this age difference, results from the questionnaires administered at Time 1 suggested that, in terms of general health ($p<0.05$) and mental health ($p<0.05$) (as scored on the SF36), the retirement community tenants were healthier than their counterparts in the local community. They also reported less pain. However, they experienced greater limitations on them as a consequence of physical health problems and were more restricted in terms of social functioning.

These findings may, at first sight, appear somewhat contradictory in that retirement community residents claim that they are generally healthier (and particularly so in terms of mental health) while, at the same time, are limited in terms of social functioning by their physical problems. Additional responses to other questions shed further light on this. Scores on the semantic differential scales show that tenants regard themselves as significantly more comfortable ($p<0.01$) and fortunate ($p<0.05$) than older people living in the locality. In terms of life satisfaction indicators, they were also more positive in thinking about and planning for the future, believing that things were getting better as they grew older. Safety and comfort were, perhaps not surprisingly, the two things that tenants liked best about living in the retirement community.

In other words, it appeared that, despite an acknowledgement of some of the restrictions and limitations on them, the retirement community tenants felt this was outweighed or compensated for by other factors. Over the one-year time period, these tenants also managed to maintain their levels of physical, mental and social functioning as measured by the SF36 (there were no significant changes in their scores). By contrast, older people living in the locality reported significantly greater difficulties in physical and social functioning ($p<0.005$ and $p<0.001$ respectively) and an increase in bodily pain ($p<0.005$). However, the trends are complex, and people in the locality demonstrated much more variability in scores and responses than did the retirement community tenants. The results suggest that while tenants may well feel healthier and more satisfied with their lives, they do not have access to the diversity of experiences or people open to respondents living in the wider community.

There is a sense then in which the tenants of the retirement community are a more homogenous group. Whether this was the case before they moved in or whether this is a consequence of retirement community living, is impossible to tell. However, in terms of health, there was certainly evidence that, while living in the retirement community could not in effect halt (or reverse) the ageing process, it did offer an environment which enabled a high degree of maintenance to be achieved. Moreover, tenants talked freely in the focus group discussions and in daily intercourse of what they felt to be a 'feel good' factor in operation. One tenant, Bea, commented that:

> "Part of it [the feel good factor] is about people worrying about each other. In this community we share our joys and sorrows. It all affects our mental health and how we feel."

Arthur, another tenant, graphically described it in these terms:

> "The other thing I've noticed in the 12 months I've been in here is that, as you are listening and taking part in general conversations with folks, in the concerts or downstairs watching the bowls, or just having a chat, you don't get continual organ recitals – which is a sign of improvement. I mean, people aren't discussing which organ they had taken out the year before last, and which organ was operated on [laughter], or, 'you ought to see the size of my scar'! That's the sign of

> the feel good factor: because people feel good, so they don't need to moan about their organs."

It appears therefore, that in terms of health, retirement community living offers considerable benefits. However, are these benefits experienced equally and in the same way by everyone? In order to explore this issue further, we reflect on what tenants said about the day-to-day experience of living in such a community.

Sociability, peer support and autonomy

It became very clear in the focus groups that participants held strong views on the 'special' nature of their retirement community, and this uniqueness was, in large part, generated through the ability it afforded tenants to live a lifestyle characterised by sociability, peer support and autonomy – or what one member termed "independence with inclusion". The retirement community is portrayed in the retirement community's promotional literature as a positive alternative to other forms of accommodation (and care) in later life. Frailty is regarded as a challenge to be overcome and tenants are expected to participate as one big team in the project of improving their mental and physical abilities.

There was considerable talk and reflection in the focus groups about how and to what extent this was achieved by tenants in their day-to-day lives. Two things in particular were notable about this discourse. First, and linked with the above comments from Arthur, there was a marked absence of illness narratives. In contrast with other gerontological literature which has highlighted how older people report on their health status, make explicit reference to chronological age and engage in painful self-disclosure as a means of structuring their interactions with others (see, for example, Coupland et al, 1988, 1991; Weimann et al, 1990), this appeared to have no currency whatsoever in the retirement community under study. Indeed, something of the opposite tendency was observed in that there were a number of stories verging on the miraculous. Ellie, for example, told about two different women:

> "Mary here started with Alzheimer's, and look at her now – absolutely marvellous! When Mary went into hospital she was in a dreadful state. Now she's come out of hospital and she holds a conversation, she plays her bingo."

> "There's some leaflets in the foyer that are worth reading. Have you read them? This one old lady couldn't speak at all and they got her to talk. She couldn't do anything. Her name's there and everything. That's what we've achieved for her!"

The second notable feature about these conversations was that participants made very clear distinctions between the effects their retirement community lifestyle had on them in terms of mental versus physical capacity. Physical disability was seen as an inevitable part of the ageing process, which could not be influenced by the retirement community culture (a view in sharp contrast with the promotional literature). It could, however, be managed by the judicious use of staff, provided that the information that was divulged in order to elicit support did not jeopardise their continued residence in the community. Moreover, staff were treated in a largely instrumental fashion and valued for the 'objectivity' and distance their training gave them, rather than for any social or emotional closeness. In our study, there was no evidence that staff functioned as important sources of recognition or self-validation for the tenants, as they have often been reported to do in traditional residential care (Booth, 1985; Wilkin and Hughes, 1987; Peace et al, 1997).

With regards to mental health and well-being, there was considerable discussion in the groups about negative well-being existing as a state of mind. Not "giving in" and "taking your mind off things" were seen as the remedies and the practical value of living in the retirement community was that it fostered this culture.

The attitudes of, and engagement with, other tenants was crucial to the maintenance of mental health. A culture of mutual peer help, mixing and the opportunity to participate in events and activities, were the factors most often mentioned in the context of discussion about mental well-being. Moreover, unlike physical health, mental health was seen as something that generally improved as a consequence of coming to live in the retirement community and was then maintained at high levels. Thus, the feel good factor mentioned earlier was clearly something that tenants were able to articulate given the opportunity to do so in the focus group sessions. It was here that an explanation of some of the rather confusing quantitative findings began to make sense. Peer support emerged as a key factor in the maintenance of a positive sense of well-being in the retirement community group.

Many stories were told of mutual support, ranging from how people "worry about each other" and "share our joys and sorrows" through to practical examples of helping new tenants to get to know the building and assisting people to get back to their flats or, perhaps, to the toilet.

This mutuality was also reinforced by the creation of a number of 'out' groups – a reaction familiar from the dynamics of other group situations. As we have already noted, staff are peripheral when it comes to day-to-day existence in the community. Family members are also seen in this light, but tenants see this as a positive choice, as a way of side-stepping family friction and freeing them from the possibility of becoming a burden on others. The personal freedom and autonomy this brings, together with a recognition of what we now term 'intimacy at a distance' (Rosenmayr and Kockeis, 1963), permeated the discussions. It also resonates strongly with other recent research which has explored what older people actually want in terms of support in old age (Phillipson et al, 1999). Lottie summed it up in these terms:

> "One of the major issues of getting older is the question of independence, and we want to be as independent as we possibly can.... If, however, I am going to be dependent at some stage, I would rather be here being dependent on trained people who are actually paid to give me assistance, than I would be a burden on my family."

Stories were also told about two other 'out' groups: about the decline in the local area and about what they saw as the 'disgrace' of nursing home care. These stories served to bring the positive qualities of the retirement community into much sharper focus. The local area was now viewed as a dangerous and unfriendly place with the 'community spirit' of earlier years having all but disappeared. Vandalism, burglary and harassment were common, while the difficulties of maintaining one's own property also lent weight to this negative image of hostile surroundings. The retirement community afforded these older people a 'safe haven' and the opportunity to begin, as they saw it, a new life. Casting out groups in negative terms acts as both a boost to self-esteem and serves as a reminder to tenants of the possible threats posed by not being part of their retirement community 'in' group.

In summary, it appears that there are a number of key themes in the value of retirement community living for health and personal well-being:

- the value of everyday peer support;
- the effect of mental well-being on physical capacity;
- independence from families;

- independence from staff;
- autonomy with security.

Discussion

Lest readers think that this study had nothing but positive things to report about retirement community living, it is important here to reflect on some of the limitations of such environments. We have already noted the sense in which members of this retirement community are a homogenous group: an 'in' group who sign up to the philosophy that keeping active is the key to living a fulfilling lifestyle. However, there was evidence from the interviews and focus group discussions that this homogeneity could also lead to the exclusion of certain people. Some tenants had particular expertise or a particularly high level of skill in a given recreational or craft activity. Jean, for example, told of how:

> "I stayed out of the ceramics class although I love it. But, the point was, having already done 14 years of pottery, I have to try and keep my mouth shut.... It's a clash of ideas see. They find that I probably talk differently, I don't know ... I just want friendship, that's all I want. I want to give back."

Irene also talked about being excluded saying: "I got froze out because I had already done computer classes". There is evidence, then, that you can be too competent at something and that this, in turn, can be used to denigrate and exclude people.

In a similar vein, the picture of peer support also had its limitations, particularly when it came to considering the situations of a number of the disabled and wheelchair-user tenants. Some of these tenants considered that peer support (and indeed staff support) was insufficient and inconsistent and, from our observations, tenants were excluded both literally (in terms of their physical location in the lounge area for example) and psychologically and emotionally (by being 'frozen out' of certain activities). Kate, a wheelchair-user woman with a powerful sense of what it had meant to be disabled over her life course, spoke about the exclusion she felt:

> "It was the council that recommended this place to me, and they said it was so good. As I say, the people who praise it up, are the people who

> can get about. You'll find that you've got 'you ain't got a pusher' [someone to push her wheelchair] in your face all the time. Molly [a friend] asked me, 'Are you going to Weston?', and I said, 'I'd like to but I haven't got a pusher'."

So, even within the retirement community, there are certain 'out' groups: severely disabled tenants and those who exceed or transgress the 'middle-of-the-road' cultural norm. Beyond this too, there were indications that even tenants who were part of the in group and regarded themselves as active and autonomous individuals, were anxious about their future status. It was not always clear how the boundaries of acceptable physical and mental infirmity were negotiated, and there was, as we have noted earlier, an effort on the part of many tenants to ensure that they divulged only as much information as was needed to elicit the support they needed. How, and under what circumstances, people left the retirement community was either not spoken about or was met with humorous or anxiety-reducing strategies by staff, evidently concerned to bring such enquiries to a quick conclusion.

Not surprisingly, this study also raises more questions than answers, such as what is the optimum size of a retirement community? How significant is the power of peer support? Does this describe a 'pioneer culture'? What is the relationship between physical and mental well-being? And whether 'out' groups are needed to form an identity. It is to these issues that we now turn.

Where do we go to from here?

The study reported above provided a wealth of valuable information about the health status of tenants, and about the general experience of living in such a retirement community. In particular, we have evidence about the ways in which health is maintained and how the positive aspects of retirement community living can be enhanced through a balanced mixture of security, sociability, peer support and autonomy. However, what we do not yet know is whether or how these aspects operate in much larger scale environments; nor what happens to people over a longer timescale. In order to explore these issues, we have been engaging in further work in a larger retirement village[3].

Preliminary analysis of the first wave of interviews with a sample of tenants suggests that there are strong parallels with some of the findings of our first study, but a more complex and varied picture of life in this retirement village is also emerging. Tenants' reasons for moving to the village are similar, with either their own, or their partner's health, being key. The attractive and safe physical environment, together with the promised availability of care and support (from neighbours and friends as much as, or instead of, from staff) is also an important factor. Many tenants also report increased participation in social activities and, in contrast with the earlier study, believe that both their physical and mental functioning has improved. The layout of the flats, the absence of stairs, their more compact accommodation, and no longer needing to engage in, or worry about, the maintenance of their homes and gardens, has had marked beneficial effects on their physical capacities. Feelings of security, the reduction in their fear of crime, and 'the peace and quiet' of this environment has also improved the psychological well-being of respondents, many of whom reported suffering from anxiety disorders or depression prior to moving to the village.

However, it is also the case that for some people this is again not necessarily the promised Shangri-la presented in the promotional material. For those who had previously attended day centres or similar services, there are indications that their previous levels of social contact have, in effect, been reduced and they feel that they are 'doing less'. For others, the environment appears to be having negative effects on their physical and psychological health: concerns about the building being too warm and poorly ventilated, and the consequences this has for people with breathing difficulties, were voiced by a number of respondents. In addition, the distances involved in negotiating the village have left some tenants feeling more incapacitated because of now having to use wheelchairs or scooters to get around. Difficulties in socialising, in having to pay for activities, and the 'bingo and karaoke' feel of much of the entertainment, has also contributed to some respondents feeling more, not less, isolated, anxious, lonely and unhappy.

This is only a very brief and partial snapshot of what life is currently like for some of the tenants. There is much more detailed information which has been and still is being gathered, and which examines issues such as the design of the village, the activities and entertainment, the care provision and whether or not people's expectations of this type of living have been realised. In the second wave interviews, there has been a much greater focus on social networks, and on people's involvement (or lack of involvement) with the surrounding community. In the third and final wave there is greater emphasis on friendships and on the use of both public and private space within the village.

The qualitative work also dovetails with a larger-scale evaluation of the village that commenced in June 2000. Funded by the National Lottery Charities Board, this project is entitled 'New lifestyles in old age: health, identity and well-being in retirement communities' and has a number of aims and objectives. It seeks to further examine how living in a retirement village may contribute to the improvement of older people's quality of life, health and well-being, explores how such a development may, or may not, become an integral part of the wider community in which it is located, and will consider the policy and practice implications, in terms of how viable such models are in helping to meet the future health and welfare needs of our increasingly ageing population[4].

The research we have undertaken and continue to do is couched very much within a participatory, action-research model, drawing both on the action-research tradition itself (Lewin, 1946; Hart and Bond, 1995) and on developments which in Britain have been labelled as 'human inquiry' (Reason and Rowan, 1981; Reason, 1988, 1994). This research orientation attempts to give primacy to the research participants themselves in both shaping and generating the material on which the evaluation of the village will be based. Throughout the collation and triangulation of the quantitative data with the qualitative material, we expect to be examining a number of continuing, but as yet unresolved, key themes. These themes revolve around three issues: strategies for the maintenance of health and whether, in the longer term, these can continue to be successful as people age; peer versus intergenerational support and whether these environments truly provide an alternative to either family- or residential-based forms of care; attachment to place and whether, and to what extent, the locality and the accommodation have an impact on the other two issues. Of course, we are not expecting to provide definitive answers. We are trying to begin to articulate what it is really like for the older people who are increasingly being encouraged to experience something popularly heralded as a new and empowering existence in later life and a radical and realistic alternative to other forms of institutional care. Whether this truly is the case remains to be seen.

Conclusion

Institutional care for older people is now an extensively researched and widely critiqued area (see for example, Goffman, 1961; Townsend, 1962; Willcocks et al, 1987; Booth, 1985; Sinclair, 1990; Allen et al, 1992). The traditional critique emphasises the negative impacts on quality of life:

ritualised and routinised interaction, inward-lookingness and an absence of active participation in internal and wider communal activities, which can foster dependency, minimise privacy and lead to a loss of personal identity (Goffman, 1961). The institutional critique has prompted a search for an alternative community-based lifestyle. Retirement communities are promoted as new living arrangements, which concentrate on an empowering, anti-institutional, safe environment, and which can significantly improve the quality of life of older people.

From the evidence collected thus far, we would suggest that although, on the face of it, retirement community life offers an opportunity to live an active, supportive and positive third age, it carries with it the (often unspoken of) fear about what may await those who become afflicted by physical and/or mental infirmity. The positive aspects revolve around a general sense of optimism and a tangible pioneering spirit that this does indeed represent a new beginning for many residents, which recaptures the sense of community, neighbourliness and security they feel is lacking elsewhere. The negative aspects or costs are a sense of uncertainty and unknowing about the future, combined with the marginalisation of those who do not somehow fit the 'norm'.

The questions remain as to what place retirement communities will take in the long-term care continuum in 10 to 20 years' time. Will they enable people to take an active part in wider society or will they become ever more inward looking? Will their image be one of homely domesticity or will they begin to look more like traditional residential care? Are they really going to be a 'third way' for the third age?

Notes

[1] We wish to acknowledge that, since 1996, the 'Keele team' has included a number of colleagues, some of whom have since moved to other posts. Our thanks to members past and present: Dr Sam McIsaac, Mr Tony Silvester, Ms Hilary Nettleton, Dr Joanna Latimer and Ms Jayne Rushton.

[2] This included the use of participant observation; face-to-face questionnaires with tenants and older people in the surrounding community (at two time periods); a series of focus group discussions with a sample of tenants; and telephone interviews with a selected sample of health professionals who had contact with the retirement community. Three validated parametric tools were incorporated in the questionnaires: the Short Form 36 Health Survey (SF36) which assesses health status in eight domains (general health, physical functioning, role limitation

due to physical health problems, role limitation due to emotional health problems, mental/psychological health and well-being, bodily pain, vitality, and social functioning), the Life Satisfaction Index (LSI) and 18 Semantic Differentials (SDs) (Osgood et al, 1964; Neugarten, 1961; Ware et al, 1993). The 10-page questionnaire took, on average, 30 minutes to administer and, in the majority of cases, tenants were interviewed in their own flats. At Time 1, only one tenant refused to be interviewed. At Time 2, we were able to complete follow-up interviews with 42 out of the original 48 and with 74 out of the original 98 older people living in the locality. Analysis of this data was performed using the SPSS data analysis package and results from the first round of questionnaire interviews were then used to inform the focus group discussions.

The focus groups were conducted approximately midway through the project and consisted of three groups of tenants with five participants and a facilitator apiece. The groups were asked to discuss three main topics: 'transitions' (why people decided to move to a retirement community; their expectations, hopes, fears and so on); 'independence and dependency' (what this meant to people, how it was dealt with in this particular environment, etc); and 'health' (what people understood by this, how living in the retirement community had affected their health, etc).

The final element of the research design consisted of structured telephone interviews with five health professionals associated with the retirement community and in regular contact with residents.

[3] The first aspect of this work involves a qualitative, longitudinal study by a doctoral student, of a sample of tenants living in the village. Tenants were selected at random to take part in repeat interviews in three waves: April to July 1999; October 1999 to January 2000; and April to July 2000. These interviews were supplemented by ongoing participant and non-participant observation.

75 individuals out of the total of 165 tenants were randomly selected to receive invitations to take part. 52 of these 75 (or 69%) agreed to participate in the first wave of interviews. At the second wave, 36 of the 52 (69%) remained in the study and, in the third wave, 32 of the 36 (89%) were interviewed.

[4] The methodology of the present study builds on our previous work and uses a multi-method triangulated design in an effort to further our understanding of what it is like to live and work in a British retirement community. Underlying the design is a committment to the notion of collaborative research in which members of the community are facilitated to determine and fashion the village's future direction. To meet these ends, a number of different data gathering strategies have been designed in consultation with tenants and staff. They include

questionnaires (in three annual waves) to all 166 tenants; interviews with stakeholders; ongoing participant observation; analysis of diaries kept by a small sample of tenants; examination of existing documentation; and three community 'open space' conferences bringing together tenants and staff with members of the surrounding community. This latter technique has been used in both Britain (Beresford, 1994) and the US (Weisbord, 1987; Weisbord and Janoff, 1995).

References

Ahlund, O., Rasberg, E. and Ståhl, A. (1998) 'Planning integrated services in a municipality: a collaborative approach', in J. Phillips, R. Means, L. Russell and R. Sykes (eds) *Broadening our vision of housing and community care*, Oxford: Anchor Housing Trust, pp 13-21.

Allen, I., Hogg, D. and Peace, S. (1992) *Elderly people: Choice, satisfaction, and participation*, London: Policy Studies Institute.

Baars, J. and Thomese, F. (1994) 'Communes for elderly people', *Journal of Ageing Studies*, vol 8, no 4, pp 341-56.

Beresford, P. (1994) *Changing the culture*, London: CCETSW.

Bernard, M. and Phillips, J. (1998) (eds) *The social policy of old age: Moving into the 21st century*, London: Centre for Policy on Ageing.

BGOP (Better Government for Older People) (2000) *All our futures: The report of the Better Government for Older People Programme*, Wolverhampton: BGOP.

Booth, T. (1985) *Home truths, old people's homes and the outcome of care*, Aldershot: Gower.

Bultena, G. and Wood, V. (1969) 'The American retirement community: bane or blessing?', *Journal of Gerontology*, vol 24, pp 209-17.

Coupland, J., Coupland, N. and Grainger, K. (1991) 'Intergenerational discourse: contextual versions of ageing and elderliness', *Ageing & Society*, vol 10, no 1, pp 1-17.

Coupland, N., Giles, H., Henwood, K. and Weinmann, J. (1988) 'Elderly self-disclosure', *Language and Communication*, vol 8, pp 109-33.

Forrest, R. and Leather, P. (1998) 'The ageing of the property owning democracy', *Ageing & Society*, vol 18, no 1, pp 35-65.

Goffman, E. (1961) *Asylums*, New York, NY: Doubleday.

Hart, E. and Bond, M. (1995) *Action research for health and social care: A guide to practice*, Buckingham: Open University Press.

Health Care Investments Analysts Inc (1998) 'Can we tap the power of NORCs?', *Perspectives on Aging*, vol 26, no 1, pp 13-20.

Hearnden, D. (1983) *Continuing care communities: A viable option in Britain?*, London: Centre for Policy on Ageing.

Hoonard, D.K., van den and Kestin, D. (1994) 'Paradise lost: widowhood in a Florida retirement community', *Journal of Ageing Studies*, vol 8, pp 121-32.

Howe, D., Chapman, N. and Baggett, S. (1994) *Planning for an ageing society*, Planning Advisory Service Report No 451, Chicago, IL: American Planning Association.

Hunt, M. et al (1984) *Retirement communities: An American original*, New York, NY: Hayworth.

Kahana, E., Kahana, B., Kercher, K., Strange, K. and Brown, J. (1996) *Exercise and wellness in old-old retirement community residents*, Cleveland, OH: Department of Sociology, Case Western Reserve University.

Kastenbaum, R. (1993) 'Encrusted elders: Arizona and the political spirit of post-modern aging', in R. Cole (ed) *Voices and visions of aging*, New York, NY: Springer Verlag.

Kuhn, M. (1977) *Maggie Kuhn on ageing*, Philadelphia, PA: Westminster.

Laing & Buisson (1998) 'Housing with care in the UK: from sheltered housing to assisted living', London: Laing & Buisson.

Laws, G. (1995) 'Embodiment and emplacement', *International Journal of Aging and Human Development*, vol 40, no 4, pp 253-80.

Laws, G. (1997) 'Spatiality and age relations', in A. Jamieson, S. Harper and C. Victor (eds) *Critical approaches to ageing and later life*, Buckingham: Open University Press.

Layder, R. (1993) *New strategies in social research*, London: Sage Publications.

Lewin, K. (1946) 'Action research and minority problems', *Journal of Social Issues*, vol 2, pp 34-46.

Longino, C. and McLelland, K. (1978) *Age segregation and social integration in Midwestern retirement communities*, Miami, FL: Southern Sociological Society, University of Miami.

Lucksinger, M. (1994) 'Community and the elderly', *Journal of Housing for the Elderly*, vol 11, no 1, pp 11-28.

Madigan, M., Mise, D. and Maynard, M. (1996) 'Life satisfaction and level of activity of male elderly in institutional and community settings', *Activities, Adaptation and Aging*, vol 21, no 2, pp 21-36.

Marans, R., Hunt, M. and Vakall, K. (1984) 'Retirement communities', in I. Altman, M. Lawton and J. Wohlwill (eds) *Elderly people and their Environment*, New York, NY: Plenum.

Metsch, L. (1996) 'Community adaptation: ageing in place in retirement communities', *Dissertation Abstracts International: The Humanities and Social Sciences*, vol 56, no 11, pp 4559-60.

Mumford, L.L. (1956) 'For older people not segregation but integration', *Architectural Record*, no 119, pp 191-4, May.

Netting, F. and Wilson, C. (1991) 'Accommodation and relocation decision making in continuing care retirement communities', *Health and Social Work*, vol 16, no 4.

Newcomer, R. (1994) 'Relationships between acute care and nursing units in two continuing care retirement communities', *Research on Aging*, vol 16, no 3, pp 280-300.

Neugarten, B., Havighurst, R. and Tobin, S.S. (1961) 'The measurement of life satisfaction', *Journal of Gerontology*, vol 16, pp 134-43.

Osgood, C., Suci, G. and Tannentaum, P. (1964) *The measurement of meaning*, Urbana, IL: University of Illinois Press.

Osgood, N. (1982) *Senior settlers*, New York, NY: Praeger Publications.

Peace, S., Kellaher, L. and Wilcocks, D. (1997) *Re-evaluating residential care*, Buckingham: Open University Press.

Phillipson, C., Bernard, M., Phillips, J. and Ogg, J. (1999) 'Older people's experience of community life: patterns of neighbouring in three urban areas', *Sociological Review*, vol 47, no 4, pp 715-43.

Reason, P. (ed) (1988) *Human inquiry in action: Developments in new paradigm research*, London: Sage Publications.

Reason, P. (1994) *Participation in human inquiry*, London: Sage Publications.

Reason, P. and Rowan, J. (eds) (1981) *Human inquiry: A source of new paradigm research*, Chichester: Wiley.

Riseborough, M. (1998) *From consumerism to citizenship: New European perspectives on independent living in older age*, London: The Housing Corporation.

Rodabough, K. (1994) 'Bofellesskab: the Danish import', in F. Edward and D. Yeatts (eds) *Housing and the ageing population: options for the new century*, New York, NY: Garland.

Rosenmayr, L. and Kockeis, E. (1963) 'Propositions for a sociological theory of ageing and the family', *International Social Science Journal*, vol 15, pp 410-26.

Rugg, J. (1999) 'Hartrigg Oaks: the early development of a continuing care retirement community', Unpublished report, York: Centre for Housing Policy, University of York.

Schwenck, N. (1993) 'Long term care trends', *Family Economics Review*, vol 6, no 4, pp 9-18.

Sherwood, S., Ruchlin, H., Sherwood, C. and Morris, S. (1997) *Continuing care retirement communities*, Baltimore, MD: Johns Hopkins University Press.

Sinclair, I. (1990) *The kaleidoscope of care*, London: National Institute of Social Work.

Stallman, J. and Jones, L. (1995) 'A typology of retirement places: a community analysis', *Journal of Community Development Society*, vol 26, no 1, pp 1-14.

Townsend, P. (1962) *The last refuge*, London: Routledge.

VROM (Ministrie von Volkhuisvesting. Ruimtelijke Ordening en Milieubeheer) (1998) *Van idealisme naar realisme*, Zoetermeer: VROM.

Ware, J., Snow, K.K., Kosinski, B. and Gandek, B. (1993) *SF36 Health Survey: Manual and interpretation guide*, Boston, NJ: New England Health Institute.

Webber, I. and Osterbind, C. (1961) 'Types of retirement villages', in E. Burgess (ed) *Retirement villages*, Ann Arbor, MI: University of Michigan.

Weimann, J., Gravell, R. and Weimann, J. (1990) 'Communication with elders', in H. Giles, N. Coupland and J. Weimann (eds) *Communication, health and the elderly*, Manchester: Manchester University Press.

Weisbord, M. (1987) *Productive workplaces*, San Francisco, CA: Jossey-Bass.

Weisbord, M. and Janoff, S. (1995) *Future-search: An action guide to finding common ground in organisations and communities*, San Francisco, CA: Berret-Koehler.

Wilcocks, D., Kellaher, L. and Peace, S. (1987) *Private lives in public places*, London: Tavistock.

Wilkin, D. and Hughes, B. (1987) 'Residential care of elderly people: the consumers' views', *Ageing & Society*, vol 7, no 2, pp 172-202.

TEN

Shaping everyday life: beyond design

Leonie Kellaher

Introduction

The idea that domestic dwellings might be conceived, designed and constructed so that the capacities, desires and needs of occupants continue to be met despite the many changes – physiological, social and emotional – that are likely to accompany advancing years appears attractive at a number of levels. Not least of these is the frequently expressed aspiration of older people themselves to avoid 'special' settings, such as residential and nursing homes, which, rightly or wrongly, are associated with loss of autonomy and agency if not with a more profound loss of self (Peace et al, 1997). Furthermore, the cost of special provision, entailing as it does the ongoing and spiralling labour costs of care assistance or skilled (and scarce) nursing care, impose a more or less explicit rationing on the allocation of places, which often extends to ostensibly 'preventative' domiciliary care (Allen et al, 1992). Together with demographic predictions, these factors are employed to justify a renaming, perhaps even a reconceptualisation, of the foundations on which the accommodation requirements of future cohorts might be constructed. Fundamentally such requirements must be inclusive of all groups in terms of gender, ethnicity, class and so on, and particularly of the whole life cycle.

Lifetime Homes, universal and transgenerational design, along with extra-care housing and assisted living, appear to offer dwelling places sufficiently flexible and adaptable to support the everyday lives of older people almost to the end of life, with or without specialist or other forms of help. That this is desirable as an ideal appears to be irrefutable since older people, along with policy makers and planners, subscribe to the importance of maintaining independence and identity, and of establishing and maintaining control in the domestic sphere (Sixsmith, 1986; Gurney and Means, 1993; Duncan, 1996). Whether this can be more than an ideal, even in the longer term, raises interesting questions. First, around the very complex nature of the relationship between people's material and psycho-social lives and their domestic environments. Second, questions arise as to the nature of architectural, design and policy interventions, and the place of personal agency in relation to the regulatory activity that has a bearing on living places.

Current discussion is conducted from the premise that we do not presently have a stock of housing (apart from experimental exceptions) that incorporates the standards by which Lifetime Homes are to be recognised (see for example, Age Concern, Debate of the Age Millennium Papers, 1999; Fisk, 1999). These standards are characterised by principles of accessibility and adaptability within and around the dwelling, and have been discussed in detail in other chapters in this book (see Chapters Three and Four). Focusing on the emergence of the Lifetime Homes idea/ideal and its associated principles prompts discussion of a number of issues that have a wider bearing on how housing design and planning should be considered for older people now and in the future. For instance:

- How do people – older people especially – use the built environment in support of their daily activities? To what degree is it central to both immediate and longer-term choices and decision making?
- What is the nature of older people's acceptance of, or resistance to, acknowledging special provision as supportive?
- Is it really the case that a stock of 'lifetime' homes does not exist? Is the nomenclature 'Lifetime Homes' simply a new label for earlier phases of thinking about housing and older people (such as sheltered housing or extra-care housing)?
- Or does Lifetime Homes hold out the promise of a new housing movement which can be comprehensive in its coverage of all groups (classes, ages, genders and ethnicities, family formation, sexual orientation, disability) at all life stages?

The following discussion draws on a number of studies that have aimed to understand how older people relate to their built environments, whether these are 'special' or 'ordinary' domestic homes. Among these studies are two interrelated research projects. The first, funded by the Engineering and Physical Sciences Research Council (EPSRC) was part of the EQUAL Programme (Extending the Quality of Life in the Built Environment) and aimed to chart and understand the transition 'from domesticity to care' in terms of the built environments which frame these states[1]. The second, as part of the Economic and Social Research Council (ESRC) Growing Older Programme, aims to understand the relationship between the maintenance of identity in later life and the built environment[2]. Both studies explore how older people themselves perceive and experience the built surroundings in which they dwell.

The built environment, daily activity, choice and decision making

Is there a significant focus or locus for everyday activity, whether this activity is of a practical or cognitive character? Or are we seeking to understand a *mechanism* through which a person relates in significant ways to aspects of the home? Rubenstein (1989) argues for a set of psychological mechanisms through which the individual becomes linked, and often embedded, in the home environment as it is made up of spatial and temporal materialities and social connections. Gullestad's (1989) challenge to the category of 'everyday life' as a slippery construction which is increasingly used to distinguish between personal relations and links with 'the system' (that is, between the private and the public) is also useful in prefacing the argument put forward in this chapter.

In addressing these issues here, a distinction is made between activity which is considered routine, and that in which a particular evaluation is entailed in deciding whether or how to act. Such an evaluation is likely to weigh the necessary effort against available energy resources. In the normal course of daily living, there is a viable balance between routine activities and those that require a degree of conscious decision making. Much of the evidence (for example, Clapham and Munro, 1990) suggests that imbalance occurs when a degree of infirmity dictates a frequent, and sometimes constant, need to negotiate how to perform tasks which were previously routine; planned and executed in relatively easy alignment with the material and built world of the home. To frame this in Powell Lawton's terms, environmental features which had exerted negligible or manageable pressure on the person begin to make themselves felt. We might then, detect environmental press (Lawton, 1980) in data which suggest that routine becomes overwhelmed by decision making. It is likely that when people speak of their move, for instance, to a residential or 'special' setting, the common explanation – 'It all got too much' – refers to a frequency and intensity of decision making about the minutiae of daily living which is felt as unremitting and ultimately unrewarding effort.

In examining which aspects of home 'become too much', however, the variation – especially along gender lines – is considerable (we do not have data which describes ethnic variables in relation to these 'breaking points'). People speak of a combination of features and factors, rather than of single problems, which overwhelm routine. For example, for both men and women, being unable to get out of the house is often given as a significant indicator that things are changing for them (Kellaher, 2000; Mowl et al, 2000). The General Household Survey (OPCS, 1994) also pointed to the association between age and getting out of the house, and showed that nearly half (45%) of those aged 85 years could not get out without difficulty. Occasionally people may refer to access problems associated specifically with steps or slopes, but more composite explanations are generally offered. People are more likely to hint at feeling vulnerable to accident or incident because of reduced agility and because of being exhausted by distances, as well as the unfamiliarity and unpredictability of external environments. Problems with keeping the garden in order are also often described as overwhelming, because of a general sense of sadness at seeing nature reassert itself after years of careful vigilance and successful gardening, rather than, for example, any specific difficulty in bending. Standards of housework are maintained for longer than gardening and this is significant for most women, and for many men. Clark et al (1998) point to the importance for many women of keeping the windows and curtains presentable because they are a representation to the outside world. The point to be made here is that no single feature of the material environment is consistently cited as responsible for the switch from routine to the struggle of decision making. The source of the difficulty is more likely to be given as ill-health, weakness and concomitant reduction in agility.

Having said this, one of the factors reported as likely to influence an older person to consider moving house is the need to live on one level; in other words, to eliminate the need to manage stairs. Moreover, seven out of the 16 Lifetime Homes standards (see Table 3.1 in Chapter Three, p 65) address the question of level. It is also obvious, as stated by Clapham and Munro (1990) writing about moves into sheltered housing, that material provision will have an impact on choices and actions: "the ability to bathe oneself can be influenced by the type of bathroom fittings ..." (p 30). They go on to recognise, however, that "there may be other ways of solving problems" (p 30). This is where great variability emerges between older people and the nature of their engagement with their material and built environment.

The range of solutions to both general and specific problems is vast. It rests not only on particular capacities but also on gender, and formal and informal social networks as reservoirs for help, the latter including proximity to networks and the locality or neighbourhood in which the home is set. Older people themselves explain a house move in later life in terms that are as likely to be social as to be environmental; for example, a difficult landlord, hostile neighbours, a move to be near a relative. Many are able to circumvent the problem of stairs and level changes through improvisation. Sometimes this may be by use of minor 'prosthetic' adaptation such as additional grips or handrails. Sometimes a major lifestyle change such as a move to live downstairs is involved which highlights the desire to stay in a familiar setting even if 'in the wrong space' in cultural terms. Older people constantly work at shaping their domestic environments, through micro-improvisations that are both material and cognitive. Thus, it is important to place observations that indicate the obstructive nature of the built environment in a broader context which takes full and subtle account of the range of social, financial and personal resources on which people can and wish to draw as they seek to retain agency in day-to-day life. There is more, much more, to the built domestic environment than stairs and plumbing and the obstacles they can present to daily living, and thus, for some, to the maintenance of identity as a competent adult.

Most – approaching 90% – of people past retirement age remain living at home in the 'ordinary' domestic setting until they die (Bond, 1993). Daily life may not be easy and the deficits that characterise much of the housing occupied by the older population – whether public or private, owned or rented – are not managed without effort. But this tells us something about the robustness of the housing stock and how it facilitates management of daily life and identity maintenance. It also demonstrates the inventiveness of older people and the people or agencies that support them at home (see for example, Campbell, 1983, on the Anchor Staying-Put schemes).

Clark et al's (1998) publication, which considers the value of low-cost preventative services for older people at home, shows how even very limited domestic assistance, along with the modest care and repair schemes available, provide levels of support which are judged 'just right' by the older people concerned. The point is made that older people's evaluations of their own independence constantly shift in relation to changes in capacity. However, as long as they continue doing those things they remain capable of, older people say they feel able to accept help – not care, but help – with those activities which have become problematic. Independence is thus a very selective, individual and finely judged evaluation. It is delicately wrought and easily undermined if others assume control over remaining capacities: "My independence is when I say 'I can do that myself, you don't need to do it'" (Clark et al, 1998, p 62). Moreover, this finding suggests that special care housing has to be just that, special and appropriate to the particular individual. In studies of homecare we have seen that even the most intricate, inventive and costly packages of care provided to support people at home, fail to match closely enough the routines and desires of the individual. This is because they are not designed and administered by those who have experience of the individual's routines and what is required for support rather than what will disrupt and undermine domesticity: "Sometimes help is not help ... I get her organised, and then, I have an afternoon off and it all goes to pot" (husband describing the disruptive consequences for his domestic routine of three hours a week respite support, to release him from caring for his wife who has dementia)(see also Allen et al, 1994).

A study by Askham et al (1999) of older owner-occupiers shows that only a minority (10%) of the sample of 100 informants in 86 households, mainly in their sixties and seventies, were seriously considering moving house. The remainder had made adaptations or would consider doing so if their house became more difficult to negotiate. Similarly, Mowl et al (2000), exploring people's concepts of becoming old in relation to the 'homespace', observe that the home is, for many women and some men, the last place where self-identity can be strengthened in spite of declining health and capabilities, which tend to be exposed by the undermining pressures from built and social environments lying beyond the familiar and manageable home.

These observations support the argument that non-special domestic environments can invariably be negotiated by the majority of older people, even when ill-health sets in; indeed, the familiar home setting may be the only remaining possibility for an accommodation between self and environment in later years. It should also be reiterated that such adjustments are highly individual and are worked out over time with intimate knowledge of the particular ageing body and the particular homespace. This does not, of course, preclude the possibility that a domestic setting built to Lifetime Homes standards might better facilitate adjustment and perhaps enhance outcomes for older people and those around them. But it does suggest that such settings would need to be familiar, comprehensible and controllable – particularly at the micro-level – by the individuals concerned.

The built environment raises difficulties and obstacles for some, albeit important, activities, for a minority of older people who face ill health or insecurity. These are likely to be those who reach their eighties – exactly the group which demographics show will increase in numbers. It must be stressed that many daily activities remain within reach of most older people as a consequence of their initiatives and improvisations, their support systems and networks. The EPSRC and ongoing ESRC research[1, 2], which explores, through more or less fine-grained ethnography, how older people make their homes work for them, indicates that the home, in its dimensions and arrangement, and its proximity to sources of support and connection, is crucial to the maintenance of identity. The analysis also shows, however, the importance of the home as a frame, or rather, a series of frames – some nesting within others – within and from which activities and connections are generated. It is these activities, choices and decisions that mediate between the built environmental frame and the person at the centre of the domestic effort.

Thus, it is argued that the character of the domestic built environment is a necessary, but by no means sufficient, condition for identity construction through day-to-day domestic living. When crucial decisions are to be confronted, especially consideration of a move, the frames of location and macro-aspects of design are brought into focus as the older person evaluates the capacity of a new environment as a frame for the continuation of the essential minutiae of daily activity. It is true that this daily activity, and perhaps the scale of activity, may change, but the judgements that people make about moving house appear to be centred on their material worlds at the micro-level; although judgements are considered within the wider frame which takes account of locality and the amount of space (if not its configuration) as the setting for the micro-activity that constitutes daily life. For example, one older woman said she would not have been able to move into a particular sheltered housing scheme if it had not been possible for her mirrors to be placed in a particular arrangement. This possibility rested on there being wall spaces for the two mirrors to be arranged opposite each other, on the scheme to permit this and on the social support which effected the installation.

At the centre is the person – the ageing body – framed by the homespace. In its material aspect, homespace is made up of area, configuration and objects. Routine interconnections between the person at the centre and the home as frame (or series of frames) are necessary for embodiment at home. When domestic routine has to be replaced by effort, it is argued that the person–homespace connection becomes fractured, identity is compromised and a new location that offers a chance of significant reconnection may be sought.

Special provision, such as sheltered housing and residential homes, are promoted as settings in which daily living is made easier through the arrangement of a 'barrier-free' environment and the availability of special support. In anticipating the possibilities for Lifetime Homes, an understanding of older people's reactions to such special provision may illuminate issues around personal agency.

Acceptance and resistance to 'special' housing

In modern western society the majority of older people, even at advanced years, continue to live at home and to say that this is what they want. It is only a minority – around a quarter of those aged 80 and over – who move into special settings such as residential and nursing homes. In the main, such moves are made with reluctance, if not protest. For the remaining majority who will never move from the ordinary domestic setting, the prospect of a residential move may also cast a heavy shadow. With the probability of admission to accommodation with care at advanced ages estimated at around 30%, the apprehension may be well founded. The move to sheltered housing appears to be less threatening to identity. Many older people have some knowledge of sheltered housing, for example from visiting friends and relatives in sheltered housing schemes or from attending luncheon clubs and other social functions, and these contacts may give a favourable impression of the comfort, security and self-containment of the accommodation on offer. There is some evidence that people's satisfaction with sheltered housing may be linked to their expectations of it and their previous housing experience, that is, whether they moved for housing or social reasons (Riseborough and Niner, 1994). In recent years sheltered housing providers have begun to market the idea of 'shelter for vulnerability', for example the 'Going into Sheltered Housing Week' initiative of May 2000.

Nevertheless, research has revealed the reservations that some people express about special arrangements, including sheltered housing (Oldman,

1986; and see Chapter Seven of this book). In terms of older people feeling 'at home' the age-segregated nature of sheltered schemes may still be unsettling for some. For example, the similar routines and lifestyles of the tenant group may result in the absence of intergenerational sounds and noise, which many older people may find both stimulating and important for making connections with the wider community. The more or less impermeable boundaries around sheltered schemes represent mixed blessings in that the security offered also serves to bring about an internalised idea of the separation of tenants from other groups – without necessarily addressing the role of the surrounding neighbourhood in increasing or reducing personal security. Structurally, the perceived role of the warden holds difficulties, both for tenants and wardens themselves, and it has changed over time. Many organisations now prefer the nomenclature 'scheme manager', which is perceived as less controlling of older people. The 'Emerging role of the warden' project, and the 'Emerging role of sheltered housing' project (both under the auspices of The Housing Corporation) have sought to address some of the issues of the purpose, future and image of sheltered housing.

Beyond the social rented sector, many people have opted to purchase supportive settings after retirement. This suggests that certain advantages are perceived and that there is a degree of acceptance of the arrangements – notably with the manageable, often compact, accommodation – although it needs to be noted that some schemes are now classed as 'hard to sell'. Recent and more successful schemes tend to be larger, generally offering two bedrooms and allowing more room for manoeuvre than was the case with earlier private sheltered schemes.

How have older people related to and engaged with these 'specially' designed environments, ostensibly constructed to match the types of mobility and support needs identified as special and appropriate to later years? If the idea of embodiment in environment through routine is accepted, we might expect that the problematic reverts to becoming routine when people move into special settings. In other words, older people no longer have to constantly evaluate their every action in detail and identity is thus maintained through an eased relationship with the environment. Two such special settings – residential care and sheltered housing – are discussed here with the aim of understanding whether such equilibrium is restored following a move. Environmental press theory suggests that when the pressure is lifted, the organism will revert to its former stasis, but we must ask whether or not new and different pressures are brought to bear in unfamiliar settings.

Research has shown that residents may have serious difficulty in engaging with the material and social environments which characterise residential settings (Davies and Knapp, 1981; Peace et al, 1997). One critique argued that residents' interactions and relationships were entirely mediated by the institution, so that they became more and more distanced from the world they inhabited (Willcocks et al, 1987). A more recent model (Kellaher, 2000) suggests that the mediating, and distancing, effect of the institution may be significantly reduced, and sometimes eliminated, if the associative links between individual residents are strongly founded on shared understandings. In other words, agency may, given certain circumstances, be reinvested in residents as individuals rather than located at the institutional level.

Turning to the built environment, which can be very exposed in the residential case since it is relatively uncluttered by 'connective tissue' associated with residents' lives, it is possible to make limited observations about the impact of different spatial allocations on residents' levels of engagement with the environment. In those residential settings where space standards are minimal (DoH, 1999), which is to say the single room has an area of around $12m^2$, residents engage minimally with their material surroundings (Kellaher, 2000). First, the restricted room size means that only essential items can be accommodated – a washbasin, a bed, a chair and perhaps a small table. One consequence is that few pieces of furniture and other possessions can be imported from the former residence. The likelihood is that items will consist of small, ornamental objects that will generally take their place as memorabilia on the walls. There is thus little with which to engage in terms of objects, although it is often the case that residents continue to care for – to order and dust – these small objects which may assume considerable significance as they recall a former, more active life. Second, the space which accommodates the person and the essentials is generally too confined for the resident to tolerate for extended periods and the individual is thus drawn into the public arena – sometimes unwillingly. Here the scope for environmental connection and association may well be even more restricted, although by the social circumstances which underpin residential living rather than by spatial allocation. Residents are most reluctant in the public arena to distinguish themselves from the collectivity by appropriating space or objects or by undertaking even such ordinary tasks as watering the plants. This, they believe, will be perceived as pushy, set them apart from the group and perhaps engender hostility. The anomie frequently associated with residential settings is then, a consequence of the social distancing arising from the process of making a residential move into a setting characterised by spatial and material restrictions.

Where space standards approach 20m^2 for a single room, residents may surround themselves with familiar, sizeable and useful objects. Engagement with the materiality of the setting tends to increase and residents are able to comment about differentiated space. They talk about the sleeping space, which is private, and the sitting area in which they spend much of the daytime and may receive visitors. Where space allows, most people go to some lengths to distinguish these areas and their functions. As a woman in her late eighties, living in a residential bed-sit remarked, "I don't want it to look like a bedroom...." (Kellaher, 2000, p 37).

At the same time, residents also explain that it is often difficult to adjust to a new way of life in the absence of those cues that make it possible to initiate contact through talk of common domestic experiences, since these are arranged by the organisation and the resident is excluded from the tasks of daily living. The preparation of food is undertaken by the institution, even to the extent that tea-making is likely to be ruled out in the resident's own room for fear of an accident with boiling water. Residents generally accept this and many certainly welcome release from heavier chores. Bathing is similarly an activity that comes to depend on institutional intervention, and human rather than material resources determine the frequency of the activity. No amount of perfectly designed bathroom features and fittings can increase either their use or resident engagement in respect of this activity if the human support is not available to assist and mediate between resident and bathroom. The almost universal 'rule' that residents should not take baths unaided or at least unsupervised also appears to be accepted by residents, along with the acknowledgement that this is what residential care is for. The habit and practice of bathing is curtailed and with it the practice of confidence in this area of self-maintenance. Older people are frequently able to judge for themselves when habitual practice, such as bathing, becomes too risky and make a safer adaptation, a daily wash rather than a bath for instance. This improvisation is possible in the domestic setting and will often support levels of confidence in the self as a competent adult, but it tends to be undermined in the special setting – even with all its aids and adaptations.

A research device employed to elicit residents' evaluations of aspects of the built residential environment (Willcocks, 1984) showed how residents rated ordinary features of the built environment over those special ones which reinforced the institution's stated raison d'être. For instance, windows that could be opened and radiators that could be controlled were appreciated, rather than features such as special baths, lifts and hoists. The scope for managing temperature and atmosphere throughout the day, which was highly valued by residents, may be interpreted as a way of connecting with the environment in its most pervasive and fundamental aspect – the air that is breathed.

Thus, the residential setting is a highly contrived and costly one, intended to accommodate the altered capacities of frail older people. Given organisational constraints, the residential 'contrivance' has to routinise nearly all daily activities, and it generally achieves this to a high degree, although individual improvisation is eliminated. Routine characterises residential living, and yet the kind of fully inhabited, embodied connections between person and material/built environment that routine is claimed to create in the domestic setting, is notable by its absence in the residential setting. The routine observed in residential homes appears to offer little comfort or ease to residents, who experience themselves as differentiated individuals only occasionally. Might it be that because the accommodation – in all senses – is not of the resident's making, but is constructed on the resident's behalf, that connection between the built environment, the daily activities and the resident as person is not possible? It is paradoxical that the professional design effort invested in the residential setting, while considerable, is responsible for the features least appreciated by the residents. Conversely, the professional effort that shapes the ordinary domestic setting is usually minimal and yet occupants generally inhabit the place they have made in a very engaged sense. A similar paradox emerges with regard to 'special' housing.

Research undertaken in the 1980s and 1990s (fer example, Oldman, 1990; Riseborough and Niner, 1994) on the acceptability of sheltered housing, notably to tenants and wardens, tended to show that tenants most appreciated the location and the warm, comfortable and convenient aspects of the house or flat. They were least interested in those features that define sheltered provision as 'special' – the provision of communal spaces, shared facilities and so on, and often the warden. As in residential settings, older people in sheltered settings appreciated the normal and ordinary features with which they could engage and which they could control, over and above those 'special' facilities geared to their declining capabilities.

In examining the 'ambiguities and contradictions' they claim are inherent in sheltered housing, Clapham and Munro (1990) argue that the fixedness or rigidity of a package of care intended to meet 'special' needs of older people is implicated. They conclude that a sheltered housing scheme can only work when a sizeable proportion of tenants does not need its special facilities. One implication is that, if all tenants are frail and use the defining facilities of communal space and other shared features and make excessive demands on the warden, a level of institutionalisation occurs. On the other hand, if a 'sizeable' proportion does not use the special facilities, an element of tacit resistance to the 'specialness' of the provision might be assumed. Clapham and Munro (1990) also argued (along with Butler et al, 1983) that sheltered housing is 'an ageist form of provision' because it is a block solution to highly variable states and associated difficulties. We might extend the argument to suggest that even quite frail tenants are intent on resistance to the stereotyping aspects of this particular form of 'special' provision. The counter point must be reiterated, however, that tenants appreciated the "small, warm and specially adapted house" (Clapham and Munroe, 1989, p 39) and many older people regard sheltered housing as the best solution for themselves. The notion of resident resistance has been discussed in relation to residential settings, but it is generally very passive, usually taking the form of withdrawal to an inner world. Nonetheless, even very frail and powerless people continue to resist block treatment (Goffman, 1961) where it tends to stigmatise rather than privilege.

A recent commentator (Koncelik, 1998) makes a strong argument around the issue of the design of special provision for older people and "knowing when to pull back from making all the design decisions" (p 128). His main thesis is that, while the 'one-size-fits-all' approach entailed in conceptualising universal design may be intuitively attractive, it is unethical insofar as it neglects variation at several levels. He makes a distinction between architectural decision and interior design and argues that, if the hand of the designer is dominant in relation to the latter, it represents an intrusion that violates the occupant's territory. A further distinction he draws is that, while universal design is unethical because of this inappropriate intrusion, transgenerational design, being information-based rather than intuitive, is acceptable since it yields 'product variation' rather than 'product universality' (p 149).

The case might be put forward that all cultures, across generations have always arranged their domestic settings in ways appropriate for all life stages, and that inaccessibility to and within the domestic setting would be counterproductive for the collectivity. This is not to say, of course, that the accommodation of older and less agile people need necessarily have had any place in the collective arrangement. Until recently the minority status of older people is likely to have precluded special design attention. Furthermore, powerful commentators (Townsend, 1981; Phillipson, 1998) have argued that the low value placed on older people's needs has frequently been a prerequisite to the smooth running of (this) society. It is, then, probably as true to say that design and architectural device has served to exclude – along class/caste, gender and age lines – as to argue that it has served the goals of inclusivity. The capacity of Lifetime Homes standards to be inclusive needs to be weighed against the case made so far, that special forms of accommodation have, with the best will in the world, frequently exerted an excluding and segregating influence. This needs to be examined further.

Lifetime Homes – a new idea?

It is undoubtedly the case that the UK housing stock is not characterised by the Lifetime Homes criteria, but does this fact lead to a conclusion that homes suitable for a lifetime of changes are in low supply? We have seen that the majority of people who reach advanced years remain in 'ordinary' homes, made special by individual action. Many make adaptations to the structure of the home or to their routines, and most are reluctant to risk a house move unless the forces for change weigh very heavily on them. Moreover, such forces for change are likely to be a combination of social and built environmental influences, and any decision to move will be made in the hope that lost ground may be regained through realignments of particular social and built environmental resources. The active engagement of the older person in such rehabilitation appears to be an essential prerequisite for a successful move that restores equilibrium. The special nature of certain settings mitigates against such involvement and subsequent engagement with either built or social environments. Older people themselves appreciate this danger – invariably associated with residential settings – and determine to avoid or resist.

It would appear then, that most older people already view their homes as 'lifetime homes' in the sense that they envisage the continuous enactment of day-to-day life in relation to the objects which support and surround them, and alongside their social networks. With regard to the macro aspects of the home, older people with the resources to anticipate future change may make precautionary moves. Many, however, do not do so in the hope or expectation that they can continue to routinely accommodate themselves and the objects which support their identity within the macro frames of the dwelling and the neighbourhood. They, and policy makers, also know that, in the absence of a minimal social support network, the most accommodating and prosthetic environment cannot support a person independently, in isolation for extended periods. The research on the long-term value of alarm systems (Tinker, 1984) has demonstrated this clearly. In making a move an older person will take social support – formal or informal – into serious account, arguably giving it precedence over the macro frame of the built environment and special features.

More recent thinking about essential environments for ageing incorporate these considerations more fully than hitherto. For example, the Design for Living Taskforce defined four cornerstones of 'design for inclusion'. While these points would foster 'active healthy ageing', they would be intrinsic to designing for *all* people irrespective of their individual characteristics. Their cornerstones are:

- *stimulation*, both physical and cognitive;
- *flexibility* to accommodate change brought about by the ageing process;
- *independence*, through choice and control;
- *social interaction*, through family, friends, neighbourhood, and the wider communities (DTI, 2000, p 7).

For many older people, their existing housing actually or potentially embodies these characteristics more organically – through personalisation and development over time – than do designed special settings.

Conclusion

Should Lifetime Homes criteria be perceived as an enhancement of those standards that are already consolidated in the building regulations and, as such, are part of the public health infrastructure? Are they to be read as elements of architectural decision or of interior design? In this respect they are intended, as in Koncelik's conception, to lead to 'product variation' (1998). On the other hand, it is possible that architectural decision can intrude on interior design. While in material terms the two cannot be entirely separated, it can be argued that older people make a cognitive separation of the macro and micro aspects of the home, only focusing on architectural and wider environmental features when equilibrium is disturbed and routine is disrupted as the environment presses on them. At the same time, the evidence presented in this chapter suggests that few, if any, older people wish to live in settings which loudly declare their special nature. They do not want this because it immobilises them and breaks their links with the environment in all its material and social aspects.

If Lifetime Homes standards are not to lead to the development of dwellings which undermine the homemaker's sense of agency in the paternalistic and ageist fashion that has marked most residential provision and much of 'special' housing, it is crucial that they come to occupy the niche – already prised open by Part M of the Building Regulations (Part T in Scotland) – that looks towards public health. By regulating rather than designing for the enhancement of basic accessibility and adaptability standards, the benefits can accrue to the population as a whole. Groups of all ages, with highly variable capabilities and cultural preferences are thus encompassed by the ideal. The segregationist outcomes in terms of age and ability that are now associated with special housing (certainly at minimum resourcing levels and in relation to 'special' features) might be avoided if the universality of both the Lifetime Homes ideal and the design for inclusion agenda becomes a serious objective. These universal features are, arguably, as important for the housing stock of the future as were the building regulations and public health measures the whole community came to take for granted in the postwar period. In other words, the Lifetime Homes standards need to become the backdrop for the social and cultural development of future decades. However, they can never be sufficient for cultural development, any more than a pure water supply, an efficient sewerage disposal system, damp proofing and insulation have been.

The notion of Lifetime Homes can be viewed, on the one hand, as an exercise in social engineering. Dwellings are to be constructed to certain standards so that they are accessible and adaptable for those who live there and to those who visit. On the other hand, Lifetime Homes can be viewed as a common sense, evolutionary response to enhanced knowledge about design, construction and ergonomics, and make daily living easier for longer. This must be an advance. However, this chapter argues that the advantage to older people is eroded if such measures are promoted purely as ideology rather than as a background context against which the range of choices and decisions that constitute life in later years, at home and out and about, are made. How, then, can the provision of built forms and services enable older people to participate in society in ways of their own choosing? There is a need to consider the realities of older people's lives and expectations, and those of people who will become old in the future. These considerations include the facts that:

- Above all, older people want to live in 'quality' mainstream accommodation, in physically good condition and within a range of social environments.
- To facilitate this, reconsidered, and higher, requirements for accessibility and flexibility in building standards should be approached as a matter of regulation rather than as special provision.
- There is a need to acknowledge the social implications of ageing as well as the physical implications.
- The notion of 'independence' is a very selective, individual and finely judged matter: older people need support in evaluating their own situation and accessing the help they require in their chosen homespace.
- Social support structures to enable inclusive, lifetime homes will have wider implications, for example in costs to transport and health infrastructures.

With such an agenda, regulators, policy makers and providers of services and of the built environment can augment and amplify the efforts that older people already make themselves, day in and day out, in shaping their home lives.

Notes

[1] 'Profiling the housing stock for older people: the transition from domesticity to caring': principal investigator Dr Julienne Hanson, The Bartlett School of Graduate Studies; co-investigators Leonie Kellaher, University of North London, and Professor Mike L. Rowlands, Department of Anthropology, University College London.

[2] 'Identity and environment: a cross-setting study': principal investigator Dr Sheila M. Peace, The Open University; co-investigators Caroline Holland, The Open University, and Leonie Kellaher, University of North London.

References

Age Concern and Debate of the Age (1999) *The future of the built environment, the millennium papers*, London: Age Concern.

Allen, I., Bourke Dowling, S. and Perkins, L. (1994) *Making it work*, London: Policy Studies Institute.

Allen, I., Hogg, D. and Peace, S. (1992) *Elderly people: Choice, participation and satisfaction*, London: Policy Studies Institute.

Askham, J., Nelson, H., Tinker, A. and Hancock, R. (1999) *To have and to hold: The bond between older people and the homes they own*, York: JRF.

Bond, J. (1993) 'Living arrangements of elderly people', in J. Bond, P. Coleman and S. Peace (eds) *Ageing in society: An introduction to social gerontology,* London: Sage Publications, pp 200-25.

Butler, A., Oldman, C. and Greve, J. (1983) *Sheltered housing for the elderly*, London: George Allen & Unwin.

Campbell, J. (1983) 'Staying put: an Anchor approach', in F. Glendenning (ed) *Accommodating the frail elderly*, Papers delivered at a seminar at Keele University, Staffordshire: Keele University.

Clapham, D. and Munro, M. (1990) 'Ambiguities and contradictions in the provision of sheltered housing for older people', *Journal of Social Policy*, vol 19, no 1, pp 27-45.

Clark, H., Dyer, S. and Horwood, J. (1998) *'That bit of help': The high value of low level preventive services for older people*, Bristol/York: The Policy Press/JRF.

Davies, B. and Knapp, M. (1981) *Old people's homes and the production of welfare*, London: Routledge and Kegan Paul.

DoH (Department of Health) (1999) *Fit for the future?: National required standards for residential and nursing homes for older people*, Consultation document, London: DoH.

DTI (Department of Trade and Industry) (2000) Design for Living Task Force: Foresight Ageing Population Panel Report, April, London: DTI.

Duncan, N. (ed) (1996) *Bodyspace: Destabilizing geographies of gender and sexuality*, London: Routledge.

Fisk, M. (1999) *Our future home: Housing and the inclusion of older people in 2025*, London: Help the Aged.

Goffman, E. (1961) *Asylums*, London: Penguin.

Gullestad, M. (1989) *From alterations in time to a quest for unity in space: The transformation of Norwegian notion of everyday life*, Paper presented at the cross-cultural workshop of the Committee of Human Development, University of Chicago, April.

Gurney, C. and Means, R. (1993) 'The meaning of home in later life', in S. Arber and M. Evandrou (eds) *Ageing, independence and the life course*, London: Jessica Kingsley with the British Society of Gerontology, pp 119-31.

Kellaher, L. (2000) *A choice well made: 'Mutuality' as a governing principle in residential care*, London: Centre for Policy on Ageing.

Koncelik, J. (1998) 'Design, ageing, ethics and the law: beauty is nowhere', in S. King-Roth and R. Roth (eds) *Ethical issues in art and design*, S&B Arts International.

Lawton, M.P. (1980) *Environment and aging*, Monterey, CA: Brooks/Cole Publishing Co.

Mowl, G., Pain, R. and Talbot, C. (2000) 'The ageing body and the homespace', *Area*, vol 32, no 2, pp 189-97.

Oldman, C. (1986) 'Housing policies for older people', in P. Malpass (ed) *The housing crisis*, Beckenham: Croom Helm, pp 174-99.

Oldman, C. (1990) *Moving in old age: New directions in housing policies*, London: HMSO.

OPCS (Office for Population Censuses and Surveys) (1994) *1993 General Household Survey*, London: HMSO.

Peace, S., Kellaher, L. and Willcocks, D. (1997) *Re-evaluating residential care*, Buckingham: Open University Press.

Phillipson, C. (1998) *Reconstructing old age: New agenda in social theory and practice*, London: Sage Publications.

Riseborough, M. and Niner, P. (1994) *I didn't know you cared! A survey of Anchor's sheltered housing tenants*, Oxford: Anchor Housing Trust.

Rubenstein, R. (1989) 'The home environments of older people: a description of the psychosocial processes linking person to place', *Journal of Gerontology*, vol 44, no 2, pp S45-53.

Sixsmith, A. (1986) 'Independence and home in later life', in C. Phillipson, M. Bernard and P. Strang (eds) *Dependency and interdependency in old age: Theoretical perspectives and policy alternatives*, London: Croom Helm.

Tinker, A. (1984) *Staying at home: Helping elderly people*, London: DoE.

Townsend, P. (1981) 'The structured dependency of the elderly: creation of social policy in the twentieth century', *Ageing & Society*, vol 1, no 1, pp 5-28.

Willcocks, D. (1984) 'The ideal home visual game: a method of consumer research in old people's homes', *Research, Policy and Planning: Journal of the Social Services Research Group*, vol 2, no 1, pp 13-18.

Willcocks, D., Peace, S. and Kellaher, L. (1987) *Private lives in public places*, London: Tavistock.

ELEVEN

Inclusive housing

Caroline Holland and Sheila M. Peace

Introduction

In this book the contributors have looked at various ways in which living environments can be designed, arranged and supported so that people in later life can maintain autonomy and remain connected with communities. Until recently, most studies about older people's housing have concentrated on issues of independence and the ability of individuals to maintain themselves, with assistance if necessary, in their own homes or in 'homely care in the community' (DoH, 1989). Concerns about independence and dependency have centred on two major problem areas. The first of these is the need of many people living in the community, often alone, who have inadequate support mechanisms to maintain their independence as their physical or mental abilities decline. The second is the position of older people living in settings such as residential care, whose independence may have been undermined by a culture of structured dependency bordering sometimes on infantalisation.

While there remains much work to be done to improve the situation in both these areas, there is at least a general recognition of the issues among both policy makers and service providers that most older people aspire to a level of independence, which may be supported by others, but which enables them to maintain control over their own lives. It is also recognised that this is essential to the well-being of older people and that it relates to the physical, social and psychological environments they inhabit. But, if there is recognition of the value of independent living, why is inclusion now an issue for older people? Could this be a reflection of social trends and changing attitudes to ageing as the 'baby-boomer' generations grow towards old age? The problematisation of old age becomes less acceptable as older people increasingly expect to be recognised as people with everyday lives that can be carried out in everyday places.

Why are older people as a group (if not individually) vulnerable to social exclusion? In an analysis of the sociology of old age, Fennell et al (1988) focused on three significant social trends: segregation, rising living standards and widening social cleavage. They gave examples of formal and informal segregation in housing as groups of households with broadly similar characteristics congregated in particular areas such as 'executive' estates, strips of 'retirement' bungalows along the coast or inner-city 'ghettos'. Alongside this trend was the general improvement in living standards which followed the public health improvements, the National Health Service and social security, and increasing national and personal prosperity. However, different sections of society experienced improving standards at very different rates, leading to increasing variation in the wealth and access to resources of different groups.

One of the outcomes of these continuing trends has been a reinforcement of the separate identity which has been accorded to older people as a group who are 'vulnerable' or have 'special needs'. Throughout most of the 20th century the significance of this group, although growing in size, could be overshadowed by other trends. But, as the baby-boomers of the 1950s and 1960s have recognised, their society is ageing, they have begun to also notice the diversity of later life. For example, there has been an increasing recognition of the difference between 'vulnerable older people' and groups of younger retired people who are depicted as fit, active, affluent and assertive. In essence these two representations of older people capture the dichotomy which Julienne Hanson (in Chapter Two) has referred to in terms of 'special needs' and 'lifestyle choices'. While the almost universal desire for independence is taken as given, the widening lifestyle differences between different groups of older people and between older people and younger groups, and their increasing vocalisation, has brought the politics of old age into the debate about social exclusion.

In Chapter One we referred to the growth of old age as more people live longer, and the difficulties of defining older people given their age range and heterogeneity. Old age is not fixed. The *biological* effects of ageing are mediated by environmental and medical conditions – we have seen how, in this society, the physical condition of retired people in general has improved over the 20th century. The *social* construction of old age has a bearing on the attention given to biological ageing – whether older people have access to rationed medical treatments, for example. At the same time it is influenced by perceptions of the physical implications of ageing and the extent to which physical and mental decline is seen to be inevitable and universal. As the proportion of the population that has reached pensionable age and is still anticipating many more years of life continues to increase, we might expect a shift in ageist attitudes, including those found among older people themselves. People may expect and be expected to remain socially engaged for longer as well as remaining independent. This leads to a number of questions. How will the interests of older people be expressed and promoted? How will we finance our greater longevity? How will we manage necessary support services? Will the experience of ageing itself change? If so, towards more inclusion, further exclusion or increasing inequality?

In this final chapter we examine the notion of inclusion insofar as it applies to housing our ageing society. We look at the issues under four broad headings: the physical and material environment, technological futures, the social environment, and resources. We take a broader look at some of the themes that have been touched on in preceding chapters, as the authors considered various aspects of environments for ageing. We then go on to consider how our society can open up choices for older people, and the role of current initiatives in supporting autonomy and inclusion as we age.

The material environment

In order to be inclusive, housing for older people needs to allow individuals to maintain an involvement with the wider community – in doing this it also helps to maintain the links between different age groups in society. Inclusive housing allows individuals to take part fully in their preferred mode of life. Housing in itself may not substitute for other deficiencies – for example in health, family or social life, spiritual or mental well-being, or transport and the wider infrastructure – any of which may affect people's satisfaction with life and their sense of connectedness. Yet good housing can provide some support in situations in which people have other problems, while inadequate or inappropriate housing can make matters worse.

In discussing housing as material we must make a distinction between ongoing property and new build. In the case of existing buildings, the issues are those of maintenance to sustain continuing habitation and adaptations to make buildings more suitable for people's changing needs. In the case of new buildings, the issues are those of regulation and specification. Existing properties encompass a wide variety of settings from different historical periods and various architectural and building styles. Although less than 1% of properties now lack the basic amenities (such as hot water or an internal WC), much of the older housing stock requires attention to rewiring, plumbing, window frames and so on. For people living in these circumstances in the private sector, access to finance, advice and practical support in arranging repairs and adaptations has long been seen as a priority. However, until very recently the coverage of care and repair schemes which provide information and support was incomplete, with some areas having no scheme in operation[1]. Within the social rented sector, while the proportion of local authority (LA) tenants who live in poor housing has been declining, there remains a proportion (around 17% in 1996) of LA housing which needs renovation (DoE, 1998).

At a conference of Better Government for Older People (BGOP), the Inter-Ministerial Group for Older People stated that:

> Older people – particularly the least well off people – are more likely to live in poor housing. For example, people aged 75 and above in the privately rented sector are more than three times more likely to live in poor housing compared with the average for all people in all tenures. Investment improvements to the housing stock will help to reduce the number of older people living in poor housing, and we are providing an additional £5 billion for housing over the lifetime of this Parliament. (BGOP, 1999, p 15)

The message from BGOP was that Registered Social Landlords (RSLs) should direct money released for regeneration initiatives towards housing choice, adaptations and physical improvements, by working with tenants associations and senior citizens' forums in bottom-up planning and provision.

Beyond the need for basic amenities, many more people would like assistance with mending, painting and gardening – caring for their property both internally and externally. Older people continue to need local support for these activities, yet, typically, the available help has been limited both financially and in terms of the work which can be undertaken within programmes, so that the adaptations or repairs on offer may not necessarily fit the occupants' own preferences. Of course, many people do things to their homes that others might see as amateur or idiosyncratic, and which would not be eligible for public funding. In Chapter Ten Leonie Kellaher has discussed some of the ways in which people naturally make their own adaptations to their environments as the need arises. Recognising and supporting these activities would allow people in the poorest housing to remain both independent and socially engaged through the process of improving their own housing. There are a variety of routes to overcoming 'architectural disability' and not all of them require professional intervention. Perhaps we should ask, Do older people need to *construct* a residence through engagement in order to own it, and for it to own them? Might this be the *home for life* rather than the 'lifetime home'?

Most older people do not live in inadequate housing in the usually accepted sense. When it is basically in good order, what housing is good enough? For much of the 20th century it was often assumed that older people could be satisfied with housing that might appear inadequate to younger people. In various studies older people stated their satisfaction with small one-bedroom homes, communal accommodation with shared bathrooms, and homes that they had become used to in spite of defects or lack of amenities (see Wilson et al, 1995). In particular, the notions of compactness and convenience were adopted as goals in specialised housing for older people.

But we know that satisfaction with one's living circumstances relates to both external and internal comparisons; reflecting among other things relative expectations, life experiences and financial necessities. However, expressions of satisfaction with present housing have been seen as problematic in some circumstances, for example, where people are worried about being made to move, or where they have no realistic alternatives.

In Wilson et al's study (1995), the physical quality of housing was the most important factor in explaining older people's satisfaction with their housing: damp, draughts and defects were the primary concerns. Contrary to some received wisdoms, large houses in themselves were not more likely than small houses to cause dissatisfaction, and increasing age did not necessarily bring increasing satisfaction; although age did appear to increase people's appreciation for well-designed kitchens and bathrooms, regular public transport and accessible shopping facilities. Older people in private rented property were more likely to be dissatisfied – but this was because it tended to be in poorer physical condition rather than because of the tenure as such. Satisfaction with otherwise 'good' property could be severely compromised by safety and security issues, especially in ground-floor properties. Neighbours and the wider neighbourhood were very important in determining older people's satisfaction with their homes (JRF, 1995; Wilson et al, 1995).

Authors in this book have also looked again at some of the factors that contribute to housing that might be good enough for older people. The first of these factors is *accessibility*. At any stage of life, and for many reasons, people may experience physical impairments that can be exacerbated by particular aspects of the built environment such as steps, heavy doors or lighting levels. As people age and the prevalence and duration of physically limiting conditions increases, details of the environment may become more significant (as, for example, in the effect of changes of level on the incidence of falls). For some people, the contemplation of these changes is worrying and environmental stress may be revealed in these interactions.

Accessibility is an issue in which the focus has moved from public to private buildings and from specialised environments to more general requirements. We have seen in Chapter Four how specifications of accessibility have varied to include different notions of visitability and liveability. In the context of needs that we all have at certain times, the ongoing debates – on universal design, generic versus specific housing, how adaptable and very adaptable environments are defined, how inclusive the definition of access is to be and who is to define it – lead us to challenge exactly what we mean by 'special needs'.

Most people will continue to live in housing that was built some time ago and generally without regard to the design specifications that might now be considered desirable, although creative features may have been added since. Advances in standards of amenity, the availability of consumer goods and appliances, and changes in the shape and activity of households, mean that there has been a continuing gap between people's lifestyles and the houses which they inhabit, for example, very few houses have enough and well-situated electrical sockets. Solutions can be complicated and made more expensive by the very variability and complexity of existing housing designs and conditions so that the adaptability of buildings is often a financial as much as a technical matter.

In theory it is much easier to make new buildings barrier free and to design in flexibility at the outset. The extension in 1999 of Part M of the1985 Building Regulations (Part T in Scotland) signalled that government was beginning to move legislation in this direction. What may be important here is that a new baseline for all will be established as a minimum standard from which creative developments can build, and we have seen how some partnerships between authorities and developers have done this. As we saw in Chapter Four, those involved in the provision, design, build and occupancy of buildings, and who may be affected by these regulations, expressed a range of reactions to the proposals. For some they went too far: for others not far enough. Some people feared that increasing regulation would impose uniformity and increase costs, while others anticipated a new release of creativity and an economy of production.

Whether and how much to regulate is a recurring problem in these areas at the public–private interface. While regulation may be resisted, so, very often, is deregulation. For example, the accessibility of spaces can be important in facilitating ongoing engagement (Kellaher, 2000), yet recent debates over the size of single bedrooms within residential care homes, as part of national minimum standards[2], have highlighted the tensions between marketability and quality of life. However, accessibility regulations may be viewed in a positive light if they can be presented as an opportunity for innovation and as a guarantee of high standards, rather than as restrictive and limiting.

The development of the Lifetime Homes standards represents another milestone on the road to accessibility in new-build housing. Lifetime Homes are premised on the idea that accessibility can be designed into buildings in such a way that the potential for environmental barriers at almost all stages of life is reduced. In order to be 'universal' or 'generic', these new homes need to be a mainstream provision – and preferably regarded as generally superior to housing with built-in barriers. But it remains to be seen how these standards will be encompassed within new-build housing. Given the financial forces within housing markets, Lifetime Homes standards could become, as Leonie Kellaher has warned in Chapter Ten, the new 'special needs' standards – making lifetime homes physically accessible, but not socially inclusive. Transgenerational designs that take account of cultural variation could be accepted by all. We need creative thinking, not the recreation of a cycle of disadvantage for some.

Another factor in making housing inclusive is *space.* The safety and comfort of homes are heavily influenced by the physical parameters of the built environment and the extent to which they can be controlled. The built environment can disable most of us at given times, as Julienne Hanson reminds us in Chapter Two, but it can be particularly disabling for people who already have difficulties in carrying out the activities of daily living. The amount and layout of space within the home makes a difference to how people of any age can organise their lives. It is more difficult to invite friends round when you live in a bed-sit; more difficult to have your family to stay when you only have one bedroom; more difficult to feel in control of your home when you cannot get upstairs. Many older people want space for the hobbies, computers, exercise equipment, collections of objects, and so on, which make for environmental familiarity. Others might want to get rid of things, although this does not necessarily mean 'disengagement', they might acquire something new instead, or simply want to get rid of clutter. Couples may want separate bedrooms in which to maintain good sleeping arrangements. People also need to be able to move things, reach things, store and retrieve things, fix things. People sometimes get bored with their interiors and want to move things around. Older people need the space in which to carry out these normal activities and space into which they can spread for activities that go beyond the bare essentials of body maintenance. Inclusive housing offers older people a range of dwelling types without making assumptions about their uses of space. Going beyond the requirements for supporting activities of daily life, it allows everyone the level of comfort which able-bodied people in mainstream housing take for granted. It supports engagement with others – visitors and guests, pets and people outside the home – and engagement with the self through continued activities, occupations and control of space.

These needs and preferences are reflected in the owner-occupied market, where most older people live in mainstream housing and a minority move down into one- or two-bedroom purpose-built housing. Holmans (2000) has also pointed to the implicit acceptance of a bedroom in excess of standard[3] in rent allowances for private tenants. Within the social rented sector, the notion of under-occupation, which long influenced attitudes to older people's continuing occupation of 'family' housing, has been undermined by these trends and good practice would now support the acceptance of a bedroom in excess of standard for tenants in the social rented sector. This leaves specialised housing, such as standard sheltered accommodation, as the main form of provision which cannot, without adaptation, provide the extra space which most older people need in order to carry on living as they want to.

Detailed studies of factors associated with older people's satisfaction with housing (see Wilson et al, 1995) also underline the importance of *sensory factors* such as warmth and draft control, sound and lighting levels (similar studies in residential settings have also looked at the roles of touch and smell). For comfort and for safety, people need to be able to adjust the temperature, airflow, humidity, noise and light in their homes. Many existing homes present barriers to these controls, especially to people with physical disabilities; but as several of our authors have shown, developing technologies offer the opportunity to return more control over the sensory environment to frail and disabled people.

However, control over the environment involves more than physical manipulation. For example, the inadequate initial construction of many buildings has allowed intrusive noise to a degree that has affected the quality of life of residents. In the case of temperature control, the cost of fuel poverty linked to inefficient heating systems has denied many older people the ability to keep themselves warm in winter. Growing concerns about the annual increase (about 30%; DETR, 2000) in the death rate of older people during the winter months led to calls for action on fuel poverty and to the introduction of cold weather payments as an increment to supplementary pension payments, although this approach had its critics (Age Concern, 1995). The Housing Green Paper, *Quality and choice* (DETR, 2000), introduced the idea of a Home Energy Efficiency Scheme (HEES), which would fund insulation and heating systems including central heating. The HEES was aimed to target "those people who are most at risk from ill health caused by fuel poverty – the elderly and families on low incomes, the disabled and the chronically sick" (section 12:15). The necessity of these measures on fuel poverty stems from both the disadvantaged economic status of many older people and the prevalence of uneconomic heating systems in houses with poor thermal properties. While the main focus of Lifetime Homes has been on design and accessibility, these issues also point to the relevance of *sustainability* for inclusive housing.

However, houses do not exist in isolation, and their *location* relative to other places and objects has a significant impact on the ability of residents to take part in activities outside the home. Older people and others have described many aspects of the near-home environment that affect their ability to get out as well as to stay in. These include infrastructural elements, such as public transport and the location of shops and health services; local elements, such as the exact location of bus stops and street-crossings, for example; and, not least, micro-environment features, such as the surface of the ground underfoot.

Technological futures

While homes built to Lifetime Homes and various mobility standards, along with 'sustainable' and 'green' homes, will continue to be in the minority for a considerable period of time, currently emerging technologies have the potential to spread more widely and more quickly than previous waves of new technology have done. They do not usually require planning regulations and may be less costly than the structural alterations that are often required to provide mobility standards. Given the rate at which people replace and acquire new consumer durables, information technology (IT) applications tend to become increasingly ubiquitous in society as a whole. Information technology solutions are more likely to be seen as empowering and 'cutting edge', than as 'special needs'; and this includes technological innovations which can be useful to older people and those who support them. In Chapter Five Malcolm Fisk outlined some recent technologies, including personal computers and mobile telephones, which are already being used in increasing numbers by older people. When technologies are genuinely useful to them, older people will readily take them on board: recent examples are the use of email to communicate with grandchildren, and using telephone or online shopping facilities to choose purchases, rather than relying on a friend to make proxy choices in-store. As Malcolm Fisk pointed out, new technologies have the potential to 'liberate' older people. Older people may find, as some younger disabled people have, that computers allow them to communicate with other computer users in a context that minimises personal physical limitations. Gender differences in the use of technologies have generally been studied at much younger ages (for example, within groups of school students), but, in the rapidly evolving technology market, it is not yet clear how older women – more numerous than older men and more likely to be self-reliant – will embrace communication technologies.

At present there are barriers to using these technologies, including the cost of equipment, the need for improved human–computer interfaces, and the need to persuade people that they are actually useful. But, as relative costs come down and the utility of equipment is improved, we may expect IT solutions to become more standard (see, for example, Rickford, 2000).

In part, the perceived utility of technologies depends on the availability and attractiveness of alternatives. We know that the immediate future promises a society with more older people living alone, and with a smaller workforce from which to draw care and support staff. We know that older people generally prefer to continue living at home with domiciliary help rather than moving into residential homes, and the government has recognised the need for regulated domiciliary care linked to support arrangements (DETR, 2000). Technologies will be an essential part of these arrangements. For example, they may enable people with dementia, who are in danger of becoming a 'very special needs group', the potential to live in places that reinforce personal meanings for them (see Chapter Six).

The ethics of these new technologies, especially when devices are used for surveillance or monitoring, are still under discussion, and several of the authors in this book have raised this issue. Older people will want to be clear about who controls the technologies and who has access to data about them. This would appear to be a matter which requires regulation, but by whom? And how can the voice of older people themselves be heard in setting ethical standards and in regulating the use of technological interventions? This could well become one of a number of quality of life issues which, viewed under the new human rights legislation (DoH, 2000), require radical rethinking.

The social environment

One of the main concerns of older people, especially those living in economically deprived areas, has been the incidence and perception of crime and their own sense of security. This has taken a heavy toll on those older people who have felt themselves to be prisoners in their own homes, and not always secure even within their own four walls. Fear of crime is a quality of life issue that can be disabling in itself, and has been a particular problem for older women living alone (Peace and Johnson, 1998). The Housing Green Paper (DETR, 2000) proposed funding a package of security measures for low-income households (that is, with at least one member aged over 60 and assisted through HEES), if they are considered to be at higher risk from crime. The stated aim was to help these households to participate more fully in the local community "and thereby reduce the risk of isolation and exclusion" (section 12.23). The Housing Green Paper also recommended security measures as part of new and refurbished housing schemes. In addition, half of the proposed investment in new CCTV equipment would be in residential areas. However, security need not be solely related to the dangers of intrusion by strangers, it is also related to feelings of social isolation and problems in reaching people one cares about, or even with whom one is familiar.

It is therefore not surprising that a sense of security may also be related to feelings of autonomy. Repeated studies have shown that older people highlight independence as one of the things that they value the most, and for many years housing providers have proclaimed it to be their aim to support older people to live independently in the community. Independence and autonomy have been seen as essential for maintaining well-being and a sense of self in later life, and their significance has been most clearly seen when people have lost elements of them, for example, in residential care and long-stay hospital wards (Peace at al, 1997). As we have seen, this emphasis on independence has coincided with the gradual but inexorable increase in separate and smaller households and a decreased tendency for intergenerational living. It is crucially important that the changing nature of the household across the life course is recognised so that the common equation of housing with the family is extended to include other forms of household.

In understanding the variability of household groupings we may also need a more subtle understanding of group- and solo-living arrangements with non-kin. Older people in particular have often seen a stark choice between living alone in social isolation and living with a group of other people not of their own choosing. Some have sought other solutions, including seasonal migration or long visits to relatives, home-sharing or lodgers, having grandchildren to stay at particular times or spending the day with friends but sleeping at home. All these solutions might be described as 'doing your own thing' alongside others.

Interdependence and companionship may play an equal part with independence in helping older people to maintain an integrated lifestyle. Older people's networks and contacts are pivotal in making social inclusion possible, and they can be supported and extended by sympathetic infrastructures. For example Malcolm Fisk (Chapter Five) noted that technological development need not lead to isolation, but can free up 'people time'. Without social relationships it is possible for people to become so isolated that independence alone cannot sustain well-being. Older people are well aware of this as they negotiate between staying put and moving. One of the challenges for housing providers and social/health supporters is to create living environments that enable people to achieve the balance between independence and interdependence which suits them best.

The 20th-century solution for older people who needed better housing, and perhaps low-level support, was sheltered housing based on small, self-contained independent living units grouped around communal facilities. These are environments within which age is the primary, and sometimes the only, point of commonality between neighbours. In some areas of the country there is a general lack of other accommodation which is affordable and which has the amenities that older people require. This has meant that some older people have moved into sheltered housing regardless of whether or not they wanted or needed warden services or an age-segregated community.

Nevertheless, others have chosen sheltered housing precisely because it excludes the close proximity of young people – the absence of noise and aggravation, especially at night, and an added sense of security are often cited as some of the chief benefits of sheltered housing. Judith Phillips and colleagues (Chapter Nine) have commented on the emphasis on security in the case of retirement communities. However, the social life of age-segregated housing varies enormously and people living in sheltered housing have also commented on their 'deadness', especially at weekends or public holidays when some residents are away visiting family and wardens may be off duty. Some people miss the everyday sounds of the mixed community, as John Percival has shown (Chapter Seven), and there can be an absence of noise and movement that leads to a lack of stimulation from listening and watching other people. In some cases, people may replace this with audio-visual stimulation – the 'virtual' community of the TV, radio and Internet. People who can get out and about and people who have a constant flow of visitors may find less need for the reassurance of neighbourly activity – emphasising again the importance of visitability in supporting social relationships.

These and other examples of age-segregated environments, such as continuing-care communities in the US (Moen and Erickson, 1999), raise issues of principle about social inclusion. They provide a model of housing which suits some older people: environments which offer the supports necessary for people to carry on living as independently as possible and with the potential for a protected social environment. In this respect the age-segregated model can help some people to maintain a level of integration and connectedness with others, which they might not manage if they lived alone in mainstream housing. In Chapter Eight Maria Brenton described another model in which residents have a pre-established base of communal interest. The residents in CoHousing Communities, who have worked at their interrelationships prior to moving in, are more likely to get along with each other than residents placed alongside each other solely on the basis of housing need. In both Europe and North America, communities of like-minded people have organised together not just on the basis of age, but also on their gender, local connections, income, religion, previous employment, education or culture.

The age-related model does not suit the taste of all older people nor, necessarily, all stages of later life. Furthermore, there is an argument that it reinforces stereotypes of older people as different from the rest of the population, with 'special needs' based on age rather than with the same needs as everybody else. There is also an argument that the commitment of older people can help to support stability within communities. Inclusive housing recognises that older people have a right to be part of the community, but it also enables the community to benefit from the contributions which older people can make. One of these contributions, for example, might be in maintaining the local community's sense of its own context through local knowledge – a sense of history and continuity. Mary Marshall has discussed the role of environmental embeddedness and context in helping people with dementia to understand and negotiate their domestic surroundings. In a similar way, communities need to be able to interpret their collective spaces, and long-resident older people can contribute to this local knowledge, provided they remain in contact with the rest of the community.

The situation of people with dementia presents particular issues for the notion of inclusive housing. People who have great difficulties with communicating and who may have a fragile sense of context can behave in ways that are often socially unacceptable (although this can, of course, apply to people of any age who do, or do not, suffer from dementia). As we have seen in several instances in this book, the conformity required by communal living arrangements may come into conflict with the notion of a home for life, testing the limits of inclusive housing (see for example Foster, Chapter Seven). This raises the need for a debate about resourcing facilities and staff to accommodate different types of people, without having to remove some of them to other, more medicalised places.

This issue also brings us to the important point about the boundaries of housing and support, and the right to be unwell and to die within a grouped setting which has become home. Judith Phillips and colleagues (Chapter Nine) raised the issue in their discussion of retirement communities in which life could be positive while people remained fit, active and engaged in occupations. But, if people are no longer able to cope with this lifestyle, do they have to move? At what point does the individual's needs challenge those of the wider group? In non-specialised housing, people live and die within their own homes, they also fluctuate between being well and being unwell – this is seen as part of life. The hospice model has also shown how environment and support can be integrated to support a person through stages of ill health right through to death (Dickenson et al, 2000). Yet, to date, the acceptance of death has been difficult for many of those who have chosen a collective lifestyle based on activities and engagement as an indicator of quality of life, and the 'good life' in these communities may be compromised by the 'social death' of obvious physical decline. Will people who have chosen the right to live alongside each other also accept each other's right to fall ill and die in the same community? Changing attitudes to ways of living may, in time, change attitudes to declining mental and physical health and death (Sidell et al, 1998). These debates need to be set alongside current efforts to develop intermediate care and rehabilitation for older people who have had to spend a long time in hospital (see DoH, 2000).

Social relationships are not the only relationships that have an impact on how older people interact with the wider community. The attitude of care and other support staff can be critical, and, indeed, for some older people with no family contacts, daily interactions with care and nursing staff will constitute their most meaningful social relationships. As Mary Marshall (Chapter Six) and Leonie Kellaher (Chapter Ten) have both indicated, in some group living arrangements the paid staff effectively hold the key to residents' interactions with the built environment. In many situations, both in residential settings and in domiciliary care, staff time is so limited and job descriptions so tightly defined that individuals are not able to make free decisions about when and how they use space indoors, go out, bathe, eat and so on. Increasing the flexibility of support arrangements would have an impact on the working lives of a body of staff who until now have tended to be poorly paid and, often, untrained (DoH, 1998; Whittington, 1999).

One of the features of specialised housing is that it allows the concentration of people with particular types of needs – say, for nursing care or for a particular level of personal care – to be housed and provided for in one location by a staff team with the appropriate skills. Many older people who need some help or support do not need these more intensive levels of personal care, but, by the same token, there are other groups including those with dementia or mental illnesses who do need specialised care. One of the consequences of inclusive housing as an ideal – and of Lifetime Homes if they became ubiquitous – is a need for a much wider range of skills among the teams staffing groups of houses. Alternatively, the activities of specialist staff would need to be dispersed within the community rather than focused on one setting. This presents further organisational challenges for health, social services and housing providers, who have for some time been aiming for a more integrated approach through joint working. To date, housing providers are still not recognised as full partners in joint planning arrangements.

Other groups within our society have also been treated as 'different' and cast into lifestyles from which they may have sought routes to 'normality'. Do older people have anything to learn from younger people who have been labelled as 'disabled' or defined in terms of their medical or social problems (see Bull, 1998; Shaw et al, 1998; Spiers, 1999). Seeing disability as the socially constructed constraint on people with a range of physical, mental and other impairments has enabled people with disabilities to effect lasting change in their life chances. For those living in 'special needs' settings, there has been a long road to 'ordinary living'. In developing living arrangements for people with learning difficulties, for example, work towards 'normalisation' and 'ordinary living' has given way to a philosophy which seeks rather to value the individual for their own sense of worth – one which is not dependent on the model of 'normal' others, but which recognises and embraces diversity (King's Fund, 1980; Morris, 1993; Brown and Walmsley, 1997). Many disabled people challenge the view that their disability must mean dependence. They see independence as being about the ability to make choices and to achieve personal goals, although this may require assistance – a form of interdependency in which autonomy is preserved (Morris, 1993) and impairments recognised (Crow, 1996). Thus, being able to live independently, with help and support rather than being cared for, is seen as a human right. The development of a social model of disability has provided a framework through which disablism could begin to be challenged so that people might exercise choice and control over their own lives.

The 1995 Disability Discrimination Act and the 1999 Disability Rights Commission Act have embodied the acceptance of the rights of disabled people – particularly in the workplace and in markets – and barrier-free environments now have to be regarded in this context. The outcomes are yet to be seen. The implications of a social model of age discrimination have yet to be tested in a similar way, but with the gradual build-up of an anti-age discrimination lobby and the implementation of the 1998 Human Rights Act we might expect an increasing movement for change by older people.

Resources

While many of the issues raised by the notion of integrated housing are dependent on our attitudes to ways of living across the life course, such attitudes are also influenced by our use of resources – nationally, locally and personally. In this chapter we have commented on issues relating to housing design and adaptations, the purchase and use of new technology and the quantity and quality of staff working with older people, all of which have implications on resources. But one of the most significant barriers to older people fully taking part in the life of the community has been their relative poverty compared to the working population. While the 20th century saw an increase in the numbers of people retiring with good occupational pensions and equity in housing, the majority of older people continue to be economically disadvantaged relative to the employed population – in 2000 around 80% of people living in poverty were pensioners, predominantly older women (Ginn and Arber, 1998; Hancock, 1998). We have already discussed the problems that this causes older people in relation to the cost of keeping warm; many also have difficulty in meeting other running costs and cannot afford essential maintenance. Yet the perception seems to persist that older people can make do on very little:

> It is ordinarily believed ... that a retired person does not need as much as a working person, on whose funds travel and perhaps clothing might make particular calls. Yet there is research which suggests that to sustain the same style of life enjoyed in employment as much as 70 per cent of income needs to be retained in retirement... (Henle, 1972). It is probably not unfair to suggest that the original opinion is influenced by a tacit belief that the retired or unemployed person *should* receive less than the worker as a matter of custom and economic law, and that the supposition that the money is not required follows automatically from that. (Midwinter, 1997, p 69; emphasis in original)

Of course there is also enormous variation between older people with regards to their economic resources. As we saw in Chapter One, variation in terms of age, gender, ethnicity and social class have profound effects on access to decent housing and the other resources necessary for a socially engaged life. In terms of day-to-day living, the most significant economic resource for most older people is their pension, and we know that women, some minority ethnic older people and the oldest older people are among the groups whose low pension entitlement has a continuing effect on their quality of life (Atkin, 1998; Ginn and Arber, 1998). Compounded with this are the effects of living in socially deprived areas – whether rural or urban – where the environment outside the immediate home base can, in itself, be disabling and discouraging. In areas such as this it becomes very clear that housing can only be made 'inclusive' within a wider social context.

In addition to diversity in terms of income, there is also diversity in the access that groups of people have acquired to perhaps the most significant form of personal capital for most people – their housing equity. Being an owner-occupier became far more common in Britain in the latter part of the 20th century, but the amount of equity held in housing varied greatly between geographical areas and types of accommodation (see Forrest et al, 1996). Regardless of the notional equity held in housing, its effect on the income of older homeowners can be marginal, indeed, in many situations, older owners may be worse off in terms of disposable income than those older people who rent from social landlords (Hancock, 1998).

In spite of this, the number of older people who have chosen to use their housing equity to supplement their income or to fund maintenance and adaptation has been relatively small (Hamnett, 1995; Hancock, 1998). At least part of older people's resistance to capitalising their housing equity has been put down to homeowners' general aspirations to bequeath capital to their family. Issues of inheritance have been quite strong within our society, relating to emotional as well as financial exchanges. The inheritance of housing is becoming more commonplace as the effects of the spread of owner-occupation continue to filter through to subsequent generations, and more complex as family change sees the impact of 'step-families' on inheritance patterns (Bornat et al, 1999). The cumulative effects of inheritance on the wealth and housing opportunities of later generations of inheritors and non-inheritors remain to be seen.

What we have seen is the distress of older people and their families who have been forced to sell houses in order to finance residential and nursing home care. In emotional terms, these owner-occupied houses had often been perceived as 'lifetime homes' – homes over which people had ownership and control for as long as they wanted, and even perhaps as more-than-lifetime homes in their potential for people to bequeath something of themselves to later generations. The funding of long-term care has become a political issue (Royal Commission on Long Term Care, 1999) with accommodation and support no longer provided 'from the cradle to the grave'. In 2000 the government announced that in England the costs of accommodation and personal care will still be means tested, while the costs of a registered nurse's time will be covered (DoH, 2000); this may work against the ideals of flexible lifestyles facilitated through varied assistance outlined throughout this chapter. The Scottish

Executive decided otherwise (Scottish Executive, 2001) and it remains to be seen what effects the differential either side of the border will have in practice and on attitudes towards the acceptability of means testing.

None of this is to deny that, for many older homeowners, the costs associated with maintaining and running their homes is a burden from which they would wish to be freed. What families may now be seeing is that, if older people want to make adaptations, buy in help or move to a more comfortable form of housing with assistance, they may need to use their housing capital for themselves rather than bequeath it. There is a relatively small but significant number of older homeowners who sell their houses and move (sometimes back) into social rented housing (Forrest and Leather, 1998). The calculations on which such decisions are made can be complex. Both staying put and moving home can make an inroad into capital and affect the disposable income available to people after taking into account their housing and care costs.

A part of this equation is often the access that people may have to informal support: here the changing nature of individual families (for example, geographical dispersal between generations) has an effect on who can offer help and how often it can be accessed. In order to 'stay put' in their non-specialised housing, older people may need to face an array of assistance costs – for gardening, home help, meals-on-wheels, home nursing, odd-jobs, transport and so on – instead of, or in addition to, help which is given free. In setting the costs of 'community care' alongside the advantages and disadvantages of 'community living', for many individual older people the decision to stay where they are, or to move into housing with care has, therefore, been a matter of economics and their own sense of family values as much as a decision about the pros and cons of specialised housing.

Opening up choices

> The more opportunity people have to decide these things for themselves, the more likely they are to feel ownership of the decision and to be satisfied with the outcome. And the more information they have on which to base their decisions, the better those decisions are likely to be. (DETR, 2000, section 9.6)

If it is about anything, inclusive housing is about giving people a living environment that supports their lifestyle choices. Universal design and specially adapted environments can make a major contribution to making housing inclusive, but they are not the whole story. As we have seen in this book, elements of the wider social environment also affect the ways in which the built environment can support people. Because older people are as diverse as any other large section of the population, it is perhaps unrealistic to think that their housing needs can be met by a 'one-size-fits-all' type of housing any more than anyone else's needs.

As we have seen, certain forms of specialised accommodation – including nursing and residential homes, sheltered and extra-care housing – became common enough by the end of the 20th century to be considered standard provision. But the clear differences which existed between these types of places and the health status of the residents for which they aimed to cater have become blurred. This is partly the result of the demographic, social and organisational changes which we have already discussed, partly the result of joint working and private finance initiatives, and partly the outcome of new thinking about the needs of specific groups of older people.

Alongside the new forms of special housing provision which have been developed, there has always been the much smaller market of niche provisions, including hotels and hostels, small residential homes and adult placement schemes, mobile-home parks, tied accommodation, grace-and-favour homes and homeshare arrangements. As a result there is currently a wide range of living arrangements for older people who cannot or do not wish to live in mainstream housing and, with the development of new technologies, there is potential for this variation in viable living environments to expand further. Therefore, settings in which people may live vary in scale from the very large (100-bed plus) nursing homes run by some of the largest providers of care in the country, to individual arrangements. In any of these situations there will be people who would rather live some other way, and people who would never consider living another way. The trick of finding your niche is perhaps to control the search for it.

In order for people to make good choices, they need *information* and a means of *communication* with providers or gatekeepers of housing. While many older people are adept at finding out information about everything from welfare benefits to medical treatments, information needs to be readily available; this is unfortunately not always the case with housing, which originates from many different providers. Older people facing problems with their homes will not necessarily know about practically available alternatives[4], let alone innovative housing communities, technological solutions or adaptations to lifetime standards – the estate agent will not tell you these things ... yet. If the options of which people are aware are unattractive, people may be more inclined to stay put.

Even when people do know, in theory, about which alternatives might be open to them in the areas where they want to live, uncertainty or misunderstanding may dissuade them. For example, older owner-occupiers may consider themselves ineligible for sheltered housing, or council tenants living alone may assume they have to take a one-bedroom flat in order to be able to move. On the other side of the coin, housing providers have tried to take the preferences of older people into account when developing specialised housing for them. However, these preferences have usually been derived from asking older people about their satisfaction with their existing housing, and/or their opinions about existing forms of housing with care: comparatively few studies have asked older people to consider radical alternatives.

Older people living within housing which could be improved may also want to *participate* and be involved in creating living places. Their consultation could be empowering for all involved. To date privatisation within the housing and care home industry has produced some niche markets that fragment the housing, care and health areas. Yet we are also seeing moves to joint working that are bringing these groups together in ways that recognise the symbolic and pragmatic importance of housing. The ways in which particular housing requirements are met may affect how people feel about their own and other people's ageing. We can see this in the common response of people to the environment of nursing and residential homes. As places where people commonly approach death, they have always had a problem in being attractive places in which to live – 'later life' environments with more emphasis on the 'later' than on the 'life'.

As a nation, we similarly need more accessible domestic homes, yet resist the suggestion of bland, unchallenging, even medicalised environments. At each stage there has been resistance to the introduction of regulations and technologies that aim to level up the accessibility of environments to make them suitable for almost everybody. Jo Milner and Ruth Madigan (Chapter Four) described some of the strong reservations within the building industry to further regulation in the area of accessibility, and Mary Marshall (Chapter Six) indicated an evident reluctance to advance pilot work on technologies to help people with dementia. However, there are examples of forward thinking on these issues – Mary Marshall also drew attention to *Just another disability: Making design dementia friendly* (Stewart and Page, 2000), from which we can start to build a new consensus. The challenge for designers and providers of housing is to create environments which do not inadvertently disempower people but which still offer stimulation, interest and the opportunity to be adventurous.

So we are left with the question, can inclusive housing be developed for an ageing society? The opportunity is there to develop choice in housing for all, which will take older people's accommodation out of 'special needs'. But will the opportunity be taken? Will it only happen when 'special needs' are just seen as a part of everyday living for all ages? We began this book with quotations from contrasting descriptions of accommodation that might suit older residents. Our vision is a future where desirable design features in general housing include planned accessibility and sustainability. Highlighted as selling points, these 'barrier-free' features will be preferred by most potential residents. For example:

New instruction

In a prime thoroughfare at the heart of the suburb, a beautifully presented home with a ground-floor extension. Accommodating three bedrooms – one on the ground floor, two bathrooms and a through living and dining area. This desirable home has a gently sloping approach, 'gold standard' access throughout the house and energy efficiency at NHER Rating 9. Designed to make living easier. Must be seen.

Notes

[1] In April 2000, Collective Enterprises Limited was appointed as the national coordinating body for home improvement agencies, which help older people and people with disabilities, taking over from Care and Repair England. Increased funding to home improvement agencies was also announced for 1999-2000 to allow their expansion from 143 agencies to 184.

[2] The DHSS and Welsh Office (1973) Local Authority Building Note No 2, 'Residential accommodation for elderly people', gave a recommendation of $10m^2$ for a single bedroom. New national minimum standards were announced in July 2000, using $10m^2$ for single rooms in existing care homes from 2007 (subject to some flexibility in defined cases). The standard for single rooms in new care homes will be $12m^2$ from 2002. Wheelchair users should have rooms of $12m^2$ and door widths of 800mm for their own accommodation and communal rooms. In addition, each resident should have a minimum of $4.1m^2$ of communal space

within the home. Shared rooms in existing homes may constitute no more than 20% of overall resident places from 2002. (See DoH, 2001.)

[3] The bedroom standard has been used as a measure of space sufficiency in Britain since the 1960s, although it does not have direct statutory force. In essence it allows a separate bedroom for each person over 21 except for 'married' couples, while people aged 10-20 should not have to share with someone of the opposite sex. The modified standard for calculating rent allowances provides for separate bedrooms for over-16s and a spare bedroom for each unit of accommodation: a lower standard than this constitutes overcrowding (Holmans, 2000).

[4] The Housing Green Paper began to address this problem with the suggestion of a general advertising system in which properties could be labelled to indicate the type of household for which they are most suitable (DETR, 2000, s 9.28).

References

Age Concern (1995) 'Affordable warmth', Briefing Paper 2395, September, London: Age Concern.

Atkin, K. (1998) 'Ageing in a multi-racial Britain: demography, policy and practice', in M. Bernard and J. Phillips (eds) *The social policy of old age*, London: Centre for Policy on Ageing, pp 163-82.

BGOP (Better Government for Older People) (1999) *In our hands*, Report of the Better Government for Older People Conference, Oxford, July.

Bornat, J., Dimmock, B., Jones, D. and Peace, S.M. (1999) 'The Impact of family change on older people: the case of stepfamilies', in S. McRae (ed) *Changing Britain: Families and households in the 1990s*, Oxford: Oxford University Press, pp 248-62.

Brown, H. and Walmsley, J. (1997) 'When "ordinary" isn't enough: a review of the concept of the normalisation principle', in J. Bornat, J. Johnson, C. Pereira, D. Pilgrim and F. Williams (eds) *Community care: A reader*, London: Macmillan in association with The Open University.

Bull, H. (ed) (1998) *Housing options for disabled people*, London: Jessica Kingsley Publishers.

Clark, H., Dyer, S. and Horwood, J. (1998) *'That bit of help': The high value of low level preventative services for older people*, Bristol/York: The Policy Press/Joseph Rowntree Foundation.

Cole, I., Gidley, G., Robinson, D. and Smith, Y. (1998) *The impact of leasehold reform: Flat dwellers' experiences of enfranchisement and lease renewal*, London: DETR.

Crow, L. (1996) 'Including all our lives: renewing the social model of disability', in J. Morris (ed) *Encounters with strangers: Feminism and disability*, London: The Women's Press.

DETR (Department of the Environment, Transport and the Regions) (2000) *Quality and choice: A decent home for all*, Housing Green Paper, London: DETR.

DHSS (Department of Health and Social Security) and Welsh Office (1973) *Local Authority Building Note 2, Residential accommodation for elderly people*, London: HMSO.

Dickenson, D., Johnson, M. and Katz, J. (eds) (2000) *Death, dying and bereavement* (2nd edn), London: Sage Publications.

DoE (Department of the Environment) (1998) *English House Condition Survey 1996*, London: The Stationery Office.

DoH (Department of Health) (1989) *Caring for people: Community care in the next decade and beyond*, Cmnd 849, London: HMSO.

DoH (1998) *Modernising social services*, White Paper, Cm 4169, London: The Stationery Office.

DoH (2000) *Social Care News*, a special publication aimed at informing people employed in the social care field about the government's new NHS plan and what it means for their work, August, London: The Stationery Office.

DoH (2001) *Care homes for older people: National minimum standards – Care Standards Act 2000*, London: The Stationery Office.

Fennell, G., Phillipson, C. and Evers, H. (1988) *The sociology of old age*, Milton Keynes: Open University Press.

Forrest, R. and Leather, P. (1998) 'The ageing of the property owning democracy', *Ageing & Society*, vol 18, Part 1, pp 35-63.

Forrest, R., Leather, P. and Pantazis, C. (1996) *Home ownership in old age: The future of owner occupation in an ageing society*, Oxford: Anchor Research.

Ginn, J. and Arber, S. (1998) 'Gender and older age', in M. Bernard and J. Phillips (eds) *The social policy of old age*, London: Centre for Policy on Ageing.

Hamnett, C. (1995) 'Housing equity release and inheritance', in I. Allen and E. Perkins (eds) *The future of family care for older people*, London: HMSO, pp 163-80.

Hancock, R. (1998) 'Housing wealth, income and financial wealth of older people in Britain', *Ageing & Society*, vol 18, no 1, pp 5-33.

Holmans, A. (2000) *Housing demand and need in England 1999-2001*, York: JRF.

JRF (Joseph Rowntree Foundation) (1995) Findings: Housing research 146, June, York: JRF.

Kellaher, L. (2000) *A choice well made: 'Mutuality' as a governing principle in residential care*, London: Centre for Policy on Ageing.

King's Fund (1988) *An ordinary life in practice*, London: King's Fund Centre.

King's Fund Centre (1980) *An ordinary life: Comprehensive locally-based residential services for mentally handicapped people*, London: King's Fund Centre.

Midwinter, E. (1997) *Pensioned off: Retirement and income examined*, Buckingham: Open University Press.

Moen, P. and Erickson, M.A. (1999) *Decision-making and satisfaction with a continuing care community*, Ithaca, NY: Ithaca College/Cornell University.

Morris, J. (1993) *Independent lives: Community care and disabled people*, London: Macmillan.

Peace, S.M. and Johnson, J. (1998) 'Living arrangements of older people', in M. Bernard and J. Phillips (eds) *The social policy of old age*, London: Centre for Policy on Ageing.

Peace, S.M., Kellaher, L. and Willcocks, D. (1997) *Re-evaluating residential care*, Buckingham: Open University Press.

Rickford, F. (2000) 'The new IT generation', *Community Care*, 27 July-2 August, pp 18-19.

Royal Commission on Long Term Care (1999) *With respect to old age: Long term care – Rights and responsibilities*, London: The Stationery Office.

Scottish Executive (2001) 'Free care for older people to be extended in Scotland', News Release SE 01/38 2001, Edinburgh: Scottish Executive.

Shaw, I., Lambert, S. and Clapham, D. (eds) (1998) *Social care and housing*, Research Highlights in Social Work No 32, London: Jessica Kingsley Publishers.

Sidell, M., Katz, J. and Komaromy, C. (1998) *Death and dying in residential and nursing homes for older people: Examining the case for palliative care*, Milton Keynes: School of Health and Social Welfare, The Open University.

Spiers, F.E. (ed) (1999) *Housing and social exclusion*, London: Jessica Kingsley Publishers.

Stewart, S. and Page, A. (eds) (2000) *Just another disability: Making design dementia friendly*, Conference proceedings of the European Conference, Glasgow, 1-2 October, Glasgow: Just Another Disability.

Whittington, C. (1999) 'Modernising the social care workforce: the first national training strategy for England', Supplementary report on the Partnership of Social Care and Health, Leeds: Training Organisation for Personal Social Services England.

Wilson, D., Aspinall, P. and Murie, A. (1995) *Factors influencing housing satisfaction among older people*, Birmingham: Centre for Urban and Regional Studies, University of Birmingham.

Index

Page references for tables and figures are in italics; those for notes are followed by n

C

D

E

F

G

I

J

K

L

M

N

O

S

T

U

V

W

Y